The Motley Fool UK
Investment Guide

Whatever is funny is subversive . . .
every joke is ultimately a custard pie.
George Orwell

First published in 1998 by Boxtree

an imprint of Macmillan Publishers Ltd
25 Eccleston Place, London SW1W 9NF
Basingstoke and Oxford

Associated companies throughout the world

ISBN 07522 2439 5

Text © The Motley Fool UK 1998

10

A CIP catalogue entry for this book is available from the British Library.

Designed and typeset by Keystroke, Jacaranda Lodge, Wolverhampton
Printed and bound in Great Britain by Mackays of Chatham plc

Contents

Rounding Up

Appendices

Welcome to the Age of Foolishness!

David B.

Who isn't a little anxious about money? Who doesn't worry that they're not saving enough or that their savings aren't growing fast enough? Who has a total and utter, rock solid, unshakeable faith in their financial adviser and in the financial professions as a whole? If none of these questions worries you, then you should probably put this book back on the shelf and leave very quietly the way you came in. Our bet is, though, that most people picking up this strangely named volume have at least some doubt in their mind on one or other or all three of these questions. It's only natural. After all, who amongst us was taught anything whatsoever about personal finance at school? Who amongst us has ever understood, *really* understood, what a financial professional was going on about? Yes, we bet the answers are pretty doubtful to these questions too.

There's a dark void in many people's lives when it comes to finance, a feeling that 'Here be dragons', that it's best not to meddle in what you can never hope to understand. Well, tosh, piffle and rubbish! We don't believe that's so at all and in this book we plan to show why. We'll show you how the financial professionals and the City are out to keep the public as ignorant as possible, how they sell investment plans which eat up 80 per cent or more of the first two years' contributions in charges and take a full seven years to break even, how they sell other plans which perform worse than even the average in over 90 per cent of cases. We'll take you on a tour of all those TESSAs, PEPs, PPPs, ISAs and BAPs (one of these is a type of filled roll, no prizes for guessing which). We'll show you what they all mean – in very simple, easily understandable terms – and then we'll show you just how you can beat the professionals at their own game. And beat them roundly. You don't need GCSEs, 'A' levels or a degree for this. Just a smattering of common sense, your feet on moderately firm ground and a willingness to challenge the orthodoxy, to rise against convention. In fact, as usual, Winnie the Pooh puts his finger right on the spot. Here he is summing up his friend, Owl:

'Owl hasn't exactly got Brain, but he Knows Things.'

Knowing Things, not very many things, is one of the keys to this whole business.

The final quality you'll need is a sense of humour. In contrast to the financial professionals, we don't believe that learning about investment has to be worthy or turgid or boring. We believe it should be fun. We have got a lot of enjoyment out of writing this book and from working to promote a sound understanding of basic financial principles, both offline and on and we hope you'll come and share in our spirit of lightheartedness. But please don't think us flippant. We understand how deadly serious is the issue of financial security; we however, simply don't buy into the mock awe and very real pomposity with which it is invested by the ranks of the professionals.

So who are we, these three strange-looking characters in silly hats? For that, we must go back to 1993, when David and Tom Gardner sat down and took a long, hard look at the investing orthodoxy which prevailed in the United States of America. The wisdom seemed to be that Mr Joe Average, as the common punter is termed in the United States, was a hopeless case when it came to understanding anything about investing; one step removed from a flatworm in fact. His only hope lay in finding a benevolent professional who would take over the burden of managing his savings and steer it through the financial minefield which, alone, he had no chance of negotiating without losing a leg at the very least. In return for this limb- and possibly even life-saving help, the professional would take a modest commission. The result? Mr J. Average could go home and sleep at night, secure in the knowledge that his savings were in good hands and the professional would make a fair living, returning to his family every evening and basking in the satisfying glow of an honest job, well done.

It was fairyland, but in this prosperous nation, with its sunstruck coasts, purple mountains, gun-toting crazies and pizzas the size of tractor tyres, all was not quite as it seemed. Mr Average, was ignorant all right, but it wasn't because money and finance were impossible, or even difficult to understand. It was because he had never been *taught* anything about them at all. Simple concepts like pensions, price-to-earnings ratios, stock market indices and execution-only brokers were not just unknowns, they were terrifying, shadowy concepts, the very mention of which might unleash malign powers. Nowhere in the entire educational system was provision made to teach this basic and vital information.

Without education, it was true that the average investor (read: 'Everybody who ever hoped to save any money for their future') had no chance of understanding what was going on and had no choice but to hand over his or her hard-earned dollars to the professionals. That was a shame in itself, because actions based on ignorance of any kind cannot be auspicious for the future. But that was far from the end of the story.

You see, the professional money managers of the United States were not stepping into the breach of ignorance and delivering a solid, dependable service as part of a public service commitment. It turned out that it was in their interests to keep the level of ignorance and confusion about money as high as possible, because the foundation of their industry was based on some very unstable bedrock indeed. It was an extraordinary but true fact that 90 per cent of the returns on offer from America's professional money managers were lower than the returns which could be made off simple, low cost investments, easy to purchase, requiring no skill to pick and with negligible charges attached to them. With a tiny amount of time and even less effort, Joe Average could outperform the professionals, precisely by being average. He just didn't know it yet. Another thing he didn't know was that in itself the stock market is not a dangerous place to invest, but is in fact one of the *safest* kinds of investments. With the financial media constantly harping on potential short-term losses in the stock market, the long-term story of reliable, outperforming growth was totally lost. Of course, short-term panic stories are what sell newspapers and lure television viewers.

America was being duped and neither its financial professionals nor its media had any real interest in the spread of mass education about their subject. They had it very cushy, which was how it had been for a long time and that's how it might have stayed. Then something happened, something which this writer, with characteristic vision, welcomed with open arms:

'What's it called? The Internet? You can talk to other people with your computer? You can get hold of information? Why on *Earth* would you bother to do that?!'

Yes, really, and at about the time that the Oracle of Bournemouth (where David hails from originally) was dismissing the greatest revolution in mass communication since the invention of moveable type, David and Tom Gardner were transferring their print publication *The Motley Fool*, started a year earlier in 1993, onto America Online, otherwise known as AOL. A small, subversive movement had begun.

The name alluded to Shakespeare's Fool – Jacques in *As You Like It* – who had an unnerving habit of demonstrating that truth often lay beyond the bounds of conventional wisdom. Fools in the olden days were about the only people who could tell the King how it really was without getting their heads lopped off for their pains. In its print incarnation, *The Motley Fool* ('Ye Olde Printed Foole', as it is now fondly remembered) had a terribly small audience, mostly of family friends, we are told, who wanted to support the boys' attempt to make a living. (And about time too, their mum was probably saying.) Things soon took off, though, with the move to the mass medium and by the end of 1995 they were the most popular site on AOL, they had added a website and were publishing a book which went on to become a best-seller. Soon, the Fool was on the lips of everyone in America who had any interest in finance, the Fool's newspaper column was syndicated in over 160 newspapers around the country and the website was registering 20 million visits a month. As the Wise grew more disdainful, so the Fools were growing ever more popular, helping people to help themselves out of financial bondage.

It was about at this time that I, a jobbing British doctor, sometime of Bournemouth as we've heard (Three cheers for Bournemouth! Hello, Mum!), stumbled across the Fool on the Web. Humour? Down to Earthness? A willingness to engage with the world and do something novel? And all this in a site about investment? Very strange.

So strange in fact that I got hooked and, well, you know, one thing led to another and while initially I only needed five or ten minutes a day of the Fool online to keep me satisfied, pretty soon I was doing cold turkey without three, four or even more hours plugged in every day. Yes, the Fool had snared another unsuspecting innocent. It was pitiful to see. And then this happened:

One day, after many hours' surfing, I found myself moving through a deep, inner sanctum of the online area, a place I had never visited before. The cavernous walls of the chamber echoed with the clicks of my mouse. It smelt damp and musty and of a sudden the stillness was broken by the distant sound of breaking glass and a woman's high-pitched scream. Then all was quiet once more. On the muted, darkened screen there was now just one gently flashing icon and it said 'Click here if you wish to become a Fool'. I hesitated, awestruck and barely comprehending the step I was about to take. There was no going back now, that at least I knew. I clicked. A message came up: 'Please Wait.' Then: 'Please be still while we upload your brain. Click here to proceed.' I clicked and sat motionless, as bidden. Of a sudden, the screen became busy with activity and it was clear that something extraordinary was about to happen. And then I felt it – as if someone had pulled the plug out of the bath at the base of my skull. My brains were leaving me and being *uploaded to the Motley Fool.* I sat still, a curious sense of ease washing over me. After a few minutes, another dialogue box sprang up through the misty haze of well-being: 'Please click here to download a test version of a Mark 1 Foolish brain.' As the Foolish brain was downloaded, I felt my skull filling up once more and my consciousness returning to clarity. I had become a card-carrying Fool.

All right, it didn't happen *quite* like that, but the brain-sucking, Boris Karloff imagery was too tempting to forgo. What actually happened was that I composed an e-mail one wet Tuesday afternoon in April to David and Tom Gardner. 'It's just the same here, you know,' I said. 'We pay outrageous charges for underperforming investments, just like you,' I said. 'No-one knows anything about this stuff and when the professionals come and sell it to us, we just gawp and nod blindly and believe it, like you do,' I said. 'How about a British Motley Fool? And soon!' I said. To their credit – and this says something about the accessibility this new medium provides, as well as their openness to new ideas and innovation – they didn't do the high-tech equivalent of screwing up my e-mail and lobbing it at the basketball hoop they have poised over the wastepaper bin.

Again, one thing led to another and by the autumn of 1997, five months after the first e-mail, the Motley Fool UK Online was launched on

AOL UK (keyword: FOOLUK), followed in February 1998 by the website (http://www.fool.co.uk). With what we hoped was a similar blend of humour and irreverence, we set ourselves the same Foolish task of pointing to the Emperor and revealing that those new clothes he thought he was wearing weren't such a bargain after all.

In the very birthplace of Folly, the United Kingdom, the Wise spin doctors had kept the upper hand for more years than anyone could remember: 'It's too complicated for you. Trust us. We'll look after your financial future. We have your *best* interests at heart.'

But as the Emperor paraded the streets on his magnificent charger, collecting tributes and dispensing blessings as he went, already there were rumblings of discontent and not a little merriment: 'That fellow might believe he's wearing a new suit of clothes and he's certainly been telling us that for more years than we can remember, but it looks almost as if he's got nothing on at all, as if he's been having us on all these years! He still believes it, though. Amazing!' With sentiments like this already circling on the peasants' rumour-mill, the soil was ripe for the Fool to sow even more seeds of revolution and, yes, even treason.

The bloke on the horse, you see, really does have nothing on. Not a stitch.

Bombast, bamboozlement, overcharging, investment underperformance, longer words where shorter ones would do: it's all here. The truth, though, is that you don't have to put up with paying through the nose to investment managers, *ninety per cent* of whom, as we've heard, will perform worse than the average. You don't have to smile gratefully as you slip most of your first two years' worth of pension contributions directly into your financial adviser's pocket. You don't have to weep tears of thanks as it takes seven years or more for your endowment policy to even *start* to show a positive return on your money.

None of what we are going to discuss in this book is complicated or intimidating or impenetrable to the average person. It's all totally simple and totally Foolish and it will give you the key to unlock the sinister mystery which investment remains for so many of us. It will also show you how, with no skill whatsoever, you can beat the professionals at their own game. And what's more, it will show you how you can do this with as little as half an hour of effort each year. Or even less.

Does that sound a trifle unrealistic? Really, it shouldn't. You see, your motivation and that of the financial professionals are very different. While your first priority is to make money for you, *their* first priority is to make money *from* you. Their second priority is to make money for you, but it comes a long way down the line. As a savvy individual, you can cut out the middleman, head straight for the best value, lowest-cost investments bringing in 'average' returns and outperform 90 per cent of the pros. Jim Slater, whose books we recommend in Appendix 4 ('Publications You Should Like'), is an experienced UK investor with a highly down-to-Earth take on the subject. He had this to say about the *Motley Fool Investment Guide* (the US version) in his January 1998 newsletter:

> *One of its main contentions, with which I agree wholeheartedly, is that ordinary private investors are in many ways much better placed to make consistently good returns from shares than highly paid professionals in the City and on Wall Street.*

And if all this is starting to sound just a little too suspiciously easy, rest assured you won't find any get-rich-quick schemes between these pages. You won't even find anything controversial or risky. All you will find is the investment good sense we should all have been learning since we were in secondary school explained in simple terms and without huge amounts of jargon. We hope that by the time you have finished this volume (a weekend of frippery and delight or eighteen weeks of tooth-grinding misery, depending on your constitution) the black cloud of guilt and unease which hangs over you as you contemplate the need to do something for your financial future will have lifted. We hope you'll feel free and light and knowledgeable and . . . Foolish.

Before I make way for David and Tom G., I'd like to hark back a few years. Some of you reading this will have spent the early 1980s as enthralled as I was by *The Hitch-Hiker's Guide to the Galaxy*, the book, radio and television series which followed the adventures of one Arthur Dent to the ends of the universe after the Earth had, regrettably, been demolished to make way for a hyperspatial express route. Printed in large, coloured, friendly letters on the snug plastic cover of the *Guide* – the most remarkable book ever to come out of the publishing corporations of Ursa Minor and containing an alarming recipe for the best drink in existence, the Pan-galactic Gargle Blaster (see Appendix 11) – was the most useful piece of advice in the universe:

DON'T PANIC

We can't pretend that *The Motley Fool UK Investment Guide* has even an atom's worth of the brilliance of the *Hitch-Hiker's Guide*. But the advice? Surely, surely no Fool can do without it.

David and Tom G.

Something had to be done about this situation.

Ah, but there we go again, starting *in medias res*, 'in the midst of things', as was Homer's inclination in the *Iliad* and the *Odyssey*, and now ours too (in a desperate attempt to appease the Homeric Society we have offended in the past). So we should back-pedal. And be brief.

A few years ago, we two brothers stayed up past midnight for a few months running, in order to pour our souls into a literary product – that's what the book salesman called it, 'product' (had to get used to that) – designed to revolutionize thinking about money in our home country. It needed to be done. Despite the tremendous prosperity of the US stock market, studies showed that the distribution of wealth was growing more and more skewed. Of course, the haves have *always* had, and the have-nots have always had not, but the situation was growing more distressing. We deduced (correctly, we still believe, despite what the haves tell us) that one of the primary reasons for the *status quo* was the almost complete lack of education about money in the United States of America. No standard study of the subject has ever been made mandatory for American ankle-biters, something which would teach them the subtly destructive power of credit card debt, something which would teach them to understand just how much better the stock market had done than any other competing investment over the entire century. It was ironic to us that we had studied quadratic equations and binomial coefficients, and yet our own schools had never taught the far more important facts about compounded financial returns. It was incredible that the example of Anne Scheiber was not shouted from the rooftops of our educational institutions. This humble New Yorker died at an advanced age in 1995, leaving a fortune of over $20 million to charity, a fortune accumulated, from a starting point of $5,000 in the closing years of the Second World War, entirely through investments in common stocks such as Coca-Cola and Gillette.

Swooping in to redress these wrongs, *The Motley Fool Investment Guide* was published in January of 1996 to some critical acclaim, went on to earn that *sine qua non* label 'best-seller', and continues to sell well several years later . . . in the United States. We checked our sales in Great Britain, and discovered we'd sold seventeen copies. That's as best we can tell – there's some question as to whether that seventeenth copy was in fact purchased or used as wrapping at Billingsgate fish market, but we'll leave that to the accountants.

Something – we repeat – *something* had to be done about this situation.

(That one was for you, Homer, and please be more understanding now, gentle Society.)

Enter David Berger. This British junior hospital doctor had been playing the voyeur for several months, peeping into our US website (http://www.fool.com) from his perch in the pastoral setting of North Devon. He grew gradually braver, to the point of contributing occasional scribblings to our communal effort. Indeed, his written stuff was sufficiently sassy that we felt we must meet the fellow. Without really even being able to afford it (we're an 'Internet startup company', after all, a phrase synonymous with 'unprofitable'), we flew David across the Atlantic Ocean to spend a week with us at Fool Global HQ. We discovered among other things that he was far funnier than we, and (as it turned out) more intelligent, and better-looking, too. (He had hair, for instance – hey, why do you think we wear the caps?) We also discovered, with his help, that the lack of education about money in the UK was at least on par with the situation in our own country, if not even a little bit worse (!) . . . and that a book speaking in plain and entertaining terms about the subject might be a valued contribution to the British literary scene.

In addition to those revelations, we spied further evidence that he could write, which mattered to us most of all. We then asked him to draw up a series of *Steps to Investing Foolishly* for a proposed UK Fool site. In typical Bergerish (his own language), Step Five began like this:

Editor's Note: Welcome to a short treatise on the importance of shares, which also happens to constitute the Fifth Step in the *Ten Steps to Investing Foolishly.* You can find the fornicating monkeys about halfway through, but we suggest you read the entire article slowly from the start to allow the suspense to build.

If that doesn't read like winning material to you, return this book to the shelf right now, as you are the proud possessor of better taste than will be on offer here. From our point of view, though, any writer capable of using fornicating monkeys to make an important point about shares was our chap.

Something therefore *has* been done about this situation.

You see, as funny as we once wanted to hope we were in our own country, we were clearly neither amusing, nor useful, nor interesting in even a superficial sense in the United Kingdom. Our answer is thus to tag along with the fellow sitting between us on the cover photo of this book, figuring that he might be.

In closing, all the blame for the appearance of this subversive text or its contents must fall on David's head (his e-mail address is FoolUKBook@ fool.com). Any spontaneous overflows of emotion, recollected in tranquillity, that tilt toward the 'praise' end of the spectrum are, however, still best addressed to TheGardners@fool.com. Bless you and thank you, Dear Reader.

How to Use This Book

Chaos often breeds life, when order breeds habit.
Henry Brooks Adams, *The Education of Henry Adams*, (1907)

Many people reading this book *will* like to start at the beginning and read all the way through and that's fine. It's even how we initially planned it would be. Others, though, will start at the end and read it backwards. Others still will skim back and forth through the text, eyes alighting here and there on a different spot of interest on each pass. Yet others will only read the one or two chapters which interest them and a few, a very few, will be so aghast at what they read in the first few pages that they will fling themselves in front of a bus in protest against the unfair practices of the financial professionals before they even get to any of the really juicy bits. While it doesn't really matter how you come at the book, we'd prefer you not to plump for the latter option as the liability implications make our jumpy American lawyer even jumpier.

Most of the chapters in the book can more or less stand on their own, although we do think they add up to a coherent story in which the total is greater than the mere sum of the parts. The way you tot up that total is down to you, but above all we hope your journey to understanding the basics of investment will be not only liberating, but fun. Please promise us, therefore, that as soon as you find yourself glazing over, and certainly as soon as you find yourself re-reading paragraphs in a desperate and increasingly frantic attempt to understand just what we're banging on about, that you'll take a break. Make a sandwich, listen to some music, hitchhike to the South of France, do anything as long as you're not breaking your head over something you don't understand. We don't actually think there's anything very complex in here – in fact, there is nothing in this book a twelve-year-old couldn't understand; in fact, we hope there *are* a few twelve-year-olds reading this – but eventually any brain which has dealt with a single subject for too long seizes up. When that happens to your brain, be kind to it and give it a rest. When you come back, things will seem much clearer.

How the Book is Structured

In the first section, we look at how and why you should invest for your future and how to go about it simply and Foolishly. Then we have a short interlude where we depart on a couple of tangents for light relief. The second section is more juicy stuff about investing in shares and the final section is devoted to the nitty-gritty of investing. It's also in this section where we dish the dirt on pensions, endowments and the like. We had to leave this until last, as the facts are so scandalous and horrifying that we couldn't bear to put them in earlier.

Finally, there's a glossary. Oh *yeah*, a *glossary*, you say. Well, don't! We went to a bit of trouble putting it together and we think it's a useful reference.

At the end are a number of useful appendices.

In fact, that's enough of an introduction. Now it's up to you to read this book and decide if it's any use or not.

Starting Out

I

Why You Should Invest

I am a Millionaire. That is my religion.
George Bernard Shaw, *Major Barbara*

Think about it: Monday matinées, Saga holidays to Scarborough, trips to the shops in a Mini Metro at 18 miles an hour. You're going to have to finance all these somehow. The money that you are earning today is going to have to pay for what you hope will be – and is increasingly likely to be – a long retirement. Whether it will be happy or not is down to you and will depend at least partly on whether you have to worry about where the next box of teabags is coming from.

That's one very important reason to think deeply about investment.

Maybe you're a bit ashamed about the other reason. Maybe you want to make some money, some *real* money, by investing. That's okay, you can admit that here and, yes, you've come to the right place. It is possible, genuinely possible for you, Arthur Smallridge of Chorlton-cum-Hardy, to take a portion of your regular income, invest it and watch it grow to monumental proportions. We've already seen how Anne Scheiber did it in the United States, but just the same is possible here. You don't have to know exactly what you'll do with the financial freedom you are going to buy for yourself in years to come, but our guess is that something will come to you. As we see it, money is like fuel. Most of us have to work fairly hard to bring in enough logs to feed the fire we need to keep us warm in our daily lives. And the curious thing is, the fire just seems to get hotter the more fuel you throw at it. One day, though, with a stockpile of enough logs to feed a reasonable-sized fire, perhaps you'll have the time to turn your creative attentions elsewhere. Jean-Jacques Rousseau, the Swiss philosopher, and incredibly enough one of the first people to point out in the eighteenth century that the Alps were in fact beautiful, had this to say of money:

Money in one's possession is the instrument of liberty.

Even today in Britain, with all the hoo-hah which surrounds the Lottery, many of us feel that setting our caps in pursuit of a large sum of money is at the very least a trifle vulgar and at worst obscene. Seeing money as opportunity, however, *we* don't subscribe to this view at all. Things have changed a lot in the last 50 years and the idea of a secure job for life isn't with us any more. Since we're all likely to change jobs and careers many times in our lives, we don't see anything wrong with earning yourself the opportunity to do what moves you. You might want to write the history of the Darlington marshalling yards, compose a masterpiece, devote your entrepreneurial skills and your fortune to working on behalf of others or maybe you'd just like to take the time to walk in the woods and hear, really hear, the wind rustling the leaves and the birds calling to each other in the upper branches. Whichever you choose, you're going to need the resources to sustain yourself while you do it.

By picking up this book, buying it and reading this far you are soaring ahead of most of your contemporaries, the majority of whom are already guaranteed to know less about investment than you do. Your future wealth is assured. So sit back, relax, make yourself another cup of tea and have a biccy – you've broken the back of it.

What Investing Means

Investment is something we do every day, consciously and unconsciously. We invest in our relationships, our jobs, our hobbies, and our lives. (We hope you've just invested £12.99 in this book and if you haven't, if you've stolen it, put it back this instant.) If we didn't invest in these things, we wouldn't get anything back, or at least nothing back of very much worth. And investment is all about 'getting back'. We invest something, whatever that may be, in the hope of a return over and above the original input. It seems so pathetically simple that you're probably wondering why we're going on about it at such length. What is interesting, however, is that while we put a lot of effort and time into, say, investing in our relationship with our partner – flowers, surprise weekends away, not screaming and stamping our feet when they smash Grandma Flo's prize fruit bowl – so often we put pitifully little thought or effort into investing for something as vital as our financial future. Oh yes, many of us are paying into some plan or other, sold us by some adviser or other, but *time, effort, interest, energy*? 'Fraid not. There are quite a few reasons for this and we'll look at some of them later on, but the purpose of this book is not to turn you into an investment geek, an anorak who is barely able to converse with their fellow human beings except in terms of earnings per share and cash flow analysis. No, instead we hope to awaken more than a spark of excitement in this thrilling and very Foolish business of investing. The business of managing your own money and guiding your financial ship towards its ultimate destination is as fulfilling as it can be simple and as enjoyable as it can be lucrative.

A Very Crafty Move and a Little Bit of History

Time was when you could expect to work all your life, retire at 65 and drop dead shortly after. The advantage of this system was that it meant there was no need for investment by the state to provide a wage for the country's pensioners. The number of people in work so far exceeded the number of OAPs that incoming taxes were more than able to cover the outgoings, a reasonable-ish pension was provided and everyone was happy. Pensioners marvelled at the enlightened, beneficent nature of the newborn welfare state, while looking back on a hard life, well lived. The welfare state paid up every week with a smile, while at the same time crossing its fingers and counting on the pensioners' imminent demise.

Now, though, the population is becoming less and less obliging and not only are people living longer and longer, they are retiring earlier and earlier. Whereas there were around 5 employees per pensioner in the 50s, there are likely to be closer to 2 per pensioner in the second decade of the next century. 'Not much dosh coming in to pay for all those pensions,' you whistle. Yes, but Mrs Thatcher was there before you. In 1981 or thereabouts.

In 1981 a crafty thing was done. We don't want to get into politics here, but whatever you think of the Lady Who Was Not For Turning, this was a crafty thing, a very crafty thing, to do. Up until 1981, the old age pension was linked to average earnings. This meant that as average earnings went up each year, so the pension increased by the same percentage amount, an arrangement which seems equitable enough. The only problem was that this was costing an awful lot of money, more money in fact than the government could afford. There was no investment fund out of which pensions were paid, a fund which was growing with time. Instead, pensions were paid – and are still paid – out of the National Insurance contributions of people in employment, and those in the know could see that one day soon it was all going to prove just a dash too expensive. The solution? Clearly it was impossible to simply cut pension payments – there would have been an outcry and this, you will remember, was a Britain still smarting from the deprivations of the 70s. No, there had to be a better way and it was this: instead of linking the pension to average earnings, link it to the Retail Price Index ('the rate of inflation' to the rest of us). This sounded all right in principle, but the fact is that the Retail Price Index appreciates on average at around 2 per cent less per year than average earnings. Effectively, this means that the state old age pension is now depreciating at 2 per cent per year in relation to average earnings. (If you don't think 2 per cent per year sounds like much, then wait until you have read the next chapter.) The result today is that the government is making a saving of between 8 and 9 thousand million pounds a year. This is great news for the Treasury, but at the time of writing, the single person's basic state pension is £3364.40 per year and the married one is £5376.80. Average earnings currently stand around the £20,000 mark. Taking the one as the percentage of the other, we end up with . . . not very much. By the next century the old age pension will stand at somewhere between 10 and 20 per cent of average earnings, or so the National Association of Pension Funds predicts.

Meanwhile, as the real value of the state pension declined, something else was happening to occupational pensions – fewer and fewer people were paying into them. There has been a decline of over 12 million from 1967 to 1991, by which time there were just 10.7 million people with an occupational pension scheme.

Something, then, had to be done about the future destitution of the nation's pensioners and, you will not be surprised to hear, the onus was put on to the individual to save for themselves. This took the form of savings incentives like the Personal Equity Plan, introduced in the mid-80s and the Personal Pension Plan, introduced shortly after. We won't go into detail here about just what these consist of – that comes later – but they are both tax-efficient means of saving which have had quite a degree of success. This success, however, has only really been among those who could afford to pay and that includes paying for the charges they carry. A report by the Association of British Insurers reveals that even people who pay personal pension contributions for 30 years can see a quarter of their final investment fund eaten up by charges.

Cough! Splutter! Gasp!

Please excuse us, tales of Wisdom always have this effect on us, but – pass the smelling salts, will you? – we are feeling better now.

This is loadsamoney and someone, somewhere, is laughing all the way to the proverbial bank. Just how hard they're laughing will be revealed later in the book.

It is fair to say – whatever pups the financial services industry has sold us to date – that governments now and in the future will have to continue to encourage personal saving in a big way, because pictures of pensioners in soup queues don't do much for the image of 'Cool Britannia'. All this, of course, is splendid news for investors.

A Foolish Investor

We hope that having read this far you realize not only how much of an investor you already are, but how much of an investor it is necessary to be in modern Britain. Some people reading this will already know a fair amount about the basics of personal finance, while others will not. Whichever is the case, most people who have a pension plan or investment plan of one sort or another do not think of themselves as 'Investors'. They just think of themselves as someone who has a pension plan or investment plan.

'So what, Fool?! You're nit-picking!'

Well, we beg to differ. If you consider yourself an Investor, rather than just simply someone who pays into a pension plan, this changes the mind-set, broadens the outlook and, crucially, it puts a level of responsibility on you to look after your investments. 'Looking after your investments' means ensuring maximum return with minimum cost in terms of charges and tax. By calling yourself an Investor, whichever investment vehicle you choose to use is simply that – a vehicle. Whereas in the other case, investments are potentially fragmented into a pension plan, PEP and a host of other things, each in its own encapsulated world. The Investor, or rather the Foolish Investor, is able to take an overview and to think in terms of Total Return. As long as an investment is pulling its weight in the Total Return scheme of things, then that's fine. If it isn't, then Out It Goes.

Total Return is (almost) all that matters. By 'Total Return' we talk here of the return after all taxes and charges of the sum of an individual's invest-ments. Very little else is relevant. Whether an investment is sold as a School Fees Plan or a Put Your Dog Through Obedience Training Plan or a Personal Pension Plan is irrelevant. Does it bring in the rate of return you expect, at a cost you are prepared to bear? It's very simple, but it involves being prepared to sweep through the suffocating layers of humbug which envelop much of what the financial services industry (hereinafter known as 'the Wise') is busy peddling to the British public. If you do this, you will soon find it simple to distinguish when you are more effectively contri-buting to the Send A Pension Fund Manager To The Bahamas Plan, than to the Retire At A Young Age And Breed Racing Pigeons/Collect Stamps/ Take Up Freefall Parachuting Plan (delete as appropriate). Sadly, many more people are contributing to the first plan than the latter types.

Think of yourself, then, as an Investor. Look,[1] you're a person, you have thoughts and ideas and opinions about all kinds of things. You can have them about investing too. Once you've been through this book (and perhaps visited one of our online areas), you will have the basic knowledge necessary to cut away the confusion and hype of so many of the invest-ment products being marketed in Britain today. We will even make a promise. Before you are halfway through this book you will know how to beat 90 per cent of the financial professionals (that's the Wise, again), with the expenditure of just a few minutes each year.

The world has never looked better for Foolish Investors. The stock markets of the Western world continue to provide the same kind of steady returns as they have done so faithfully for the last 70 years or more, standards of financial reporting and regulation have never been higher and

---

1 Look, we borrowed this habit of saying 'Look' from Tony Blair. It worked for him, didn't it?

the UK government is firmly committed to principles of tax-efficient investing for the reasons already outlined. Most importantly of all, perhaps, the Internet is in the process of bringing information and opportunity to the average citizen which was previously the province only of the professionals. Anyone who has ever kept hold of the remote control in the typical British family's Saturday night telly scrummage will testify to the fact that:

(S)he who controls the flow of information controls the flow of life itself.

Very shortly, it will be the common person who controls the flow of life and boy, are the Wise in for a nasty shock.

2

The Miracle of Compound Interest

Oh wonderful, wonderful, and most wonderful wonderful!
and yet again wonderful, and after that, out of all whooping!
William Shakespeare, *As You Like It*

Not all investment years are created equal. The strange thing is, that people who really ought to know this often don't. The *Financial Times* has a 'write in and ask the expert for advice' section in its weekend Money Supplement. In one edition in February 1998, the first question was asked by two parents concerned that their daughter, aged 30 and living in the USA, had no pension provision. They wanted to start her off with a gift of £6000 (what marvellous people!), but where should they invest it on her behalf? A reasonable question from two savvy and obviously loving parents. It is clear from the answer, however, that the expert in question had not the first appreciation of the Miracle of Compound Interest, for he started his answer by saying: 'The age of 30 is not very old, particularly if your daughter is getting valuable qualifications which could lead to high earnings as her career progresses. So, do not worry too much.'

Do not worry too much?! Do not worry too much?! Eeek! The age of 30 is definitely not very old, in life-years, but we're not talking life-years here, we're talking investment-years. You calculate dog-years by multiplying human-years by seven (although why Yorkshire terriers and Great Danes have the same exchange rate, we've never quite figured out), but invest-ment-years are altogether more complicated. To investment-years must be applied a complex formula, integrating expected lifespan with current age, shoe size and favourite 60s rock group into a fractal geometry based, chaos-driven equation. This is all then fried and served with a sprig of basil and a drizzle of olive oil on a bed of financial advisers. For lesser minds this can be summarized as signifying that, early on, investment years are worth a great deal more than they are later on. A huge amount more, in fact.

Welcome to the Miracle of Compounding! It is the bread, the water, the mead of the investor. It sustains and nurtures in times of famine and exalts in times of plenty. It is the carrot and the stick; it keeps us Playing the Game. Without a firm faith in this particular miracle, Fools are lost souls, doomed forever to bang at the oaken gates of Investment Plenitude, but never to pass those self-same, hallowed portals.

Let us turn back the clock, back to an era you may, or may not, prefer to forget. Already the focus is dissolving, the camera pans to the round window, a trill of gurgling music escorts us through and we burst into . . . into the past!

You are thirteen years old and sitting in Miss Doublebottom's classroom. It is late May, almost lunchtime and you are coming to the end of a double maths lesson. Through the open window wafts not only the gentle scent of spring flowers and the embracing warmth of an almost summer afternoon, but the lazy drone of a lawnmower and occasional disembodied snatches of the groundsmen's conversation. It all seems so peaceful and the soporific voice of Miss Doublebottom so comforting as she rambles on and on and on, that very soon . . . ZZZZZZZZZzzzzzzzzz . . .

And that, unfortunately, was your big mistake (and quite possibly also the mistake made by the *Financial Times* expert). In the 20 minutes between your falling asleep and the bell going for lunchtime, Miss Doublebottom dealt with and dismissed the crucial topic of compound interest. Oh, go on, why don't you? Why not blame Miss Doublebottom for it? You can if you want, but it was not entirely her fault. Perhaps she should have stressed it a little more. Perhaps she should have gone over it again, but the truth is that even teachers aren't all that clued up about personal finance and investment and, like the rest of us, they are just a teensy bit frightened of it. Now, this is understandable and the astonishing implications of compound interest are so far-reaching that it is not surprising she wished to gloss over the whole affair. In maths textbooks, interest in general is always looked at in terms of debt: *Johnny buys a motorbike and borrows X amount of money at Y rate of interest, to be repaid over Z years. How much must he repay in total? Answers to be given in the form of x* $\times 10^y$. We find questions of this sort are at once tedious and terrifying and it's only natural to want to shy away from the subject as much as possible.

Don't be too hard, then, on Miss Doublebottom. Instead, start to assume some Foolish responsibility – after all, it was you that fell asleep, wasn't it? And, by coincidence, that's just what you're doing: having reached the age of majority you are about to put right the ignorances of the past, a Foolish course of action indeed. You are going to embark on a voyage of mathematical discovery, one of wonderment and awe. You are poised to change the way you look at life and, quite possibly, you are about to become a party bore on the subject of compound interest.

Like everything in the world of Foolish investing, there is no magic to compound interest, merely a few basic principles which we shall derive as we progress. If you fell asleep in most of Miss Doublebottom's other lessons, too, don't worry, as the mathematical knowledge required for full participation in this compounding extravaganza is so minimal as to be derisory. In fact, there really isn't any, so sit back and enjoy the Foolish Laws of Compounding, with inspiration from Mr Hilaire Belloc. Yes, the *Cautionary Tales* of Hilaire Belloc were the moral guides of generations of British children. Who can not nod sagely at such instructional verses as: 'Sarah Byng, Who could not read and was tossed into a thorny hedge by a Bull', 'Charles Augustus Fortescue, Who always Did what was Right, and so accumulated an Immense Fortune' and 'Jim, Who ran away from his nurse and was Eaten by a Lion'. Now we shall hear some modern cautionary tales . . .

The First Foolish Law of Compounding, or *Ferdinand, Who Frittered Away His Twenties and Suffered Dreadful Agonies*

Fay, a Foolish young woman of 20, decides to save £100 per month from her secretarial salary. She puts this into an investment plan which gives her an average return of 14 per cent per year on her money. She does not give this another thought, but presses on contributing throughout her twenties, year in and year out, all the while living a life of independence, modest excitement and everyday pleasures. At the age of 30, she meets Ferdinand, a rake who has frittered away his twenties, but who nevertheless captures her heart. Shortly after meeting, the two decide to have children (whether they marry or not in this modern tale we do not know – that is left up to you, the reader, to decide). Fay decides to stop working and bring up the children (again, fearing accusations of prejudice, we would like to affirm that this is a decision she felt free and happy to make). With no income, she must now stop contributing to the investment plan, something she does with a heavy heart. Ferdinand, however, now takes his responsibilities seriously and starts to contribute £100 per month into a similar plan of his own, something he continues until the age of 60. The numbers look like this:

	Fay (£100 per month age 20–30)	Ferdinand (£100 per month age 30–60)
Age 20	0	0
Age 30	£26,453	0
Age 40	£98,069	£26,453
Age 50	£363,562	£124,522
Age 60	£1,347,806	£488,084

Ouch! Extraordinary, isn't it? Ferdie thought so too. By the age of 60, Fay is still almost three times ahead of Ferdinand, although she has not contributed anything for *thirty* years. Now, Ferdinand retires and they both let their nest eggs grow for the sake of their grandchildren. At the age of 100, Ferdinand is worth the staggering sum of £92,191,098, but Fay is still worth almost three times as much: £254,578,320. And all because she started a paltry ten years earlier, and yet she contributed only a third as much.

We were going to continue this model out for another few hundred years, but the numbers became too huge. There was an ear-splitting explosion and smoke started pouring from the Foolomatic supercomputer's overheated main processor. Seconds later, the ground outside Fool headquarters was littered with the groaning, writhing forms of baled-out Fools, begging for mercy from the God of Compounding.

Anyway, this sacrifice was not in vain and neither were Ferdinand's squandered twenties, for from them we derive the **First Foolish Law of Compounding**:

Start early, Fool!

The Second Foolish Law of Compounding, or *A Foolish Female Who Learnt Too Late about the Building Society and Was Burned to Death as a Result*

In this next Foolish example, we follow the fortunes of a Frippery of Foolish *Femmes*, five in all. They all, at the age of 20, agree on the importance of regular, long-term investment, but they disagree as to which type of investment is the best. Each opts for a different one, ranging in long-term return from a building society deposit account, to a volatile, yet lucrative, share-buying strategy. Some of the investments they choose carry hefty charges. For the sake of argument, the returns range as follows: 5, 8, 12, 15, 20 per cent per year. They each contribute £100 per month from the ages of 20 to 60 and the numbers look like this:

	Fennella 5%	Felicity 8%	Freda 12%	Faith 15%	Florence 20%
Ground Zero	0	0	0	0	0
5 Years	£6,962	£7,603	£8,538	£9,304	£10,716
10 Years	£15,848	£18,775	£23,585	£28,019	£37,381
15 Years	£27,189	£35,189	£50,104	£65,661	£103,731
20 Years	£41,663	£59,308	£96,838	£141,372	£268,831
30 Years	£83,713	£146,815	£324,351	£599,948	£1,701,909
40 Years	£152,208	£335,737	£1,030,971	£2,455,145	£10,575,155

What interests us most here is the last line. Look how the return increases at each stage. Now, these women are only 60 and have only been contributing £100 per month, yet some of them have managed to accrue seriously alarming amounts of cash. What has made some of their piles double or treble the size of their nearest neighbours is a paltry difference in return of a few per cent.

This leads us, inescapably, inexorably and ineluctably to **The Second Foolish Law of Compounding**:

Small differences in investment return matter. A lot.

They matter far, far more than the uninitiated could possibly think. Two to three per cent simply does not sound like it could matter very much, but it does. It matters so much it hurts. It matters so much that Fools have been known to cut off vital body organs in anguish at the investment return they have lost through heavy investment charges. That's how much it matters.

And while we're on the subject, the Second Foolish Law of Compounding also allows us to conclude that the British government of 1981 was familiar with the ins and outs of compound interest (well, you'd hope they would be – they are the government, after all). Two per cent per year relative lack of increase in the state pension doesn't sound like much, but as we can now see, over time it most surely adds up. That's why the Treasury now saves £9,000 million per year and pensioners are unable to heat their houses. This shows at the same time just how painful and how lucrative a mere 2 per cent can be.

You will be wondering when we get round to the 'Burned to Death' bit. It's only natural and, go on, be honest, that's what's kept you reading this far, isn't it? Aye, 'tis a sad tale, that's for certain and it concerns 'Fennella Five-per-cent'. Labouring under the sad misapprehension that the building society was the place to save her hard-earned cash, poor old Fennella

---

The Rule of 72

Now consider the Rule, dear Fool. Consider it a labour-saving, convenience aid to modern living. If the Fool is the food processor of investing, then the Rule of 72 is the natty little attachment which grinds the coffee beans. The Rule of 72 lets you estimate with a fair degree of accuracy how long it will take your lump sum investment to double at a given rate of interest, and it couldn't be simpler. Divide 72 by the rate of interest and you have approximately the number of years of doubling of your investment:

$$72 \, / \, x\% = \text{years to doubling}$$

Like any rule of thumb this one has its limitations and in this case, it is increasingly inaccurate once you get much above 15%, but actually even then it's pretty good. Frankly, if your investments are regularly above 15%, the minor errors here are irrelevant anyway.

Here's an example:

£10,000 invested at 11.4% will take 72/11.4 years to double = 6.3 years

---

entered retirement ill prepared for what was to come. She found herself with little more to live on than – *frisson* of horror! – the **state old age pension**! Unable to pay her electricity bills, she was forced to live in a single room, huddled up to a one-bar electric fire. One cold day she fell asleep, slipped forward and *whoof*! Within minutes there was nothing left but the charred remnants of a flowery housecoat, some pink, fluffy slippers and the uneasy, cordite-like tang of burnt human flesh.

And that, Dear Fool, is what happens to those who put their faith in the building society.

The Third Foolish Law of Compounding, or *Ffyona*, Who Squandered Her Inheritance and Came to Grief

---

Now, one final example. Let's take our Foolish gels again, debs one and all, and add another, Ffyona. At the age of 20 each of them has come into £50,000 from an aged great aunt. They are still a sensible crew and each of them decides to invest all the money in their chosen investment vehicle, choosing to continue with their jobs and live off the small salaries they provide. All that is, except Ffyona, who has decided she is going to live what used to be called, so quaintly the 'High Life'. Within six months, yes, you've guessed it, there is nothing left. With no money and now no job, poor old Ffyona finds herself a Fallen Woman, earning her living in a way Too Terrible for the ears of Young Children. For the rest of our Foolish friends, however, the future looks like this:

	Fennella 5%	Felicity 8%	Freda 12%	Faith 15%	Florence 20%
Ground Zero	£50,000	£50,000	£50,000	£50,000	£50,000
5 Years	£63,814	£73,466	£88,117	£100,568	£124,416
10 Years	£81,445	£107,946	£155,292	£202,278	£309,587
15 Years	£103,946	£158,608	£273,678	£406,853	£770,351
20 Years	£132,665	£233,048	£482,315	£818,327	£1,916,880
30 Years	£216,097	£503,133	£1,497,996	£3,310,589	£11,868,816
40 Years	£352,000	£1,086,226	£4,652,549	£13,393,177	£73,488,578

Look at the last line again. Ooooh, doesn't it make your eyes water? From this last table we progress naturally and seamlessly to **The Third Foolish Law of Compounding**:

Don't squander your inheritance on sex, drugs and rock 'n roll. (Unless you want to, that is.)

The Fourth and Fifth Foolish Laws of Compounding, or Two Davids and a Tom Skimp on the Numbers, but Are Saved by the Benevolence of a Foolish Public

Lavish numbers and spreadsheet Foolery were the order of the day for the first three Foolish Laws of Compounding, but now it may seem as if there's precious little to support the final two. A swizzle, says you! Quite possibly, says we, but we hope you will see that the essence of these final two Foolish Laws is encapsulated within the previous three and that by now you will have us down for an honest bunch of fellows. Here, then, without further ado, are our two final Foolish Laws of Compounding, every bit as vital as their predecessors, even if a little shorter on the padding:

The Fourth Foolish Law of Compounding

Over time, regular saving of quite small amounts can build up to an astonishing sum of money.

The Fifth Foolish Law of Compounding

Time and patience are the friends of compounding and, therefore, of investing.

Coming Soon to a Fridge near YOU!

We hope that with the Foolish Laws of Compounding rattling around in your head, you are starting to settle into the mindset of Foolish investing. Maybe you are starting to dream, to realize that you do not need a huge sum of money to begin profitably investing for the future. In short, you're limbering up for what is to come. The key, though, to successful investing is regular saving and keeping your investment objectives in mind. It can be tough to maintain that sort of resolve over a long period, but to aid you in your Foolish quest, you will see that on the next two pages we have duplicated the Laws of Compounding in a super-deluxe, easily digestible form and we've also thrown in the Rule of 72 as a free gift. For no extra charge you can cut out the right-hand copy along the dotted line and stick it up somewhere visible, somewhere where its elegant simplicity and timeless beauty will be a lasting complement to your home. Why not the fridge door? From now on, every time you reach for a pint of milk or the liquefying remains of last Thursday's quiche, the Miracle of Compound

Interest will enfold your grey cells with a most gentle and wondrous awe, inspiring you to new heights of saving and investing.

In fact, with this constant reminder of the power of compounding to change your life, we're confident that you will be a millionaire within twenty years of reading this book. And if you're not? Then feel free to sue us.

If you can find us, that is.

The Motley Fool UK's Laws of Compound Interest

The First Foolish Law of Compounding
Start early, Fool!

The Second Foolish Law of Compounding
Small differences in investment return matter. A lot.

The Third Foolish Law of Compounding
Don't squander your inheritance on sex, drugs and rock 'n roll. (Unless you want to, that is.)

The Fourth Foolish Law of Compounding
Over time, regular saving of quite small amounts can build up an astonishing sum of money.

The Fifth Foolish Law of Compounding
Time and patience are the friends of compounding and, therefore, of investing.

The Rule of 72
72 / x% = years to doubling

The Motley Fool UK's Laws of Compound Interest

The First Foolish Law of Compounding
Start early, Fool!

The Second Foolish Law of Compounding
Small differences in investment return matter. A lot.

The Third Foolish Law of Compounding
Don't squander your inheritance on sex, drugs and rock 'n roll. (Unless you want to, that is.)

The Fourth Foolish Law of Compounding
Over time, regular saving of quite small amounts can build up an astonishing sum of money.

The Fifth Foolish Law of Compounding
Time and patience are the friends of compounding and, therefore, of investing.

The Rule of 72
72 / x% = years to doubling

3

All That Glitters Is Not Gold

It is not that pearls fetch a high price because men
have dived for them; but on the contrary men dive for
them because they fetch a high price.
Richard Whateley, *Introductory Lectures on Political Economy*

We're moving on, slowly but Foolishly. In the introduction we learnt what
the Motley Fool was all about and whence it sprung. In Chapter 1 we
learnt why we need to be an investor and in Chapter 2 we were thrilled and
awestruck by the Miracle of Compound Interest. Now, we're raring to go
and, er, invest.

But in what? If you're like most people, you'll have already flicked through
the Table of Contents and a few of the later chapters and have figured out
that the Fool loves shares. No, it doesn't just love shares, it eats them, it
breathes them, it savours them, it caresses their smooth, yielding . . .

Okay! Okay! That's enough! (Sorry about this, Dear Readers, but
some of us get a little carried away at times. Normal service will now be
resumed.)

No, shares aren't the only possible investments in this wonderful world
of markets and market makers and we'd like to take just a little time
now to examine some of the other investment options facing us, before
devoting the rest of this book to shares. Down, boys, down!

Invest in Yourself

Why not? You are your best potential money-making asset. Take the time
and the money to invest in yourself. New skills or a new outlook could well
propel you into a newer, more highly paying job and one which is more
rewarding. If you are running your own business, then investment in that,
an enterprise whose value and potential you are uniquely placed to assess,
could be your best move. Don't neglect yourself or your talents – it won't
pay off in the long run. Of course, if you don't have any talents or
you don't think you have much scope to increase your money-making
potential, then don't throw good money after bad. Concentrate instead on
saving as much as you reasonably can and developing your sense and
knowledge of Foolishness as far as you reasonably want to take it. Looked

at in that way, your purchase of this book is one of the best investments in yourself you've ever made. Now, who says you don't have any talents?

And Invest In Your Family, Too

We talked in Chapter 1 about investing in yourself and your family on a personal level and we stand by our assertion that it ain't no good being a Fool if all you're going to be is a lonely Fool. So, take the time out to stroke your spouse / partner / kids / dog / rabbit / motorbike and we'll meet you back here in a few minutes . . .

> *Tum tee tum tee tum tum . . .*
> *One banana, two banana, three banana, four . . .*

Welcome back. It's time to explore the world of non-equity investment,[1] and oh what a chequered world it is!

Britain's Favourite Investment

Is it the chance to watch Dale Winton, Bob Monkhouse or Anthea Turner on the telly on Saturday night? Is it the desire to contribute to the Good Causes? Or is it the opportunity to dally with Fate and perhaps, just perhaps find ourselves the grinning subjects of a *News of the World* spread: 'I'll still be going into work on Monday, honest. It won't change nuffink!' Sadly for the egos of Dale, Bob, Anthea and the Lottery Good Causes, we play the National Lottery because we want to win. No matter that the chances against are fourteen million to one, it could, it just could be us.

Ever made acquaintance with Schrödinger's cat? This unfortunate feline has spent the last 60 years since his invention in a sealed box. Inside with him is one bowl containing cat food and one containing poison. Until we open the box and see which one the moggy has chosen to eat, we cannot know whether the cat is alive or dead. It exists in an indeterminate, multi-potential state, neither dead nor alive. Herr Schrödinger invented his cat to illustrate some fairly way-out concepts in quantum mechanics, but he could just as well have been talking about the Lottery. Until the balls start to roll out on Saturday night, each of us who has bought a ticket is neither a winner nor a loser. And it's a thrill!

It's also an investment, just not a very good one. At odds of fourteen

---

1 A share means the same as an equity which means the same as a stock. We'll talk about what exactly all this represents later in the book.

million to one against winning (and frankly who cares about anything else?), this is not smart money. Granted, the stake is only a pound, but we'd be fools (note the small 'f') indeed to dream too long or hard of what we'll do with the cash when we win. No, if you just want a delicious shiver at the other-worldly possibility that you may win, then play – there aren't many thrills you can get for a pound these days. But if things have gotten out of hand and you spend the second half of every Saturday night punching holes in doors with the soggy remnants of a Lottery ticket protruding from a contorted, foam-spattered mouth, then maybe you need to think again and almost certainly you need to get out a little more often for some fresh air.

History's Favourite Investment

In the last section a poor feline explained, with reference to quantum mechanical theory, why we play the Lottery. In this section, we will be looking at the philosophy of value. Heavy stuff, hey? But don't worry, this isn't going to be too intense. We're just going to wonder why we value one of our oldest commodities as highly as we do. Or did. For gold, store of value since before the Phoenicians were plying the Mediterranean and mincing through the Hanging Gardens, is looking a little tarnished these days.

Since the beginning of recorded history, gold has been the 'gold standard' of value (you see – it's so enshrined in our language that it is now totally synonymous with value). As a mediaeval merchant, you would have taken gold coins with you on your travels. Gold was the only universal currency and was prized for its beauty, malleability and, above all, its quality of remaining untarnished down the years. None of this would have meant much, of course, if the stuff hadn't been scarce as well, but with all these qualities gold was set to be the US dollar – the 'greenback' – of its age, universally convertible and universally valued. Unlike the greenback it's not so easily forged, but that didn't stop a lot of people trying, including our own Sir Isaac Newton who incidentally spent far more time on alchemy than he ever did on classical physics. Tsk, tsk, Sir Isaac.

Today, though, everyone seems to be losing faith in gold. The gold price has fallen from $850 per ounce in 1980 to around $300 today and some of the world's central banks, the national banks of each country, are starting to sell some of their huge gold stores. They reason that they can hold US government bonds (Treasury Bills) instead and earn interest on them.

Amazingly, the banks can earn interest on gold bullion too – by lending it out – but it's only about 1 per cent per year. As long as the gold price has been falling, it has paid speculators to borrow gold, sell it for dollars and invest those dollars in Treasury Bills. Then, when it came time to give back the gold, they were able to buy the required amount at a cheaper price than they had sold it, making a profit on the deal in that way too. The low rate of interest they received wasn't too much of a bother for the banks as they didn't have to pay the cost of storing and guarding it. Neat, hey? As long as the gold price keeps falling, that is ... As of 1997, though, even the Australians, one of the world's gold-producing nations, had had enough of this horse trading and sold a large proportion of their gold reserves. The Swiss, too, in mid-1998 are proposing selling off half their gold reserves. This kind of trading based solely on price speculation obviously worries them. It worries us too.

There we have it then. We say:

1. If the world's central banks want to put their faith in them good ol' boys in the US government rather than an off-yellow metal of indeterminate value, then we'd be fools to argue.
2. If you're after a store of value when the nuclear winter finally draws in, invest one third in tinned food, one third in petrol and the final third in guns to protect the first two thirds with. If things are that desperate, Mad Max probably won't be interested in your gold.
3. No gold bars for these Fools.

The Gee-gees

Got a tip for the 2.30 at Newmarket? No? Oh well, never mind. Like the Lottery, this business is too uncertain for Fools interested in the business of wealth accumulation. It can be fun though and if you're looking for an excuse to wear a dickie bow or a silly hat, this could be your answer.

The Building Society

How many times have we heard it? 'Put your money in the building society – that'll keep it safe.' It's not true and, as we'll see shortly, the Bible of the Long-distance Investor (see Chapter 4) shows us why. Long-term building society returns just about match the long-term rate of inflation after you've taken tax into account. This means that creaming the interest off and using it to buy a new frock occasionally actually shrinks your money. Putting your money in a building society deposit account is marginally better than putting it under your mattress, but that's about it.

Other than for shortish periods when you need somewhere accessible to put your money, building society accounts are most unFoolish places to stash the cash. Avoid!

The Bank

Just as for the building society, you ain't going nowhere but standing still by keeping your long-term money in a common-or-garden bank deposit account. In fact, for short-term rates of return with your money easily accessible, a High Street bank would be doing well if it beat some of the supermarket banks now springing up.

National Savings Certificates

'I'm from the government, I'm here to help you.' Remember that one? It usually comes along with 'The cheque is in the post' and 'Bend over, this won't hurt a bit'. The strange thing about this one, though, is that when we're talking about National Savings Certificates, it's true. The British government, bless its cotton socks, sells a range of savings certificates, many of them tax-free, which are totally safe and reasonably good value. Strangely, you can buy these things through your local post office: 'Good morning, Mrs Wiggins, and how are Deirdre and the baby? Oh, how lovely! That'll be a book of second-class stamps and £100 worth of the 13th issue index-linked savings certificates, please. Ta very much. See you next week.'

Simple as that. If you have a granny who, in the parlance of 1990s investing Britain, is totally 'risk-averse' and keeps all her money in the bank or building society, then tell her this:

- She can buy these government investments in the post office and can put between £100 and £10,000 into them.
- They are currently growing at the rate of inflation plus 2¼ per cent.
- They are tax-free.
- At the end of five years she'll get her original money back, plus a sum to account for the effect of inflation, plus all that interest at the rate of inflation plus 2¼ per cent.
- If she sells in the first year, she won't get any interest, but after that she will.
- If she tries washing out the teapot, she may find her tea no longer tastes of five-day old haddock. (Only add this last if you are on exceedingly good terms with your granny and can truly bear her tea no longer.)

Index-linked gilts work in much the same way as the index-linked savings certificates referred to above, although many have much longer terms than five years. There is still no Capital Gains Tax to pay on the profits, but the price of gilts does fluctuate and if you want to cash them in before their time is up, you may lose money.

One thing, though. Please don't think that the unfair and stereotypical portrayal of the nation's grannies which we have used in describing government savings vehicles means that they are suitable only for female nonagenarians. No, they can be useful for any old Fool who needs a pot of medium-term cash. As we shall see later on, you must consider stock market investments to be locked away and unavailable for a minimum of four to five years. Money needed within this time should be stored elsewhere and this isn't such a bad place at all.

For the detailed gen on index-linked savings certificates and gilts, talk to the very helpful people (for they are) at National Savings on 0645 645000. If you're super sweet, they'll even send you a leaflet all about them. Alternatively, stop by the website, http://www.open.gov.uk/natsav, which is rather well laid out.

TESSAs

TESSA stands for Tax Exempt Special Savings Account and since they are due to be abolished in 1999 we won't spend too much time talking about them. They're a form of tax-free savings account and they're Not Very Exciting. You were able to put £9000 into a TESSA over five years and get a reasonable-ish rate of interest (around 7.5 per cent), with no tax to pay if the money stayed in for the full 5 term.

Our opinion is that if you can lock up your money for five years, then there are much more exciting places to put it. Can you guess where we might suggest? If not, smack yourself on the bottom for not paying attention, go back to the beginning of this chapter and start again.

Well, honestly.

Corporate Bonds

As we'll see later on, if you buy shares in a company – and here we'll use Swallow and Honk PLC (yard of ale manufacturers, as certified by the Campaign for Real Ale) as an example – then you effectively become a part owner. If one day the market for yards of ale dries up (say, if the world's rugby players were eliminated at a stroke by a mystery virus) and the company goes bust, then you as a part owner will be one of the last people to see any money back. Everybody the company owes money to will get paid off first and then, if there's any money left from selling off the remaining stock cheap to nurseries and convents, you might get a look in.

It's called capitalism – you staked your money directly in the enterprise, it might have paid you back handsomely, but it hasn't and that's just too bad. Not all companies are as risky an investment as Swallow and Honk, of course, but some are.

Being the owner of a corporate bond, on the other hand, puts you in a different relationship to the company whose bond you own. What you have actually done is to lend the company a sum of money to use as they will. They agree to pay you the money back at a specified date in the future, plus a yearly amount of interest, say, 8 per cent. Bonds have different safety ratings, but mostly they are pretty safe. If you wait until the bond's term is up before cashing it in, you will get your money back in full, but if you try to sell it on in the mean time, its value will vary with the prevailing yields on bonds and the time remaining to the redemption date. In the highly unlikely event of the multinational company whose bond you have bought going under, then you, as one of the company's creditors, will have call on the remaining assets long before the unfortunate company's shareholders.

Nothing comes for free, of course, and you have to pay for this almost absolute assurance of safety with far lower long-term returns on bonds than on shares. That said, corporate bonds are another Foolish store for medium-term money.

Property

Property as an investment? Well, yes. It's a special case, complicated by the irksome need imposed by the British climate for Fools to keep a roof over their heads. We'll talk about this in much more detail in Chapter 21 ('How to Buy Your Own Home, But Do it Foolishly').

So There We Are Then

So there we are then. (Is there an echo in here?) We've had a skirt through the major non-share investment vehicles. Some are no more than a bit of a flutter, others provide real, safe long- and medium-term returns and in some circumstances are even Foolish. We'll be looking at just where index-linked gilts and savings certificates, deposit accounts, corporate bonds and bricks and mortar fit into the *grande projet de folie* later in this *magnum opus*, this only investment guide you'll ever need, this mother of all self-help manuals, this curry-monster's finance extrava— (That is most definitely enough! Ed.) In the next chapter, however, we will be enthusing about shares, the only class of investments which has Fools leaping out of bed in the morning, crying: 'To arms!'

4

The Bible of the Long-distance Investor

Steady boys, steady;
We'll fight and we'll conquer again and again.
David Garrick, 'Heart of Oak'

Welcome to this, the fourth chapter. It may not sound like much to you, but to us it means a great deal, for this fourth chapter isn't just any old fourth chapter. It's more thrilling than *The Compleat Taxidermist* Chapter 4 'Dealing with the Entrails', it's a dimension beyond *A Guide to Icelandic Nightlife* Chapter 4 'Thorvald Sigmundsson's Friday Night Country Music Hoedown' and it has more surprises than *Banking* Chapter 4 'The Cheque Book'. Chapter 4 in the *Motley Fool UK Investment Guide* is the reason we are here and it reveals the truth about shares. It is the heart of our humble book and we can't help but get rather excited about it.

In fact, cut to:

> *A jester being driven along crowd-lined streets in an open-topped limo, waving happily. Fools thronging the route cheer and shout. Belled caps are thrown in the air. Some Fools, overcome by emotion, begin to hyperventilate and require calming by the St John's Ambulance Brigade. Others start to go lobster red as they fail to protect themselves from the sun's burning rays, while here and there along the roadside, a child expires in delight from an overdose of vanilla ice cream and '99' flakes. It is the kind of picture we are more used to seeing when a victorious task force returns from trouncing another, usually smaller, nation.*

All right, all right, all this frivolous stuff can get tedious. We realize that. From now on, it'll be straight down the line, deadly serious stuff on investing. Honest. But we really *do* like shares.

What Many People Think about Shares

Stocks and shares. Equities. The stock market. The Footsie. Wall Street. The Dow-Jones. It sounds impressive, but what does it all mean? What image does it conjure up? For many people who are not familiar with investing in shares (and some who are), it probably looks a little like this:

A skyscraper in the City of London with mirrored windows. Black Jaguars swishing back and forth. An immaculate receptionist with razor-red nails and shoulder pads jutting out as far as the Essex end of the District Line. Somewhere in the depths of the building, men in shirt sleeves (stripy ones) and red braces screaming into telephones and tearing out tufts of hair by the handful as they peer intently into television screens: 'BUY!!! SELL!!! Is that Tokyo? Get me Higginbotham, dammit! I'll flay him within an inch of his life!' With year-end bonuses of hundreds of thousands of pounds, the Wise never, ever leave their desks at Arrow, Gant and Lowd (motto: 'Profit or Die!') before ten at night. When they do get home to their trophy houses and spouses, they crack open the champagne as they celebrate another evil day in the service of Mammon, before spending the rest of the night torturing small, furry animals on a shrine specially dedicated for the purpose (in the children's nursery – snare 'em young). Sometimes they don't go home at all, but sprout hair on the backs of their hands, fangs in the corners of their mouths and patrol the streets of London in search of the blood of young virgins.

If this is the concept you have of investing in shares, and it would not be entirely unreasonable if you did, then odds-on you probably don't think it is something in which you should be dabbling. 'Best leave it to the experts', you've probably told yourself for so many years.

But investing in shares does not have to be like that. It is possible, for Fools, to make a great deal of money in shares without needing to perform regular human sacrifices. Not even when the value of your investments goes for a Burton, as it will do occasionally. Let's examine some of the evidence, and pretty stunning evidence it is, too.

The Bible of the Long-distance Investor – the *Barclays Capital Equity-Gilt Study*

The most thrilling read in Britain today is not to be found on the shelves of any bookshop, it's not in most libraries and it's not even on the Internet. Possibly there are some out there who have never heard of the *Barclays Capital Equity-Gilt Study*, but they should not fret, for this is a good thing and means they still have the joy of that discovery ahead of them. This 90-page booklet is not a snip at £100, but the information it contains within its pages is priceless. Published every year since 1956, this study looks at the returns of British shares against gilts and cash since 1918. Getting interested yet?

You would be forgiven for thinking we had temporarily taken leave of our senses. There *is* nothing interesting in the movement of share prices over the last 80-odd years. OK then, punks, tell us that after you've rolled your eyeballs across this graph:

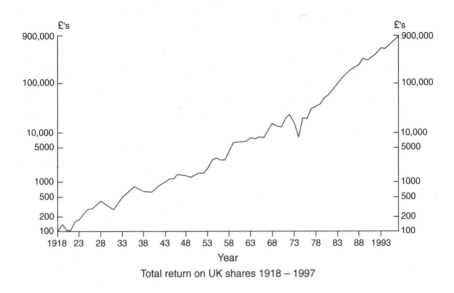

Total return on UK shares 1918 – 1997

Source: Barclays Capital Equity Gilt Study

This graph shows the total return of shares on the London Stock Exchange from 1918 to 1997. Look at it again and notice four things.

1. The scale of returns is logarithmically compressed. If it were not, we wouldn't be able to fit it on the page.
2. Notice the direction it goes.
3. Notice that it doesn't proceed in a straight line of perfectly algebraic proportions.
4. Notice *once again* the direction it goes.

You know[1], if the financial media and commentators would simply apply this basic 1-to-4 approach to thinking about the stock market, the world would be a much better place. Some of the most experienced financial journalists do their readers a constant, ongoing disservice by causing them to focus on the short term. Talk about losing the forest for the trees. This is what we refer to as 'the journalistic approach to the financial markets'.

The *Equity Gilt Study* tells us that shares have, on average, returned 12.2 per cent since 1919, and that is including the Great Crash of 1929. Gilts, which you will remember are government bonds, have returned 6.1 per cent over the same period, and cash in a deposit account, just 5.4 per cent. From

---

1 Tony Blair says this a lot, too.

1945 to 1994, property returned 8.5 per cent. At the same time, inflation has been 4.1 per cent on average from 1919–97 and 6.2 per cent from 1946–97.

All roads lead back to compound interest. If we had had a solvent ancestor with sufficient foresight and compassion to invest for his grand-children back in 1919 and he had decided to invest £100 in the various available options, how would he have fared? The table below reveals all:

	Dec 1918	Dec 1997	Dec 1997 Real terms
Cash	£100	£6,521	£324
Gilts	£100	£10,652	£528
Equities	£100	£884,714	£43,891

Source: BC E–G study
(NB Real terms = taking into account the effect of inflation)

There is no competition. If only great-grandfather had had a spare thousand or two back in 1919, we can hear you sighing, but let's flip back to reality: no-one in 1919 had a thousand pounds to spare. The First World War had just finished, millions were dying in the flu epidemic, the outside privy was standard in much of Britain and the principles of Foolish investing were still several generations distant. It's no good wishing: we're going to have to create our wealth for ourselves, but the example of history gives us strength for the future.

People – misguided people – often say that a building society account or gilts are safer than putting your money in shares. Long term, very long term, we've just seen that that isn't so. But what about in the shorter term? You won't be surprised to hear that it isn't so there, either. Back to the Good Book . . .

Taking all the four-year periods since 1918 (1918–22, 1919–23, 1920–24, you get the picture), equities have outperformed cash in 82 per cent of them. For gilts, the number is 84 per cent. For consecutive ten-year periods, the numbers rise to 97 per cent and 96 per cent, respectively. In other words, since 1918, money in equities has stood a greater than 80 per cent chance of outperforming cash and gilts over *any* four-year period and a better than 95 per cent chance of outperforming them over *any* ten-year period. Commenting on these figures, Michael Hughes, Chief Economist at Barclays Capital, had this to say: 'The greatest risk for most investors would therefore be to have too much money in cash.'

Later on, when talking about investment planning and the types of holdings to have in an investment account, he says:

> *It is clear that* equities have higher real returns than gilts over *all holding periods* and for holding periods up to ten years, also carry higher risk.

However, for longer holding periods, equities have lower risk character-istics than gilts. *For the long-term investor therefore, equities are a safer bet.*

The italics are ours and probably not necessary, but we tossed them in any-way. The evidence, the incontrovertible evidence, is that the stock market *per se* is not a risky place to put your money. And yet, ask most people in Britain whether their cash is 'safer' in a bank deposit account or the stock market and you'll almost be able to see visions of the sort we described earlier (werewolves, virgins, power-dressing secretaries) flashing through their minds. These'll be followed by the instinctual memory of the 1929 Crash and investment bankers falling from skyscrapers like tiles off a roof in a high wind and then they'll come out with the supposedly 'obvious' answer: 'A bank deposit account – what do you think I am? Stupid, or something?'

Why is this? Well, take a look at the first line of an article entitled 'A quick guide to market basics' in the Weekend Money section of the *Financial Times* of the weekend April 11–12th 1998: 'The stock market is a dangerous place and small investors may be confused.' If no less a body than the *Financial Times* is telling you the stock market is a dangerous and confusing place, you'd have to be a fool to argue, wouldn't you? Nope, you'd have to be a Fool. Oh, there's danger a-plenty in the stock market alright, if you're going to approach it in a reckless and impulsive manner, but the same goes for the M25 on a Friday night. The thing is that the media, that self-same media which is unable to follow the simple 1-to-4 approach, doesn't find the true story behind the stock market newsworthy. What the financial media wants you to think about is fear and change and specifically what happens NEXT (and 'next' here refers to any time period up to six weeks). What happens NEXT is what sells newspapers, but the unfortunate result is that many adults are turned off the thought of investing in the stock market because it is *so* risky and *so* volatile and *so* treacherous that they feel they couldn't ever keep up with it.

Look back at the stock market graph. There are groups of several years where it zags more than it zigs. If it zags for deep enough and long enough, (1973–4 springs to mind) then that is called a 'bear' market. Those who sell out during these times, losing large amounts and swearing off the market forever, in most cases deserve what they get. If they're going to take that sort of approach, they're fools, not Fools. Anyone who invests in the stock market with an ultra-short-term time-horizon – less than five and definitely less than three years – is spinning a roulette wheel. Which brings us to a point we want to be extremely clear about:

We have no idea where the market is heading over the next three years. Neither does anyone else. DO NOT LISTEN TO ANYONE ON TV, ON RADIO, OR IN THE PAPERS WHO PRESUMES TO BE ABLE TO FORETELL THE SHORT-TERM MARKET DIRECTION. THIS

PERSON IS MOST LIKELY AN IDIOT. If you're convinced otherwise, research all his or her previous market predictions. Compare those to the actual moves in the market and you will discover we're right. If you discover we're wrong, immediately e-mail us at FoolUKBook@fool.com. We'll probably try to hire this oracle (or if they're female, marry them off to Tom G.), even though we will almost certainly have lost out to a large City firm first.

Interestingly, even if this person were fairly consistently right about the market's short-term direction, it wouldn't be a good move for you to follow along. To play the short-term game involves jumping in and out of a lot of shares. The amount you'd pay in commissions, stamp duty and, potentially, Capital Gains Tax as you jumped hither and thither could well leave you with fewer profits (and more headaches) than just buying and holding good companies.

And that's not all. The degree of volatility, the fluctuations of the market itself, can actually increase our investing profits. The more volatile the market happens to be, the more a regular saver can earn from that volatility through a mathematical quirk known as pound-cost averaging. It's neat, it's tidy, it's very, very Foolish and we'll talk about it again in Chapter 7 'A Tale of Two Professions', in which we learn how to buy into the market as a whole, follow its ebbs and flows and beat 90 per cent of the professionals over time. For many, this type of investment – an index tracker, which aims to 'track' the market's growth over time – will be the beginning and end of your investment career. Nothing further is necessary to ensure a life-time of Foolish and profitable investment.

Some of you, though, want to beat the average, beat the index trackers, beat that zig-zagging line and we think we know some ways to do just that. In fact, we take it as a personal challenge to beat the market average, because we believe it can be done by people like you and us who *don't* get to sit down with the Chief Executives of the companies we invest in.

But let's close with a question, one which is often asked. How far can it go? When will it stop? Is 'growth' eternal? Will the market continue to rise on and on and on, until the ultimate cessation of the human race?

Good question. Please let us know if you have a definitive answer to this. For ourselves, we have a few thoughts on the subject, but which ultimately lead to no firm conclusion, except that we keep coming back and throwing our money into the market.

Over the long term, the market reflects the growth of business. (Over the short term the market moves for an assortment of other, usually far less consequential, reasons.) So, the first question is, will business *always* grow? Now, obviously it doesn't always grow, because there are bad years and good years, but what this question means is could there ever be a pro-longed period – say, as long as a human lifetime – in which business and thus the stock market fails to grow, or even shrinks?

Well, what sustains business? A large number of factors, primarily things like population growth, environmental conditions and government stability (and, since we're out-and-out capitalists, we'll also add here lack of excessive government interference). Increasingly, advances in science and technology which are changing the way we live are also fuelling the growth of business. The question now becomes, do you at present perceive conditions which would lead to 70 years of stagnation or decline?

It is very easy to *create* scenarios in which that would happen, but most of those scenarios involve catastrophic events (nuclear war, asteroid impact, alien invasion, lethal airborne flesh-eating viruses – or all four at once). We put it to you that in each of these situations, the investment returns of your portfolio would be the *least* of your worries. Each of these situations could bring about the end of civilization.

Thus, our own best guess is that as long as our civilisation is still around, you will continue to see long-term growth in business and in the world's stock markets.

5

You Have More than You Think

Now is not the time to misuse money.
Advertising slogan for an Indian insurance company painted
on a rock on the mountain road to Darjeeling, 1993.

Now, we're ready to invest. No holds barred, we are *serious*. Stand back, the City of London, this is Darren Normal-Bloke of Scrimthorpe and he's coming through.

But what, Darren, have you got going for you? Who are you, anyway? And where *is* Scrimthorpe?

Brain

This may come as a surprise to you, but you're pretty well stacked in the grey matter department. You've picked this book off the shelf, after all. Somewhere in the depths of your psyche, filed in the 'Dread Department' between cancer, AIDS, a comet striking the Earth and Mrs Tucker, your moustachioed form teacher when you were in Class 1A, is the topic of your financial future. Most people have elected to shut out what they perceive as a far distant era and the financial demands which may be made on them when the cash flow has dwindled to zero. Yet you, Fool, have identified the questions of how you're going to pay the electricity bill and/or the grand-kids' bail money in 2028 as issues of not a little importance and have elected to educate yourself. This is the act of a supremely rational human being.

'All men by nature desire knowledge', wrote Aristotle. How remarkable it is, though, that we can elect to cast our essential nature aside when it comes to something as basic as money. This stuff is important. We do not live in a barter economy. Trading half a dozen leeks for a knitted woolly hat is not an option outside of a couple of communes in the west of Wales and even the British winter can be distressingly chilly without suitable headgear, as we all know. We need money and we use money and we think about money many times a day. Why do we allow a steel curtain of despair and panic to drop down (*clang!*) every time we need to think rationally about it? Fear. Gut-wrenching fear. It's only human to want to shut out the unpleasant, but the consequences can be disastrous.

You, reading this, with your Mark 1 Foolish brain, are now going to do a simple sum:

$22 - 14 = ?$

Now, let's see . . .

This little piggy went to market, this little piggy . . . No, that's not it.

One banana, two banana, three banana, four . . . Nope, not that either.

If you have 22 Motley Fools in a row and you take one away and you do that 14 times, that leaves you with . . .

13?

No.

10?

Warmer.

8?

Now you're talking! Move over, Stephen Hawking, we have a Brain here. Yes, 8 is the answer we've been grappling for. Eight is the amount left when you take 14 away from 22. For want of the ability to perform this simple calculation (or else wilful and shameful ignorance), large swathes of the British population have cast themselves into bondage, the bondage of irredeemable debt.

Twenty-two is the number of per cent you may pay back every year on the running total of your credit card debt. This is already far more than you pay on your house (around 8 per cent at the moment) or on a personal loan (say, 12–14 per cent). The average investments in the stock market have made 14 per cent every year over the last ten or so years. Now remember that shares are the highest returning of all investments and then muse that people who are carrying credit card debt who nevertheless decide to invest in the stock market are effectively borrowing at 22 per cent to invest at 14 per cent.

We'll come back to credit card debt later, but you don't have to be the winner of Mastermind to realize that the credit card companies have hit on a great money-making scheme. We'll call it the Mushroom Plan because it involves keeping the herd in the dark and feeding them . . . well, you know what mushrooms get fed. The thing about the Mushroom Plan, though, is that it relies on the herd staying in the dark because they like it there and it's warm and it's cosy and it smells right good!

Yes, Darren, you have a brain and you're using it. But most people don't when it comes to anything financial. Let's take a look at a couple more examples. Do you have friends who are invested in PEPs? Ask them (politely and with a look of humble, yet eager interest) to explain exactly what a PEP is and how it works. Chances are they won't have the foggiest. What about acquaintances who have bought shares on the basis of what they heard down the pub, or read in the newspapers? Do they really have the faintest idea how these businesses work or what the companies' products are? We bet they don't.

There is a short-circuit here somewhere – it's the only explanation – and it enters the loop the moment the words 'Finance' or 'Investment' are uttered. No sooner has your average normal person started to utter the word 'Fin— ' or 'Inv— ', than he finds himself saying, 'Ah yes, sounds reasonable. I'll take two of those. Ten thousand, was it? Oh, twelve? Yes, that's fine. Thank you, good day.'

It's incredible. How much effort would you put into buying a washing machine or a camcorder? Would you really just plonk the money down and run? No, of course you wouldn't. You'd compare prices and lists of features and haggle with the salesman and not emerge happy until you had knocked £35 off a £400 consumer durable and the salesman was sobbing into the phone that, no, Marjorie, there'll be no food for the children this week because all the commission has been eaten up by a tungsten-hearted punter, may he die happy with his miserable Zanussi and may all his teeth fall out before he's 50. Even then you'd still be convinced he'd ripped you off, but at least honour would have been satisfied. What about that self-same honour when it comes to your investments? Instead of a measly few hundred pounds of instantly *depreciating*, enamelled white junk, we are talking here of thousands of pounds dedicated to your future which are designed to *appreciate!* Phew.

The thing is, we've made up our minds that our investments aren't something we are capable of being involved with. We think they're boring, or too complicated, or too much of a gamble and as a result we try not to think too much about them. It's an awe-inspiring prospect. *Moi?* Making decisions on investment? *Mais non*, Sire! Many people with these kinds of feelings turn to the financial advisers we've already talked about, people who work in an industry in which their bread and butter depends on fostering a climate of uncertainty and despair and replacing it with a fug of comforting, 'Come to Daddy' warmth. Part of growing up is learning that mum and dad don't always have all the answers and so it is here.

We will hear in Chapter 6 ('Be Your Own Financial Adviser') how some of the professionals who advise us operate and this question should always be in our minds: 'How do *you* make money?' Once we've asked that, we should then move on to the follow-up: 'How do you make *more* money than that?' Most of us have a sense of fair play which does not object to people earning a living if they do a good job on our behalf, but the scales are so stacked in the direction of the financial professional, that it is only natural to be uneasy at the business relationship involved.

If nothing else, walk away from these Foolish pages with the simple understanding that:

- Financial advisers working on commission earn their daily bread by selling you endowments, PEPs, Personal Pension Plans and Free-Standing AVCs and they make more money by selling you the investment plan which pays them the highest kickback.

- Stockbrokers earn commission every time a share is bought or sold on your account and then make more money by trading on your behalf more often.
- Unit trusts take a portion of the funds you give them to manage and then make more money by attracting as many other people's money as possible.

'Nothing astonishes men more than common sense and plain dealing', wrote Ralph Waldo Emerson. Employ this common sense, this quality so integral to the survival of the human race, and astonish yourself as you reflect on how each of the ways that the entities listed above make *more* money is ultimately detrimental to the punter's interests. (That's YOU!)

We will talk later and in more detail about financial advisers and stockbrokers and the conflict of interest is obvious. Briefly, though, let's talk about advisory and discretionary stockbrokers. If you have an advisory or discretionary stockbroking account, this means that you have deposited a sum of money with a stockbroking company and entrusted them with the task of rendering you wealthy. Their aim and your aim, of course, is for them to buy good investments on your behalf. But while simply buying and holding good investments may make money for you, it won't make money for them. The incentive to trade and trade and trade again, earning healthy commissions each time, is hard to resist. Further, this frenetic activity is likely to make the customer think that this is a horribly complicated business which only a *stockbroker* could understand and aren't I lucky to have such a nice man working on my behalf? *Au contraire!*

Unit trusts spend the 5 per cent or so you give them upfront to promote themselves and invite more people to the party, thus giving them more money to manage. It's a bit like one of those backpacker's guide books. No sooner have they written about João DaSilva and his family who run the nicest little guest house on the beach in Goa where three months' stay costs 50p, including three delicious meals and free use of João's motor-scooter, than the place is overrun by hordes of hippie wannabees and the party is spoiled for ever. To put that in financial terms, the more money a unit trust has to invest, the less nimble it becomes; the clumsier it is, the less likely it is to outperform the stock market.

The easiest way to understand things is to ask very simple questions, very slowly and then wait for the answers. Unfortunately, many of us feel afraid to do so, because we worry we may look stupid. In reality, we only look stupid when we try and hide behind presumed knowledge. By contrast, thinking we ought to be able to understand these things, even though we've never really given them much of our attention before – now that *is* stupid!

To return to our theme: we have more than we think. We have the power of reason, our mundane, everyday common sense, and the capability to bring it to bear on what may seem at first to be an intimidatingly complex subject. Reason's simplest tool is the asking of questions, something many financial professionals don't want you to do.

Finally, the very act of sitting down to read this book already demonstrates you have taken the decision to move from servitude to freedom. The heart of Foolishness is a fundamental belief in rationalism, in the idea that we can and should bring our powers of reason to bear on financial matters. In fact, the application of reason is the only way to succeed with finances and your employment of your reasoning faculties will mark you out from the majority of other people in the marketplace. If you're not using your brain, you're using something else: someone else's advice, the daily horoscope, or just plain luck. Don't let yourself down. Instead, use your most powerful asset and the cheapest aid to investing yet invented: your brain.

Time

You also have more of this than you think. Even if you don't think you have very much of it, you have more than you think.

In this context 'Time' means a couple of things. Firstly, it means the seconds and minutes and hours we cobble together into the daily hullabaloo we call life. We can squander these through precipitate action, or we can husband them and cherish them and use them – Aha, you think we're going to say 'wisely', don't you? – Foolishly. Use time to your advantage. Do not, ever, agree to anything immediately, particularly if it's an investment which someone else wants you to buy. Stall, stammer, feign an epileptic fit if you must, but don't get bullied into signing anything the first time around. This also goes for people who are allegedly on your side, like your financial adviser. Ultimately every financial adviser is a salesman. Every salesman knows that if you put a client skilfully enough into a position of pressure, the temptation is to simply agree to get out of an uncomfortable situation. This is a dangerous thing to do. Use time to your advantage by deferring any decision and researching it and any possible alternatives. If you do that, you may find yourself calling your financial adviser back and saying: 'Felicity, I see the unit trust PEP you want me to buy has a 5 per cent initial charge and has significantly underperformed the market average over the last five years. Now tell me why I should buy it.'

It's funny. If you've scanned the cover of this book, you'll have figured out that two of the authors are American and one British. It was Winston Churchill who referred to us as 'two nations separated by a common language' and we can attest that it is true. Only, the difference isn't just in language, it's in approach and style as well. Here in Britain, we nurture a reticence, a desire not to rock the boat and above all not to create a scene, which seems, at least to the British author's eyes, to be lacking across the water. Cultural stereotypes are a dangerous thing to bandy about in the 90s, but what we're trying to say here is that this kind of challenging approach seems to us far less natural for a British person than an American. A British friend of one of us, a doctor, was on the verge of being sold a clutch of high-commission products by a financial adviser. Following some discussions of the type you have read here, she returned to the adviser fully armed with a series of questions concerning the performance of these investments as compared to the stock market index, their flexibility, alternatives at lower cost, etc. Unfortunately, she was not able to get past the adviser's secretary. On hearing the kind of thing our newly Foolish doctor was going to be asking, she rolled her eyes and said, 'Oh, he's going to love talking to you. I'll get him to phone you with an appointment.' And that was it. She never heard from him again. The point is that this kind of approach was not something she felt comfortable with and she had to steel herself to do it. When she finally got over that hurdle, her attitude cut through the layers of obfuscation and blather like a knife through warm butter. It is so important to train yourself to take a hard-headed and firm line. Practise polite but emphatic refusal and delaying tactics in front of the mirror. This is your future you're dealing with, after all.

There are also other ways to use time when you decide to start out investing on your own, as we hope you will by the time you have finished this book. At all costs, do not rush headlong into the stock market, convinced you are going to make a killing. That kind of attitude leads to large stakes in aggressive shares and big gambles. It is far more likely that *you* will be killed, lose a significant amount of money and be turned off investing forever, with sad consequences for your financial future.

Instead, practise. Just practise. Create a paper portfolio which you go on to track, leaving your stack of crisp fivers safe and sound in the bottom drawer of the freezer (you didn't know we knew, did you?). Follow the ups and downs of the shares you would have invested in. Rejoice as they plummet and groan as they rocket skywards – it's the exact opposite of what you'd be doing if you'd staked real money in them and it's all the more useful for that. Do it for a year if you like, or longer. This may sound like it contravenes the First Foolish Law of Compounding ('Start early, Fool!'), but it doesn't. Compound interest is your friend and it's an especially good friend if you hug it to your bosom early enough, but compound depreciation can have as devastating an effect on your investments as compound interest a miraculous one. So, start early on the Foolish investing ladder and don't squander time with unFoolish investments. Use that time instead to set up the habits for a lifetime of savvy investing. You have years and years to invest – don't spoil it all right at the beginning.

The other obvious thing 'Time' means is the years (hopefully) you have left before the band starts to play and St Peter's asking if you'll be taking the full board or demi-pension option. We touched on this in Chapter 2, where we saw the effect of time and compound interest demonstrated before our very eyes. It was inspiring, was it not? Salt away your stash, make a regular contribution to it and turn up in 30 years to collect the abundant proceeds. But time alone isn't enough – you need to combine it with patience. And faith.

Over the years, the stock market produces a reliable return, but there are times, such as in 1973–74 when it loses ground, a lot of ground. If you lose faith at times like this, you will scupper all the hard work and patient effort you have put into your investments thus far. In fact, market downturns can be to your advantage if you're a long-distance investor and we'll be looking at how this can be a little later. One person who had patience was Anne Scheiber who we mentioned in the introduction. This was the humble New Yorker whose $5000 investment in shares on the New York stock exchange in 1944 grew, by the time of her death in 1995, to $22 million. She left all her money to Yeshiva University, also in New York, and the resulting media splash was the only reason we ever heard about her. Through good times and bad, Ms Scheiber plugged away, all the while her investments growing at a steady 18.3 per cent per annum, far above the average of 11 per cent per annum for the US stock market as a whole during that period. Some years, the value of her portfolio doubled. Others, it halved. No matter, she pressed on. What was running through her mind as she left the Wall Street professionals gasping in the far distance behind her? We will never know, but we can speculate that she spent many of those years bathed in a quiet satisfaction. The reasons for her ascent to such heights were that she had patience a-plenty, she bought common, well-known shares, she held onto them and held onto them and she had faith in her approach. If anyone knew the value of time, it was Anne Scheiber.

Someone else who talks about faith is Peter Lynch, the former American mutual fund manager who has written two best-selling books on investing in common stocks. (You'll find them listed in Appendix) Among many other things, he talks about developing and nurturing an image of the 'Big Picture'. An appreciation of the Big Picture is what stops you selling all your shares when things may, superficially, look to be heading down with little or no prospect of coming up again. At times like this, the media latches on to a heaven-sent story – 'SHARES MELTDOWN! MARKET COLLAPSE! STOCK MARKET SELL-OFF!' – and things start to look very black indeed. Peter says that he would have sold his stocks 39 times out of the last 40 market downturns ('Corrections', they're called) and been sorry. We're not sure we really believe him, but he has used his humility to make an eloquent point.

The fact is, as we saw in the graph of UK share performance in Chapter 4 (and will see in the US graph later in Chapter 17), that the majority of downturns are followed relatively rapidly by an upturn. Downturns didn't worry Anne Scheiber, and they don't worry Peter Lynch. Back to the Big Picture. So, things aren't going well and the Big Picture is that the world is in crisis. Economic disaster is looming, the oil is going to run out and a comet may strike the Earth, annihilating half the population. The mood is bad, bad, bad. You feel terrible and pessimistic and hopeless along with everyone else. This really *is* it. This is 1929 all over again. Oh me, oh my . . .

Now, whip out the Even Bigger Picture. This is the one you have sitting in your greased Foolomatic Even Bigger Picture Dispenser™, attached to the belt on your waist and available for a mere £49.99 from our online areas (P+P included). You've been nurturing and building up your Even Bigger Picture during the good times for just such an occasion as this. This is the one that says the Western World will still be here in the morning; that the comet may miss and if it does you've wasted a great buying opportunity; that your average person isn't as lazy as he's portrayed and does want to go out and do a good job of work; that as some companies wane, other good ones will spring up to take their place; that over the last 79 years shares have returned 12.2 per cent annually, far outstripping all other investments. Peter Lynch identifies the cultural memory of the 1929 Crash as being the major factor in scaring people born many years later away from investing in the stock market. If that is the case, then people today continue to lose out as a result and it has been far more costly than the simple financial cost of the sell-off all those years ago.

So, time, patience and faith. They all go together and they are all indispensable to the successful investor.

What about the 75-year-olds reading this? All this talk of time means this can't be a party they're invited to, surely? No, we think the points we're making apply to everyone. These days, you probably *do* have more time left than you think. Even if you don't, you will likely be looking to pass your invested pile on to your descendants in your bid to obtain Most Favoured Ancestor status. Of course, if you really want to leave them a worthwhile legacy, you will not only be investing Foolishly on your and their behalf, but encouraging them to learn about the subject for themselves. As we see it, if you get up in the morning and, despite careful scrutiny of the obituaries column fail to find your name, you are set for another day of Foolish investment.

Other People

As with our brain power and the time we have, so we often overlook the value of other people to us.

Sadly, not all people are valuable to us all the time. When your flatmate throws out your 20 year (*twenty year!*) collection of *Motor Sport* magazine, because he thought those were the recycling boxes, he loses value to you pretty quickly. (I've been waiting over ten years to make this confession in a national medium. Sorry, Kirk. D.B.) Or how about when your toddler pours Ribena into your computer keyboard? Or you discover years later that your financial adviser has sold you one of the worst performing, highest-charging pensions there is? Sometimes it's enough to make you want to declare the Republic of MacFool on a rocky Hebridean outcrop and repel all invaders with clods of peat and solidified porridge.

But don't do it.

Turn the tables. *Learn* from other people. Learn from older brother Arthur's venture into Venezuelan coffee futures. Profit from Aunt Edith's experience with the cowboy plumbers (£800 for an hour's work on a blocked pipe at a weekend – it got a full page spread in the *Sun*). Reflect on the poor financial planning of your friend Ted ('Lend us 50 quid till the weather breaks'), who was born with hands curiously unable to keep hold of coins and banknotes, especially when approaching a Turf Accountant. If you lecture them from a tone of high financial rectitude, you'll get the come-uppance you deserve, but try showing them some of the numbers from this book.

There will be other people in your life who you can turn to for positive lessons in how to look after money and make it grow. Perhaps another friend has negotiated a cheap mortgage deal or you have an uncle who has always been a sound investor. Take him out to dinner, pump him for information – it's an investment which may repay itself many times over. (It may not, but you'll have healed the rift in the family dating back to when your dad pushed him down the stairs for pinching his tricycle.)

You can't make use of any of this huge repository of financial experience, though, unless you and they are prepared to talk about the subject. It's strange how in our age when just about anything else is fair game for general conversation, money and investment is still a taboo topic. Loosen up and try and get your immediate circle to do so too. The professionals are out there to profit from our ignorance and the best weapon we have is ourselves and our pooled experience. Let's use it.

If you like, we'll help you. Start a dining club of half-a-dozen friends or so who meet once a month to discuss money and investment strategies. Put on jester caps, call yourselves the Motley Fool UK Dining Club (Hartlepool Chapter) – we're always on the lookout for licensing deals – and let the Foolishness flood out.

You might want to go even further and start an actual investment club. These are groups of friends, neighbours, business partners and a sprinkling of very smart gerbils, who invest a pooled sum of money in shares and track their performance over time, buying and selling according to the conclusions of the regular group meetings. Some clubs seriously out-perform the professionals and many investment club members actually find the club's investments outperform the ones they hold on their own. It's something to do with the centring effect of a group of Foolish people discussing investment, or the effect of rhubarb crumble and custard on the decision-making centres of the hypothalamus – scientific opinion remains divided. Whatever the explanation, it's a real effect and an organisation called ProShare, whose aim is to promote share ownership in Britain, has a sheaf of information on the subject. Details of how to contact them are in our Foolish Glossary under 'Investment Club'.

We admit that what we have written so far in this section could have been sponsored by BT in its ongoing effort to urge us all to contact our friends and family more often. (It wasn't, but it is a thought for the future.) The universe of investing knowledge does not end, though, with friends and family. There are other people out there who have something useful to say and some of them are people who write books on investing. Naturally, we think you've bought the most important book on investing already, but you'll find some other favourite books of ours in Appendix 4 ('Publications You Should Like'), and among them you'll find the names Slater, Fisher, Buffett and Lynch. Some investing books are ridiculously complicated and some are numbingly boring, but we think the ones we have listed are indispensable to the Foolish investor. Not only that, but they're a good read. Adventure? There's plenty of that in the stock market. Disgrace? It's there too. Humour? Yup. Scandal? Absolutely. Success? Yes, some of that winkles its way in as well.

Finally, we would not be Fools if we left this section without mentioning our online world. Without it, the Motley Fool could never have had such a popular success in the United States and it would not have been featured prominently one day in the *New York Herald Tribune*. Without that kind of global coverage, it would never have come to anyone's attention in Britain and the plot to bring Foolery back to its birthplace would never have been hatched. Without that plot, this book would have wandered the ether of unconceived ideas for all eternity, patiently waiting for a patron who was never to come. So, even though you may never have been online, 'Online' is the very reason you're reading these words.

It's people who have made the Motley Fool and who continue to make it what it is. Out there, on the Web, on AOL, is a community of people who are interested in the same subject as you are: how to increase their savings and have an enjoyable time doing it. Only, this isn't one or two people getting together for a chat occasionally, this is tens of thousands of people, all with specialist knowledge of one sort or another, stopping by regularly and helping each other out with advice and suggestions. Any mistake you're about to make, someone else will have made before you and will be prepared to give you the benefit of their experience. It's a community like no other. If you like what we've been saying here, then come and visit – it could be the most profitable and enjoyable free thing you've ever done.

That you're prepared to mention in public, anyway.

Money

We reckon that the people reading this book are perfectly capable of deducing that if they give up smoking 40 cigarettes a day they'll have plenty of money left over for investment, or that if they cycle instead of taking the bus the pennies saved will soon add up. Mrs Thatcher told poor people not to go shopping when they were hungry and obviously thought she was dispensing pearls, but the fact is we all have to figure out for ourselves where we can make economies in our lives. Most of us, if we look hard enough, will have some cash-draining activity or other we could happily live without and may even be the better for it.

A lot of this money thing is down to priorities. Investment isn't such a priority for most of us, because it's not something we *want* to do. It's something we *have* to do, something we feel compelled to do. As long as investing isn't fun, as long as it remains a remote, incomprehensible business, then figuring out how to save more money to put away isn't going to be high on the List of Enjoyable Things to Do This Month. Simply having a little knowledge about the basics of investing, though, and knowing the awesome might of compound interest can alter the whole way you look at investment and make it a lot more real.

We all need targets of some sort and quite a good one to start with is to aim to save 10 per cent of your income. This may be way too much or way too little for your personal circumstances. It doesn't matter – it's just a tool. Take a look at your finances, ask yourself if you're saving 10 per cent of what you make and if you aren't, look at the reasons. It might be illuminating.

We've promised not to present you with a series of money-saving ideas here, but we are going to mention just one. Consider very carefully whether you want to spend fistfuls of cash on a new car. A friend of one of us bought a new MG sports car with borrowed money. Within a year it had depreciated to just over half its initial value and she was now carrying more in debt than the car was even worth. Spending large amounts – and, worse, borrowing large amounts – on a new car is one of the surest ways to savings penury for the majority of us who don't have unlimited incomes. These things are expensive! There are some out there whose life aim since the age of twelve has been a Ferrari sports car with leather seats and the acceleration of a Saturn V rocket. That's fine, but to the rest of you, we say: take a critical look at what you're paying for your wheels and you may find you want to spend some of that money more fruitfully elsewhere.

6

Be Your Own Financial Adviser

Never give a sucker an even break.
W. C. Fields

'Wait a minute!' you're saying, 'this is getting out of hand. You people – Fools, you call yourselves – are making some pretty outrageous claims here and you tell me there are more to come. I'd like to hear what the professionals have to say about you upstarts.'

Look, this is fine with us, it really is. In fact, the urge to seek independent, impartial advice could hardly be considered anything but Foolish. Entering the world of investment is an intimidating step. It is intimidating because, firstly, the Wise like to make it so. There is seemingly a large amount of information to be digested, jargon to be deciphered and swish brochures with impressive-looking graphs to be waded through. The Wise like it this way because it gives them the drop on the punter. (That's you.) Secondly, it is intimidating because it quite obviously is, dummy! Look, you're taking on the sole responsibility for investing for your and your family's future. You are effectively saying that you will invest your available funds more effectively than a highly trained professional. By your own efforts your retirement will be spent either living on bread and jam in the one room you can afford to heat, or snapping your fingers at the waiters in the Grand Hotel in Cannes. Scary stuff, indeed.

By reading this far, though, you have proved yourself to have some Foolish mettle. You're not the run-of-the mill punter, you like to ask questions and are prepared to engage with life. You'll take on responsibility, but are also aware that by doing so you may reap benefits and satisfaction far higher than if you hand over this most important aspect of your life to someone else. Watch out, you're turning into a Fool!

Now, where are you, a Fool, going to go for impartial, independent advice? Good question. There are two types of financial adviser: Tied financial advisers, and those who style themselves 'independent'. Tied financial advisers are employed by a particular company and can only sell you the financial products – pensions, endowments, PEPs, unit trusts – of that company. They may work on a salaried or a commission basis, but they cannot be independent or impartial. When your bank phones you up to ask if you'd like to see one of their advisers, this is probably the type of person they want you to see. They are salespeople, whose brief is to sell you a product they think you need. Avoid them as if your life depended on it. Which in a way, it does.

The second type are the independent financial advisers, or IFAs. Independent by name, independent by nature? Not necessarily. IFAs work for themselves or as part of a larger corporation. They all have had to take and pass financial planning exams and their activities are now far more regulated than ever they were. However, there is one small fly in the ointment: your hopes and aspirations and theirs do not absolutely, 100 per cent coincide. As long as this is the case, it is hard to see how you can both move in the same direction. You wish to invest for your future in as profitable a way as possible, while remaining as flexible as possible and incurring the smallest costs possible. They, on the other hand, have to make a living. They also have to make sure they don't 'mis-advise' you, which means they are likely to keep more or less within the boundaries of financial wisdom and conservative investment planning.

Let's take a look at how they make a living, first of all. Mostly, they pay their household bills through regular remittances from you. When you buy an investment product from them, a portion – sometimes a very, very significant portion – of the payments you make over the first couple of years and beyond will go into the pocket of the IFA. As we shall see later, there are significant differences between the sizes of commissions which the various types of investments pay IFAs, and it is a fact that those charging the highest commissions of all perform the worst. We'll see in the very next chapter that 90 per cent of managed unit trusts – pooled investments in shares – *underperform* the average and since they carry far higher charges than those which simply mimic the average, known as index trackers, they are far more likely to be recommended by IFAs. With IFAs only being human and us being suspicious Fools, we suspect that there is just a teensy conflict of interest here.

Stop the book! Fade the focus! We're going on a fantasy journey . . .

You're an IFA. A client, Mr Alan Average, sits in front of you. You lean back, feet resting on your imitation mahogany desk with leather writing pad and muse that two types of investment might be suitable for him, both in your opinion equally appropriate. One pays pitiful commission, the other a hefty whack over the first two years, followed by a healthy trailing commission over the next twenty. They're both as good as each other, you think, so I'll sting him with the heavy commission, you think. He won't be disadvantaged and I have to make a living. Is this so wrong? Well, is it?!

Change the scene slightly. The hefty commission-paying investment isn't quite as good as the other one, but you've got the Child Support Agency on your tail for maintenance payments for your children, Doris and Edna. Also, Edna wants a pony in the way only a twelve-year-old can and Doris wants to go on the school ski trip this winter. Which are you going to choose now, given that you're only a human being?

It's obvious that the potential conflict of interest is very great indeed. If you then consider the incentive a commission-based IFA has to sell you an investment in which you are financially penalized for leaving early (thus keeping you in and paying commission), the plot thickens.

Some IFAs do work on an upfront, hourly-fee basis, while others will undertake to rebate a percentage of the commission they receive from any company whose investment they sell you. Some of these people will even recommend the index trackers we have just talked about. There *are* good IFAs about and engaging one at an hourly rate is far more likely to avoid any conflict of interest. If you phone this number – 01179 769 444 – provided by *Money Management* magazine, you'll get the contact details for three fee-based IFAs practising in your area.

Unfortunately, even fee-based IFAs suffer from the paradoxical disadvantage of being accountable. If they give you misleading advice, or sell you a totally inappropriate product, you have redress. You can go to the Personal Investment Authority (PIA) and complain and will likely get a satisfactory result. Isn't Britain an enlightened place, compared with, say, Chechnya or Sierra Leone? How can this be a disadvantage? Well, it can. For the majority who wish to place their trust entirely in another's hands, it is obviously crucial that the people in whom they place that trust are highly regulated. The effect, however, on those who are being watched over, is to make them conservative and conformist, prepared to choose between the stale clutch of products on offer by the Wise, but not prepared to step outside those narrow confines into a wider world. By offering the control of your finances to someone whose horizons are already limited, you are closing down the spectrum of your investment universe before you've even started. More, these people are slick-talking, charming, convincing and compelling. They have to be – their survival depends on it. Don't expect to convince them of your point of view either. It's as hopeless as Galileo trying to convince the Pope that the sun didn't go round the Earth and can attract just as violent a response. As a Fool, you are accountable to no-one but yourself. That sets you apart from the teeming masses, giving you independence of action and an invaluable edge. Take advantage of it.

While we will make the point once more that there *are* good independent financial advisers out there, we'd like to propose a name change for the group as a whole. You see, 'adviser' somehow implies impartiality, and what we've seen is that the nature of the commissions business means that it is extremely hard for them to be that. For the rest of this book, we will refer to them as Independent Financial Advisers (salespeople) or IFAs (salespeople). We don't mean to cause any offence, but since that's clearly what they are, let's call a spade a spade.

So, if you wish, seek independent, impartial advice and do your utmost to verify that it really is. Do so, however, in the awareness that the only person who truly shares your aims, hopes and aspirations is yourself. By reading this book and devoting just a small amount of time to learning about Foolish investment, you are setting the scene for a lifetime of fulfilment, Folly and wealth. In short, get educated, get Foolish and be your *own* financial adviser!

7

A Tale of Two Professions and Basic Foolish Investment

All professions are conspiracies against the laity.
George Bernard Shaw, *The Doctor's Dilemma*

Tales of Amateurism

In the last century and early years of this century, there was a strong tradition of amateurism in Britain. It was generally reckoned that being a professional was somehow underhand, that it was a trifle vulgar and that there was really nothing a professional could do which an amateur couldn't do better and with more aplomb. Sometimes this was true. The early Everest mountaineers thought training was for cissies and that smoking cigarettes was a cure for the altitude sickness caused by the lack of oxygen at great heights. In 1924 Mallory and Irvine puffed their way to the stupendous height of 28,000 feet and were last seen going strong for the summit. Maybe they reached it. Nobody knows for certain, because they never returned and it wasn't for another 30 years that Everest was finally climbed with the help of bottled oxygen, a stunning testament to the stamina and endeavour of these amateurs. (It wasn't climbed without oxygen for almost another *sixty* years.)

In the nineteenth century, many of the greatest linguistic works were compiled by amateurs. One of the major contributors to the forerunner of the *Oxford English Dictionary* was a Dr W. C. Minor, an inmate at Broadmoor with a persecution complex and a conviction for murder. When you look up a word in the *OED* today, you may well be reading an entry penned by an insane, Victorian murderer.

So, don't knock amateurs because they can sometimes turn in surprising performances.

Let's see how amateurs fare against a couple of professions in the late twentieth century – the heart surgeon and the investment fund manager. How well can the 'know-nothing' hope to perform against these two groups of professionals, each of whose jobs is highly skilled and requires years of training? The answers may surprise you.

A Tale of Two Professions

The Heart Surgeon

You gasp at *Your Life in Their Hands*. You're a *Casualty* and *ER* groupie. You've been studying these programmes for a long time now, you've picked up the terminology and you're starting to say to yourself that it really doesn't look that difficult. Thoughts like this are starting to arise more and more frequently in your mind: 'I've got a 'C' in biology O-level. I could do that.'

Come up close and we'll let you into a secret – it isn't that difficult and you don't even have to be very good looking or drive a red sports car. Heart surgery is a hobby you can develop in your own garage, at your own pace. If it takes off – and there's no reason why it shouldn't – you could find yourself with a part-time job which is more lucrative than selling water filters door to door and so much more satisfying. Interested? We think you should be. Here, let's show you how to get started.

First, clear out the accumulated junk of lifetimes from the back of your garage and take it down to the car boot sale. The proceeds from the sale of jam jars full of nuts and bolts with Imperial threads and Great Aunt Doris's collection of Victorian thimbles will fund the next stage of your self-improvement programme. Next, scrub down the inside of your garage with a hard bristled broom and a bottle of Domestos. (We consider the importance of antisepsis in surgical procedures to have been overplayed, so this is not strictly necessary, but the smell does impress future customers, er, sorry, 'patients'.) Next, cover over the inspection pit with some planks, borrow your neighbour's Black and Decker Workmate and place it end to end on the planks with your own. The operating theatre and operating table are now ready for use. Some Fellows of the Amateur Cardiothoracic Society of the Royal College of Surgeons (FACSRCS) do advocate sound-proofing the garage to mask the screams of ungrateful clients, but we have found Radio 1 played at full volume works just as well and is much cheaper.

Now you are ready for a trip to the DIY Superstore. Load the kids in the car, leave the dog in the garden and off you go. You're looking for a pair of garden shears (go for a good make, as these do tend to work loose other-wise), a large cool box (the purpose of which will become clear), a length of garden hose (five metres should do it) and a pair of bellows (you may have to make a side trip to the ironmonger's for these). Oh yes, and you'll need a pig, a bucket, some bailer twine and a pair of jump leads (you may have these already, in which case, so much the better).

Back home again, turn the pig loose in the garden and cut your hose up into two equal lengths, one of which you now insert into a hole you have cut in the side of an empty, plastic lemonade bottle. Now, make a hole in the bottom of the bottle and plug your other length of hose into that. This can be a bit fiddly, but do make sure the seal is tight, as otherwise you will have blood running all over the garage floor and seeping down into the inspection pit, which is a nuisance. Into the top of the bottle, insert the bellows. Your basic, but functional, cardiopulmonary bypass machine is now ready.

It remains only to fill the cool box with six packets of frozen peas and tether the pig to a convenient spot and you are ready for action.

If no prospective patient has turned up by word of mouth, then an advert in your local paper will usually bring in a number of possible punters. Be sure to peg your rates at around half of what the local private hospital is offering to ensure a good response.

Greet your client at the front door and offer them a glass of sherry. This always breaks the ice as they may be feeling a little nervous. After some small talk to put them at their ease, escort them through to the operating theatre and invite them to lie down on the operating table, all the while keeping up the flow of chit-chat. If you think you may be disturbed by screams and wild flailings as you operate, take the opportunity at this point to disable your patient with a swift but clean blow to the head with a trolley jack.

The scene is now set for operation. Open the chest with the shears directly through the sternum. This should be the work of just a few moments and now part the ribs to expose the heart (you can identify this as it is the only thing moving). Identify the inflow and outflow tracts of the heart – it's worth mugging up on this beforehand – and, cutting small holes in them, insert the lengths of garden hose. Again, make sure the seals are tight. Now, instruct your youngest child to commence pumping the bellows. The patient is on cardiopulmonary bypass.

You will have noticed that there is a fair amount of space within the thoracic cavity and into this you empty the frozen peas, thus slowing the heart down and eventually stopping it.

At this point, send your next youngest child out to slaughter the pig and get them to bring back the heart in the bucket, while you open the patient's own heart and extract the diseased heart valve. Then, exchange the pig valve for the patient's valve, sewing it in with the bailer twine.

You are now ready to restart the heart. Disconnect the patient from the bypass machine, sew up the holes and, connecting one end of the jump leads to the battery of your car which your teenage child has started in the driveway, apply the other end to the heart. This should, usually, start it beating again.

Finally, scoop out the peas and sew up the chest wall. (If you don't manage to locate all the peas, it doesn't matter too much.) The operation is now over and by this time the patient should be waking up from the blow on the head and a strong cup of coffee is indicated.

It is only courteous to call a taxi to take the patient home, as they do not generally feel like taking the bus. We usually pay for this from our own funds and add it to the bill later.

Some budding amateur heart surgeons worry about the legality of garage cardiac surgery, but we can genuinely assure you after enquiring at the Royal College of Surgeons of London that it is entirely legal. As long as you do not label yourself as something you're not and the patient gives their consent, the law of the land takes no position on operations carried out by people without officially recognized qualifications. The same is not true for animals, however, and since, in this instance, a licence from the Home Office will be required for the pig, we suggest you consider starting off with coronary artery bypass surgery instead. Simply become competent at sewing together two pieces of soggy macaroni without any leaks and you should be all set.

Having mastered the intricacies of DIY heart surgery, you are now set to become your own investment fund manager.

The Investment Fund Manager

While we have to admit that you will be doing well in your first year or so at amateur heart surgery to outperform 90 per cent of professional cardiac surgeons, we are confident that as an amateur fund manager you will be able to achieve this level of expertise. Not only that, but the degree of preparation required is less, as is the clearing up afterwards.

How so? How can the amateur, 'no brain' (no offence intended) investor hope to outperform 90 per cent or more of the professional unit trust fund managers who have spent years training for their jobs and spend twelve hours a day or more living, eating and breathing shares? They earn hundreds of thousands of pounds, drive fast cars and wear flashy suits. It is hard to imagine how Alan and Cynthia Average in their suburban semi in Middlesex are going to better them. This is a complicated business, after all, and not one the layperson should really get involved in. Not unless they want to lose their shirts, that is! (Guffaw! Guffaw! Guffaw!)

Not.

The truth, as we are about to see and you have correctly guessed from our appallingly irreverent attitude, is somewhat different. Are you ready for this? Over 90 per cent of unit trusts underperform the market average over five and ten years. Let's read that again: over 90 per cent of the professional fund managers did worse than the average performance of shares over that period. That's 90 per cent *below* average. Unit trusts are often advocated as the 'safe' way for investors to enter the stock market. Give your money over to a professional who will buy and sell shares on your behalf, thus minimizing the risk involved and providing you with a safe, consistent return. Who says adults don't believe in fairy stories? Look at these numbers, derived from an article in the *Investors Chronicle* on March 22nd 1996:

How few UK unit trusts (equity growth, growth and income, and income sectors) beat the market

Value of £100 after ...	1 yr	5yrs	10yrs
Average UK Unit Trust	£118	£169	£289
All-Share Index	£129	£200	£380
	1yr	5yrs	10yrs
No. of UK Unit Trusts in existence over the period	362	312	203
No. of those Unit Trusts beating the All-Share	16	25	15

The figures are from Micropal and show the value of £100 invested with dividends reinvested. UT returns are after costs and on an offer-to-bid basis.

The conclusion from these figures is that only 15 out of a total 203 UK unit trusts succeeded in beating the market average over ten years. That's just 7.4%, leaving 92.6% *underperforming*.

This is an amazing statistic and is probably sufficient in itself to fill a whole investment book (we tried to pull that one on our publishers, but they insisted we pad it out a bit, hence the other three-hundred-odd pages). It means that all the effort and money which goes into running these underperforming unit trusts is totally wasted. They could have done better by not having tried to beat the market at all and merely by putting their efforts into mimicking it. All the snazzy offices and complimentary coffee and tea dispensers, hordes of staff and latest computer systems, expensive research materials and daily meetings – all for nothing.

No, we had better correct ourselves here. They are not totally wasted, they are only wasted from the point of view of the client who is paying through the nose for a service which he or she could get better and more cheaply elsewhere. You see, it doesn't really matter to the unit trusts how well they perform as long as the money keeps rolling in. Of course, they all want to do well, because that's a draw to new investors, but as long as people can be bedazzled by glittering prospectuses and cleverly reported statistics, then just how well isn't crucially important. It is a fact that few unit trusts report their results as compared to the performance of the market average. You don't have

---

1 The All Share Index is a collection of 900 shares representative of the market as a whole. The FTSE 100 represents the 100 largest shares. We'll talk about them in more detail later in "A Share Primer".

to be a heart surgeon to realize that it sounds much more impressive to say '74 per cent growth over five years' than to say '74 per cent growth over five years, versus market average growth of 125 per cent over the same period'.

All we have to do, then, is invest in the market average. Is that complicated? Nope. It's very simple.

We have an exception to our rule of not investing in unit trusts and it's this: we advocate investing in *index-tracking* unit trusts as a first step on the path to Foolishness.

Index-tracking unit trusts have as their sole aim the mimicking of the stock market index, the market average. The index in question may be the FTSE 100 or the FTSE-ASI (the All Share Index), but it doesn't make much difference as they return similar rates over the longer term. Index trackers are dull things. There is no flair to them. Their sole *raison d'être* is to be average, to be unremarkable. In fact, the more unremarkable they are, the better they are. The closer they mimic the performance of the market average, the more successful they become. The last thing you want is an index tracker which posts returns *greater* than the index, as this shows a high degree of error in following the average and implies they may be even farther *under* in future. By the very fact of being unremarkable, index trackers shine as beacons to the investor who wants to outperform the professionals with the expenditure of precisely no cerebral calories and almost as little effort.

Average is best? Run-of-the mill rules? Standing out from the crowd ain't chic? Yup, it's a topsy-turvy world.

Remember, the stock market has returned, on average, 12.2 per cent every year since 1918. Since the Second World War it has been over 13.5

-------- FTSE All Share Index
——— Gartmore UK Index Unit Trust

Source: Gartmore

per cent and in the last 10 years even more. If you take out yearly management charges of around 0.5 per cent and allow for a degree of inaccuracy
in tracking the index, you may be looking at an average return of around
13 per cent per year or more from an index tracker. Above, you'll see what
the return of an index tracker looks like, as compared to the average return
of the market. This example uses the Gartmore Index-tracking Unit Trust,
first started in 1989:

The straight line follows the dotted line pretty closely, which is the idea.
In fact, the FTSE All Share Index gave an average annual return over the
period of 14.39 per cent and the Gartmore index tracker of 13.87 per cent.

Now see below how the average British unit trusts – the ones where fund
managers are buying and selling shares as they try to *beat* the index – compare over the same period. This shows what would have happened back in
1989 if you had invested £1,000 into unit trusts of the equity growth class,
the income and growth class and the Gartmore index tracker.

To us, this graph is one of the most remarkable sets of statistics in
modern investing. We have to keep pinching ourselves to make sure it's
real. It is so hard to believe that all that fire and fury which goes into active
fund management really counts for less than nothing. The Emperor's
shivering in nothing but a pair of shoes here as we reflect that the average
return of UK equity growth unit trusts over this period – the ones which
are supposed to be the most aggressive of all – was 10.33 per cent. UK
income and growth unit trusts managed a little better with 10.83 per cent,
but still over *3 per cent* behind the index tracker. Think back now to the
Second Foolish Law of Compounding: *Small differences in investment*

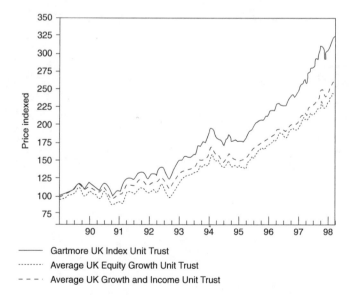

Gartmore UK Index Unit Trust
Average UK Equity Growth Unit Trust
Average UK Growth and Income Unit Trust

Source: Gartmore

return matter. A lot. Even after just nine years, the investor in the index tracker has an investment fund which is fully 25 per cent larger than the person who was seduced by the glossy literature and stumped all their savings into an equity growth unit trust. After the 40 years which a 25-year-old investor might have before they retire, the £1000 in the index tracker will have grown to a massive £180,500, while in the UK growth unit trust it will have managed only a measly £51,000. 'Nuff said?

We think so.

Can it really be so simple that all you have to do is to make regular contributions into an index tracker, keep breathing for 30 or 40 years and you'll come out at the end with a bulging pile of cash, for which you have paid very little? Yes, indubitably it can be and that is why in a single week in May 1998, Unilever, Zeneca and Sainsbury's took over £2000 million away from the various active fund managers who had been managing the money on behalf of the companies' pension funds – and doing a shockingly poor job of it – and placed it into index trackers. (One of the greatest *Financial Times* front pages of 1998 had the announcement of Unilever sacking Mercury Asset Management, sitting directly next to an almost quarter-page advertisement for – you've guessed it – Mercury Asset Management!) In the same week, the Treasury proposed that the only unit trust investments in the new ISAs – the government's latest tax efficient savings scheme, which we'll discuss later – which would qualify for a government-approved quality stamp would be *index-tracking* unit trusts. The message is clearly that the performance of the active fund managers has been so poor and their charges so high that the government isn't going to allow the public to squander their savings by investing in them if they can at all help it. It's hard to imagine a more damning indictment.

It will come as no surprise to learn that others still have seen the potential of this kind of investment before you. Richard Branson, the bewhiskered, balloon-piloting, retiring self-publicist of Virgin fame is one. It was he that brought index trackers to the forefront of the public imagination with the launch of his Virgin UK index-tracking unit trust in 1995, although the idea is not new at all. As we've seen, Gartmore have been running one since 1989 and the Vanguard 500 fund in the US has been in existence since the early 1970s. The numbers below show just how impressive a mere £100 per month can be if it grows at a rate of 13 per cent every year:

After 5 years	*£8,787*
10 years	*£24,977*
15 years	*£54,806*
20 years	*£109,764*
25 years	*£211,020*
30 years	*£397,578*
35 years	*£741,299*
40 years	*£1,374,583*

To reiterate: there is no catch to this. We're not suggesting you send us five pounds and then write letters on to 20 of your friends telling them you've got a great new money-making scheme and why don't they do the same? (Although, if you do have a spare fiver, you can always send it our way.) No, this is kosher, bona fide, straight up. Anyone can do it. If you stop at this point in the book and read no further, you have set yourself up with the only investment information you will ever need (besides having been pointed in the direction of a lucrative and fulfilling new hobby).

Profit From a Falling Market

And as if that wasn't enough, there's even more to this amateur exercise. Perhaps you have followed the steps to be outlined in the final section to this chapter and have gone out and started investing in an index tracker. Perhaps you're feeling pretty good about yourself and are even starting to be a bit of a loud mouth at parties: 'Oh yah, I'm in trackers, actually.'

Well, hang on, you don't even know just how clever you are. Take a look at this:

You contribute £100 per month into an index tracker. At the time you start, each unit of the index tracker costs £1, buying you 100 units a month. Then the market falls after six months to half its value, cutting the cost of the units in half to 50p. After twelve months – six with units costing £1 and six with units costing 50p – what is the average price of the units you have bought? Common sense would tell you that half the time you bought the units at £1 and half the time at 50p, so the answer is 75p. Common sense – and why did you know we were going to say this – is leading you up the garden path. The real answer is 66⅔p. How?

> *For 6 months at £1, £100 will buy 600 units. Total cost £600.*
> *For 6 months at £0.5, £100 will buy 1200 units. Total cost £600.*
> *Over 12 months, therefore, 1800 units have been bought at a total cost of £1200.*
> *Cost per unit*   = £1200 ÷ 1800
>   = £0.666666
>   = 66 ⅔p

By putting a regular pound amount into the index tracker, you have bought into the index over twelve months for an average price of 66⅔p, when the *actual* average price of the units was 75p (half the time at 100p, half at 50p, giving an average of (100 + 50) ÷ 2 = 75p). Magic? Yes, in a way, and it's called *pound-cost averaging*.

In this example, we assumed that the index dropped in value by half from one six months to the next, but it would have worked just as well if the index had instead been highly *volatile*. If the units of the index tracker had instead fluctuated from £1 to 50p on alternate months, the effect would have been just the same – six months buying at £1 and six months buying at 50p. Pound-cost averaging doesn't just work in a market which is turning down, it also works in a market which is simply volatile. Look back at the first graph of the Gartmore UK Index Tracker against the index to see what we mean. It's volatility – the fluctuations in share price from day to day and thus in the value of the index – which often scares people out of the market. They can't bear the thought of their holdings darting up and down in value from week to week, but as long as they're net purchasers of shares – and most of us are, since we don't yet need to live off our holdings – pound-cost averaging can make volatility into their very best friend. Radical, very radical.

And Then Profit Even More

Okay, that was *passive* pound-cost averaging, now consider *active* pound-cost averaging. If the market were to turn down after six months and the index, and thus units in your index tracker, were to halve in value as we've just seen, what would happen if you *increased* your contributions each month? This, of course, presupposes that you can afford to do so, but let's just suppose you can. You see, you consider that the market now presents such a bargain, with solid British businesses being so undervalued by a neurotic marketplace, that you're prepared to cash in the two front row seats you had booked to see Barry Manilow on his comeback tour at the NEC in Birmingham and BUY, BUY, BUY! (Wow, you *are* convinced, aren't you?)

Here are the numbers:

For 6 months at £1, £100 will buy 600 units. Total cost £600.
*For 6 months at £0.5, **£200** will buy 2400 units. Total cost £1200.*
Over 12 months, therefore, 3000 units have been bought at a total cost of £1800.
Cost per unit   = £1800 ÷ 3000
                        = £0.60
                        = 60p

You doubled up your contributions when the market took a dive – all it needed was a call to the tracker managers and a letter to the bank – and actually reduced even further the price at which you were buying units in your index tracker. What if you tightened your belt even more?

For 6 months at £1, £100 will buy 600 units. Total cost £600.
*For 6 months at £0.5, **£300** will buy 3600 units. Total cost £1800.*
Over 12 months, therefore, 4200 units have been bought at a total cost of £2400.
Cost per unit   = £2400 ÷ 4200
                        = £0.57
                        = 57p

If you read the financial press, you will occasionally find investing gurus quoted as saying: 'Buy low, sell high', 'Buy when the blood is running in the streets, even when it's your own', 'Buy as you are slowly disembowelled and roasted on a spit'. (We made the last one up.) This is actually good advice and pound-cost averaging, or better, *active* pound-cost averaging, into an index tracker is an easy and practical way to do it.

None of this stuff is very sophisticated and it's certainly not new, but it's amazing how few people really understand what pound-cost averaging is all about. You do and that puts you into a very select minority. Go ahead, now you really are justified in playing it up at parties: 'Oh yah, I'm in trackers and *actively* pound-cost averaging, don't you know?'

Don't expect anyone to linger and chat, though.

Getting Started

But how do you actually go about buying an index tracker? How do you physically do it? Where do you start?

Relax, we're nice guys, we've made it easy for you.

In Appendix 7, you will find a list of all the companies selling index trackers in the UK we could dig up and their contact details. Sit down in your most comfy chair with a cup of tea, the telephone and a stout heart. Start at the top of the list and dial the number of Company A. The exchange will probably go something like this:

VULTURE FUND MANAGEMENT. Hello, Vulture Fund Management, 'Carrion is our game', how can I help?

YOU. Umm, hello. Can you tell me about your index tracker, please?

VULTURE FUND MANAGEMENT. Ah, you mean our Vulture Footsie Fund?
(*They often have a fancy name for it and you may have to ask a couple of questions to make sure it really is their index tracker you're both talking about.*)

YOU. How long has the 'Vulture Footsie Fund' been in existence?
(*If they give a time less than three years, say 'thank you very much' and hang up. You can't really assess the accuracy with which an index tracker follows the market over such a short period.*)

THEY. Five years.
(*Excellent.*)

YOU. Can you give me the annualized return on an offer to bid basis since it started? And also the percentage tracking error?
(*Hey, impressive, Fool.*)

THEY. Certainly. It has returned 13.8 per cent, with an average tracking error of 0.4 per cent.
(*Reasonable enough.*)

YOU. Right, and how much are the annual charges?

(*If they're much more than 0.5 per cent and certainly if they're more than 0.75 per cent, think carefully.*)

THEY. 0.5 per cent, with no initial charge.

(*That's good and means they don't take a slice off the top of your wad at the beginning for the privilege of having them invest your money.*)

YOU. Uh-huh. And what about an exit charge?

THEY. No exit charge.

(*That's good, because some companies have a sliding scale of exit charges if you withdraw your money in the first five years. We are long-term investors, yes, but we don't tie our hands unnecessarily.*)

YOU. And is it possible to hold this investment within a PEP or ISA? If so, how much will it cost me?

(*To tell the truth, they will probably have mentioned this by now, but if they haven't, then ask at this point.*)

THEY. Of course and it costs no extra / a little bit extra.

(*Delete as appropriate.*)

YOU. Well, that sounds very interesting. I wonder if you'd send me all your bumf?

THEY. Of course, what's your address?

(*Etc. etc.*)

By the time you've been through the list, you'll have eliminated a goodly proportion of the candidates. Now, sit back and wait for the A4 envelopes to start clogging up your letterbox. (Strike from your candidate list any companies which take more than five days to send you a brochure: if they're not prompt and efficient at responding to potential customers, do they have the acumen to manage your money over the next half-lifetime or so?)

Once you've got all the prospectuses in front of you, draw up a table covering all the points we have talked about and make your selection. It is now simply a matter of filling in the form and sending off a cheque to get the ball rolling.

At this point, you can sit back and breathe a sigh of relief as the nagging guilt which has plagued you – for oh so long! – that you really ought to tidy up your financial affairs and learn something about this whole bally business, starts to lift. It is a blissful feeling and one to be savoured.

As you sit and bask in this warm glow of a job well done and an onerous task completed, perhaps you'd also like to give a thought to other Fools around the country. If you're online, why not come along to one of the Motley Fool UK's online areas and post the information you have gleaned about the various index trackers to one of the message boards? That way, others can take advantage of your endeavours and the net sum of Foolishness and co-operation in the world can be increased. A noble aim, we think, and hope you do too.

Finally, you will have noticed that the book does not end here. Far from it. There is still a good half inch to go. What will we be talking about from now on? A hint: we think index trackers are an excellent first step on the path to Foolishness, but that the Foolish investor with even a passing interest in the subject can do better than the mere average, impressive though that average may be. Most of the Foolish activity you'll find online revolves around this aspiration, so read on for a diverting interlude and then an introduction to the exciting and Foolish world of single share investing.

Interlude
(Two, Actually)

We all need a break from the heavy stuff now and then and this point seemed like a suitable time. Here, you'll find two pieces which we think make interesting reading. The first was actually written by a Motley Fool UK reader and is the candid and painful story of his experience in attempting the high-risk game of derivatives trading, the thought of which makes us shudder. The second is a whimsical look at the exciting new world with which the Internet is providing us.

8

A Foray into Some Very foolish Futures

Fortune's a right whore:
If she give aught she deals it in small parcels,
That she may take away all at one swoop.
John Webster, *The White Devil*

You may be thinking that our copy editor has slipped up and failed to capitalize the 'f' on 'foolish' in the title to our interlude. You know by now what a wealth of difference there is between 'foolishness' and 'Foolishness' and you're thinking we should sack our publishers for doing a sloppy job.

You're wrong, though. This is most definitely a 'foolish Futures Foray' rather than a 'Foolish Futures Foray'. Mark Kelly wrote to us in the early days of the Fool UK with a story which he has courageously offered to the world. We think it shows very eloquently why a Fool turns his back on any sort of trading which involves forecasting of short-term market trends. In this case it was index derivatives which turned Mark's world upside-down for a short period, but it could just as easily have been share options or simply day trading in shares – buying and selling on the basis of what you think the share price will do that day, or afternoon, or minute.

Before we let Mark tell his story and once more praise his courage and candour for doing so, we must issue a health warning. This is not for the faint-hearted, those recovering from major operations or psychiatric break-downs. Have a box of tissues handy and if these do not prove sufficient, trained operatives are on hand 24 hours a day at our website and AOL online areas to provide counselling and trauma support.

Mark, the floor is yours:

> *The news from the front line of idiocy is that a fool and his money continue to enjoy a short acquaintance. Only a few months ago I was reading a* Sunday Times *article about spread betting on sports events. A throwaway line there suggested that spread betting on the financial markets was best left to the experts. I recall feeling certain that I knew better. I had, after all, been paper trading the FTSE 100 Index for all of a month, using as my guide the live prices published on the City Index website. Out of twenty-five trading days I had shown a profit on all but two. Betting £10 a point, I was already £10,000 ahead. On paper, that is.*
>
> *I don't know what rush of blood to the head or hormonal imbalance led me to believe that I could turn that notional paper money into the folding, bankable variety. The impulse was strong enough, however, for me to resign*

a well-paid, if boring, career to risk my Christmas bonus on the pursuit of serious riches.

Equipped with a futures pager and a mobile phone, and with accounts opened with two financial spread betting companies, I was ready to start throwing my money at the market. I had no clear strategy – merely an unshakeable belief that I could spot the trends at an early stage, jump on to their coat tails and ride them to a quick profit. I laughed at the very idea of using the limited risk products offered by both companies, namely traded options and limited risk futures. The cost of the option premiums or additional futures spread looked like so much wasted money.

The outcome was sadly predictable. I could have foreseen it myself had it been anyone else who was approaching the business this way. On Day 1, I was late into the market on the morning of a huge rise in the FTSE 100. I bought near the top, over-committed by betting £20 a point and spent all day sweating it out to come out only £80 in front. A late surge by Wall Street saved my bacon. Even at this stage the numbers were frightening. Around £500 down in the UK market and £580 up in the US. A lot of money had been at risk for the eventual paltry reward.

Day 2 was somewhat better, with another strong finish by Wall Street leaving me up by around £350. Again I had taken a pounding in the FTSE contract and was beginning to doubt my innate ability to read market directions. I was also beginning to see how misleading paper trading could be. Both of the financial spread betting companies set their quotes not at the current level of the index, but rather at where they think the index is heading. The result was that by the time I thought I had spotted a trend, they were ahead of me by 10 or 20 points. Adding that to the normal spread between buying and selling prices of between 6 and 8 points meant that there had to be a substantial market movement just for me to break even.

On Day 3 it all began to come apart, with me giving up almost all of the previous day's gains. Again I was pacing the floor until the close of the US markets at around 9 p.m. This time Wall Street didn't come to the rescue. Even at this stage it didn't occur to me that maybe I wasn't cut out for the life of a trader, this knife-edge balance between elation and despair. Nor did I think of starting to use limited risk products. Instead I simply thought that tomorrow would be the crunch day and I would have to make up for my dismal performance to date.

I was right that the crunch would come on Day 4. The market was waiting for the latest interest rate pronouncement from the Bank of England and I correctly guessed that it would stay unchanged. As a result, by ten o'clock in the morning I was showing a profit of £580. At this stage I should have gone back to bed. Instead a greedy notion came over me that the London market might be given an extra boost by any early gains in Wall Street, which were indicated by the direction of the futures markets. I hadn't exactly played a cautious game up until this point, but now I really lost the plot. By using up my credit limits with both companies I was able to place a total of £40 a point on both the FTSE 100 and the Wall Street Dow-Jones index. Within minutes of opening, Wall Street had indeed soared to new heights. However, perversely, the London market seemed to be slipping. Unknown to me, Merrill Lynch was taking advantage of the market conditions to offload a *large number of March FTSE futures. As the effect of this sell off took hold, first the FTSE, then the Dow began to slide down, with me on the wrong side of the market. At this stage I should have panicked and sold, taking the loss on the chin. Instead I calmed myself down, reassured myself that the market would turn around and watched it plummet for the next five hours. A kind of fear-induced paralysis came over me. I was terrified to close my positions, because it would mean taking the losses. At the same time a residual optimism was telling me that the markets must surely turn around again and that I could still end up with a handsome profit on the day.*

Head in hands, I bowed to the inevitable at around 8 p.m., with just an hour left of trading in the USA. I started ringing around, closing positions and counting the cost. Which was huge. To close out all of my positions left me with a net loss of just over £8000, wiping out a large portion of my bonus and completely annihilating any illusions of my possessing the ability to trade in the futures markets.

Bizarrely, one of the people whom I instructed to close my account, who had just told me that I owed his company £6000, asked me whether there was any particular reason why I was closing the account. I guess they must have people throwing money at them like this on a regular basis. And coming back for more. I told him that I had passed my personal pain threshold by a sizeable margin and didn't want to have the mechanism open for me to repeat the experience.

So four days into my career as a financial speculator, I resigned. I wouldn't say that it's impossible to make money in that way. What it does take is a certain discipline to know when to let your profits ride and when to cut them, when to take an early loss to avoid a later larger loss. A sensible approach to the management of risk, including the use of the range of limited risk products available. And a lack of naïve optimism.

Ah well, back to the grind. Anyone know of any vacancies for an unexpectedly available senior audit manager, with extensive experience in derivatives risk management?

9

This Online World

How much a dunce that has been sent to roam
Excels a dunce that has been kept at home.
William Cowper, *The Progress of Error*

c. 55,000 years ago, Tunbridge Wells, Kent

Hew and his brother, Blok, are out hunting deer in the forest. The forest covers almost the whole of that part of the peninsula which will one day be called 'Angle-land', for no better reason than that 53,000 years later a people from Germany called the Angles would sail up, show themselves to be the most frightful boors and thenceforth behave as if they owned the place. What Hew and Blok called it, history does not record.

Ignorant of the momentous events to come, Hew and Blok were concerned only with catching a deer, but were not having much success. Every time they came close, Blok would sneeze, or stumble, or snap a twig and off the deer would go, tails bobbing through the undergrowth. Hew became increasingly exasperated and Blok, sensing this, grunted and whined in apology, for Hew and Blok did not have the gift of language.

By the third time this had happened, it was starting to get dark and Hew knew if they did not return with meat by nightfall there would be trouble at home. He became more and more angry and frustrated until, instead of the enraged grunt and blow on the back of the head which he had intended to deliver to Blok, he came out with this: 'Look, dunderhead! If you can't keep quiet, then at least go up to the head of the river, make a noise and drive the deer down towards me. I'll hide behind this tree and spear one as they go past. Now, move!'

Well, Hew was as surprised as Blok and clasped his hand to his still open mouth in horror at what had come out. Blok, by now picking up the general drift of what was required and having been thinking along the same lines himself, decided it might be wiser to absent himself up to the head of the watercourse. In due course, down came the deer, followed by Blok. Hew took aim at a plump doe and the rest, as they say, is history.

Hew and Blok returned to camp, where they deposited not only a month's worth of deer meat, but also the gift of language. Before long, they had set themselves up as itinerant language teachers, giving lessons in basic and advanced Cro-Magnon and Neanderthal for the price of a week's board and lodging. Their invention was taken up across the whole of Europe and soon people were discussing everything from the state of the market in wild boar futures to the latest fashions in sabre tooth tiger jewellery.

c. 5500 years ago, 42a Hanging Gardens Terrace, Babylon, Mesopotamia

Tetiphet is one of the entrepreneurs of his age. It was he that supplied the pot plants for the Hanging Gardens and he holds the state-wide monopoly on amphora production. Recently, he has started a bread delivery service, running 24 hours a day and delivering slabs of unleavened bread, topped with optional olives, tomatoes or curd cheese. An idea which was over 5,000 years ahead of its time, it has taken off in a big way among the elite of ancient Babylon. Tetiphet is thinking not only of a new chariot and team for his wife, but perhaps an executive reed boat which he plans to moor on the Euphrates and with which he'll take his more important business clients on cruises.

Things are generally going well, but there is a fly in the ointment. Shrewd businessman that he is, Tetiphet is worried by all the unpaid bills which he fears are eating into his profit margins. Every time he says to one of his more troublesome customers, 'You haven't paid', they say, 'Yes, I have' and he has no means of proving it one way or the other.

He goes home and thinks. And thinks and thinks. Finally, he has it. The clay he uses in his factory to make amphoras – when it's wet you can scratch the surface. He will scratch marks in wet clay to show who has paid and who hasn't. Then there'll be no argument.

Tetiphet's scheme is a roaring success and soon all the businesses in Babylon are using a similar system. From there, the news spreads around the known world and it's not long before even the bards and storytellers are writing their stories down so they don't forget them.

c. 500 years ago, Germany

Johannes Gutenberg, a metalworker, has diversified into the Bible-copying business. The hunger for Bibles in Christendom is insatiable and Johannes has 25 scribes copying away in his scriptorium, night and day. Yes, Johannes makes reasonable money, but the rate of production is so painfully slow, the scribes have such large, expensive appetites and they make so many mistakes. He tries to hurry them up by increasing the speed at which the head scribe dictates to the rest, but it backfires and first one, then another, and another, leaves. Before long they're all gone, leaving their manuscripts torn into shreds on the desks of the scriptorium. Johannes wanders through the now silent room and, sighing, is about to start scooping them into the bin, when he notices that this is no random pattern. His departing employees have torn the pages up letter by letter and rearranged them into rude messages directed at him and his mother and . . . what's that . . . his donkey? (The exact content need worry us no further here; suffice to say that Middle German of that period was rife with choice expletives and insults.)

Hang on, thought Johannes, I'm on to something here. Suppose instead of wood block printing, which is a time-consuming, irritating business, I was to make letters out of metal and then move them about to make the words I wanted? Just like this shower of no-goodniks has done. Hmm, it could just work . . .

Soon, Johannes was devoting the entire output of his metalwork shop to moveable type and printing presses and before the decade was out, a Bible wasn't a Bible if it wasn't a printed, *Gutenberg* Bible.

And what of the dissident scribes, without whom the printed word may have been delayed by another hundred years or more? Certainly Johannes never mentions them again.

c. 75 years ago, Edinburgh, Scotland

John Logie Baird has had enough of sitting in the 'three and nines' to watch the British Pathe News every day. It would be all right if the children who were waiting for the main feature would just sit down and be quiet while the adults catch up on what's happening in the world. No discipline these days, that's the problem. In fact, wouldn't it be splendid if you could watch the news in your own home, just as you listen to the wireless?, muses Mr. Baird.

Shock! Another aniseed ball thrown by MacDonald minor, the notorious delinquent from 24 Stirling Street, bounces off his balding pate. 'Right, that's enough! I'm going home to sort this out once and for all!'

For weeks he doesn't come in for meals, sometimes working continuously for 24 hours at a time. Mrs Baird peeks anxiously through the net curtains. From the garage comes the sounds of banging, crashing and curses. Occasionally, the door flies open and aerials, valves, cathodes, rays, tubes are ejected, before it closes again and the ferment continues.

Finally, a dishevelled Baird, red hair in wild disarray, the fire still in his eyes, storms back into the kitchen, sweeps his wife's embroidery to the floor and plonks down in its place a wooden box, with a dirty window at the front and an aerial on top. 'Aye, Morag, this is the answer to those pesky brats!'

And we've been watching the news at home ever since.

1996, Bill Clinton's acceptance speech following re-election to the White House, Washington D.C., US

'When I entered office in 1992, only nuclear physicists were surfing the World Wide Web. Now, my cat Socks has its own Web page.'

The Internet is about communication

Five pivotal shifts in the way human beings communicate. Five turning points in history and the last of these we are living through right now. As products of the Internet age ourselves, perhaps you'll forgive us our embarrassing enthusiasm for a few moments and let us show you what we think this astonishing new medium has to offer. (If you're already an Internet enthusiast, whether you're using it for the odd bit of serious research or are spending the wee small hours with your face basking in the blue reflected glow of your computer screen, then please bear with us. By all means, read on for a spirited and light-hearted account of what you already know, or else skip to the next chapter.)

As with many things, Internet usage in the United States has taken off far more rapidly than in the UK, but we are fast catching up. In our experience, most people have some idea of what the Internet is in physical terms – a network of computers around the world linked up through the phone lines – but don't really know what it has to offer them personally. Obviously, the best way to find out what it is all about is to go and have a look yourself and if you have a friend or relative who is online, then ask them to budge up and let you have a gander. (One Foolish bit of advice: ask them to let you wield the mouse. Otherwise, they'll zap around all over the place and, apart from feeling a bit sick, you won't quite know what's going on.) We hope that by the time you've finished this book you'll have decided that one place you *must* be is online.

When you hear people talking about the Internet, you often hear them talking about 'information' and the 'Information Superhighway'. You would have thought 'information' was the last thing we would have needed more of in our lives. It sounds so unattractive, doesn't it? What are you going to do with this 'information' you've just received, anyway? File it away in the recycling pile with all the other 'information' which comes through the door? Add it to all the other 'information' which is beamed at you night and day through the television and radio? Perhaps this is the image you have of the Internet: 'Oh, bother! Looks like we're running low on information again, darling. It really is the most terrible nuisance. Hey ho, off to the computer to stock up.'

Banish these thoughts from your mind. The Internet is not just a hypersonic Encyclopaedia Britannica, set to come flooding out of your computer screen at the touch of a button. It is first and foremost a means of communicating and is a natural successor to the endeavours of Hew and Blok, Tetiphet, Johannes Gutenberg and John Logie Baird which have so shaped human history.

Words, words, words. What are we actually talking about? Let's have an example, one totally unrelated to investing. (Come to think of it, we're already 1500 words into this chapter and not a word on investing yet. Yikes!)

One of us (D.B.) is an enthusiastic Telemark skier. 'A what?' Indeed. A Telemark skier. Unless you are yourself a Telemark skier, a disciple of the arcane art of skiing in the style of the original skiers from Telemark in Norway, you are unlikely to know much about it and there aren't all that many of them around. Not in North Devon, anyway. But you can find them on the Net and they are talking. Phew, are they talking! It was November 1997 and D.B. had £500 burning a hole in his pocket, one hundred, crisp fivers which he was going to spend on a new pair of Telemark skis and bindings. So far, so good, but how on Earth to decide just what equipment to buy?

Bring on – you've guessed it – the Internet. A quick search on the Internet revealed a website devoted entirely to Telemark skiing, called Telemarque.com and describing itself as a 'Resource for the Telemark skier'. Besides articles, listings of Telemark events across the world, listings of suppliers of Telemark equipment and information (Ugh! that word again) about Telemark races, there was a large section devoted to 'Discussion'. This section contained areas where, among other things, people were swapping hints of good places to ski, hair-raising stories of Telemark derring-do and the ins and outs of Telemark gear. Getting warmer.

A click on the Telemark gear discussion folder and D.B. was soon immersed in a world where people were buying, using, testing and manu-facturing the very equipment he was thinking of buying. In response to a few initial questions left at the discussion board, replies were received from people who had bought the skis and bindings that DB was interested in and were skiing on them every day. Their advice – not always agreeing – was noted, as were the thoughts of people using different equipment, but who felt they had better ideas about what might suit this lonely British Telemarker. Finally, a tentative decision was made to purchase a particular ski and binding combination. Then, in reply to a question about suitable ski length, the very person who had *designed* the skis replied with what he felt was appropriate and in reply to a technical question about mounting the bindings, the very person who had *designed* the bindings came up and offered his advice. Finally, another British Telemarker passing by the site dropped off the link to the website of the only shop in the UK selling these particular brands of equipment.

Now, *that's* information!

But that's not all. Over the next few days, D.B. was able to offer advice to another person on a particular ski boot/binding combination he had experience with and joined in a useful debate on the prevention of injury among Telemark skiers, directing other respondents to a website run by a physician with a special interest in the subject and who was conducting an online survey of Telemark injuries. He also gave advice from his own experience to people coming to the Alps to ski and advanced some rather forceful opinions on the advisability of using safety bindings when Telemarking. There also followed an interesting discussion with a skier in Alaska on Telemark skiing in America's last frontier, which eventually turned into a more private exchange of e-mails and heralded the birth of an Internet friendship.

So, it's not just information we are talking about here: this is interacting and engaging with your fellow human beings for mutual benefit. The group of people congregating at Telemarque.com is a community of people united by a single, great enthusiasm – for Telemark skiing. Only, this isn't a community which could exist in any other sphere beyond the virtual one. Even if you could gather together, say, half-a-dozen people in the whole of Devon who were interested in Telemark skiing, you'd be reduced to meeting on the third Thursday of each month at 7.30 p.m. under a single 60-watt light bulb and a leaky roof in the 14th Sea Scouts Meeting Hall in Exeter. Telemarque.com has over *ten thousand* visitors every day. You can join in the comings and goings of the community as and when you want and – if you have a laptop computer – from wherever you want.

Now are you starting to see where we're heading? Contrary to how it may seem, you have not stumbled on a 'How to' manual for Telemark skiing, cunningly disguised as an investment guide. There is rhyme and reason and rhythm to our musings, for while there may not be many Telemark skiers in the green fields of Devon, there aren't many investors either. Let's put it another way. There are a great number of investors – all those with personal pensions, PEPs, endowments and what-have-you – but relatively few who are actively investing in shares on their own behalf. If you wanted to stage a get-together of these active investors, you'd be looking at a relatively small club which would meet, perhaps on a regular basis, to talk things over. In fact, we favour these sorts of gatherings, whether they are informal dining clubs or actual investment clubs, where the members pool a sum of money and invest it in shares they have researched. However, they still involve relatively small numbers of people – ten or twenty at a maximum – and can hardly be termed a community.

Enter the Fool!

Ever since its inception in 1994 on AOL in the United States, the Motley Fool has been bringing investors together and forging its own, unique online community. Now its offshoot, the Motley Fool UK, has arrived to bring the same spirit of Foolishness to Britain. If you come and visit the Motley Fool UK, as we hope you will, you will find not only inter-esting articles, ideas and musings on Foolish investing, but useful reference material and one of the most enjoyable parts of the site – the message boards. In the same way as Telemark nuts at Telemarque.com swap advice and information and knowledge about Telemark skiing, so the Fool UK message boards are teeming with Fools jawing about investing.

They're not talking about skis and bindings, but companies, managing directors, whether Laura Ashley has a future or is nothing more than a brand name, the ins and outs of PEPs and ISAs, investment strategies, painful (and wonderful) investing experiences they have had, whether Pizza Express's pizzas are really good enough to justify such a phenomenal expansion . . . the list goes on. Instead of the people who designed the skis and bindings responding to others' queries, it's the people who work for these companies who are coming on to give the world (or at least Fooldom) the benefit of their unique experience. Instead of ski owners coming on to tell you how they give a 'great ride in the powder, man', you have purchasers and users of companies' services coming on to tell you where they shine and where they need to pull their socks up. You have professional share analysts from the City of London giving their opinion on a potential investment and steel importers, doctors, accountants, teachers all giving their unique points of view. Independent Financial Advisers (salespeople) – yes, they grit their teeth and stop by too – will provide useful perspectives on endowments, Personal Pension Plans and tax, among other things. Others will interject pithy comments and witticisms into ongoing discussions and the feel is one of a hurly-burly of ideas and opinions and advice erupting around you. Every level of investing skill and experience is represented, from the total novice asking what 'PEP' stands for, to the seasoned investor of many years' standing. Whatever level of investing experience people have, we hope they will feel free to ask or comment on anything they like, or, if they're feeling shy, to lurk awhile, not saying anything and simply lapping up the atmosphere and Foolish good sense.

So, the Internet brings together communities of like-minded people, but is that all? No, not on your nelly. It is the most responsive of all media to individuals' ideas and beliefs. Remember all those science fiction stories from the 50s and 60s? Some of them were pretty strange, but in any collection of short stories you'd always be able to find one in which there was not only personal transport by aerocar or gyrocopter, but democracy via the television: they were voting every five minutes from their living rooms for something or other. (You don't remember? Believe us – there were loads of these stories.)

Well, it's here. It's the Internet. We've tried it. We've tried putting up articles on our site which weren't entirely correct (for that, read: 'Contained stupid errors') and it wasn't a pretty experience. Within minutes the e-mails started flooding in to tell us just where we'd gone wrong. While this may be momentarily uncomfortable for us at times, we actually welcome it. There is no other sphere in which the relationship between the people doing the writing and the people doing the reading is so equal or so fluid. It's not like a newspaper where there are journalists and readers and the two seem separated by a barrier as impenetrable as the Berlin Wall – before it came down. At our site (and as we've seen, ours is by no means unique in this), the readers are writing – on the message boards and often formidably well – and the writers are reading what the readers have to say. Confused? You soon will be.

Most of our writers here at the Fool were actually recruited from among active participants on the message boards. We are always talent-spotting, because we understand that no-one understands this new means of communicating as well as the people who are using it all the time and who are enthusiasts for it. That doesn't mean professionals or journalists, but you, sitting in your bedroom in Accrington Stanley and tapping away on your computer keyboard. The Motley Fool UK itself came into being as the result of an e-mail one wet April afternoon from David B. to David G. and Tom G.

Being connected to the World Wide Web (the part of the Internet most of us use most of the time) brings us all together and puts us all on the same footing. Reading an e-mail from someone, you cannot tell what they look like, what sort of house they live in, what accent they speak with and often even what part of the world they're in. It's a great leveller, giving everyone the same opportunities to advance themselves on their merits.

Another example of Internet democracy. In the United States, large companies have what they call 'Conference Calls'. In these calls, companies give briefings to the analysts who monitor them on their current performance and expectations. Mostly, these companies will now allow members of the general public to participate. After all, if the professionals can have a slice of this information, why shouldn't we? The stocks we hold are just as valid as the stocks they hold. You will note that we said 'Mostly'. One day in 1996, Starbucks, the coffee shop company, was holding a conference call and refused to allow a representative of the Motley Fool to participate. This information was put up on the Motley Fool's website and within minutes the company had relented.

Okay, okay, here endeth the lesson on the Internet meritocracy. We don't want you to think we're a trio of nutcases, about to unfurl the Motley Fool flag, sing the Motley Fool national anthem ('A-jesting we will go!') and recite the Foolish motto ('Live Foolishly or cry') with tears in our eyes, hands on hearts and jester caps jingling. At least, we won't do any of these things in public. (Unless the money's really good.)

Having talked about how the Internet isn't about information, it's about communication, we reckon you're now sufficiently indoctrinated to be able to cope with what comes next.

The Internet *is* about information

We admit it: it is about information as well. There is loads of it, unimaginable expanses of the stuff, everywhere you look and on every subject you can ever think of. Everything those scaremongers have told you is true: you can overload yourself with information via the Internet, but equally there are resources available out there which will make you gasp in wonderment.

As an investor connected to the Internet, you'll be able to access company news as it breaks, read company reports, obtain share quotes, buy and sell shares, consult the financial press, set up a portfolio of shares whose price will be updated every fifteen minutes (allowing you to keep track of your investments), and, of course, have the resources of the Motley Fool at your disposal.

All this information is there on your desktop immediately. There's no penning of letters – 'Dear Sir/Madam, I would be very grateful if you could send me your latest . . .' – and no licking of stamps. There's just raw, useful data – as much or as little of it as you like.

Information is often wielded in surprising ways on the Web. Take Amazon.com, for instance. This American company bills itself as 'The World's Biggest Bookstore', with over 2 million titles available to order. Go and visit the website when you get online (http://www.amazon.com), it is an extraordinary experience. Not only will you find summaries of the books sold on the site, but readers are encouraged to write reviews of books they have read and to e-mail them in. It works like this. You read *Shares for Dogs: a simple guide to equity investing for the genus Canis*, and you like it, so you write in 'An excellent starter book, although goes into a little too much detail on financial analysis at times. Enjoyed the section on "Buy What Everyone Knows: buy dog food companies". Arf! Arf! John D. Pinscher, Barking, Essex'. This review then appears below the book on the website, along with other readers' reviews, which may strike a chord with you or not. Finally, when you decide to buy the book, you are presented with a list of books bought by those other dogs who bought this book: *Rubber balls 1945–95, The History of the Dog Collar, Sniffs and Smells of an Alsatian's Life: a career with the Metropolitan Police*, and so on. Neat marketing trick this may be, but it is also very useful and is another way of narrowing down the amount of information you have to sift through to find something relevant. If you like this book and so do they and they also liked the other books in the list, then there's a good chance you may do too.

Some people are worried by what they might find out on the Web and it is true there are weirdos out there, but if you don't bother them, they won't generally come and bother you. A few websites are pretty nasty, but to be honest the really nasty ones aren't easy to find. If you reckon that 99 per cent of the stuff on the Web is harmless and you have to go out and actively search for the other 1 per cent, you won't be far wrong.

More on information

Remember the Wright brothers, the two bicycle mechanics who flew the world's first controllable aircraft? Of course you do. Some of you will even remember the name of their aircraft – the Wright Flyer. But do you know the name of their next aircraft, or their next? Chances are you don't.

The Wright brothers first flew in December 1903 and then retreated from the public eye for the next two years. Partly, this was to perfect their invention, but partly it was because they were afraid of others stealing their ideas before they had them adequately patented. The only place they would allow coverage of their machine was in a not surprisingly little-read journal run by a friend of theirs entitled *Gleanings in Bee Culture*. During this time, countless other people around the world were trying to fly, but having very little success. One or two made uncontrolled hops of a few tens of metres, but for the most part they ended up on their noses in ploughed fields, lakes and what have you.

When the Wrights did finally emerge and started giving flying displays in the United States and in Europe, they were still streets ahead of their contemporaries, but more and more they were obsessed with their patents. As time went on, they were putting less and less of their creative energy into their machines, instead spending a large part of their time fighting lengthy lawsuits. Even as early as 1910 the Wrights' aircraft were practically obsolete.

So what's the point here? The point is that they were on a futile mission from the start. There was no way they were going to be able to patent the process of flying, which was essentially what they wanted to do. By trying to keep a tight hold of information which was so powerful it was destined to change the world irrevocably, they lost their lead. Perhaps, just perhaps, if they had said to the world 'Mimic us if you will, but we don't care for *we are the Wrights!*' then we would be crossing the Atlantic today on the Wright Flyer Mark 86.

So what's the *real* point here? The real point is that we're seeing a similar phenomenon today with the Internet. For a long time, a lot of people have made a lot of money from hanging on to large masses of information and letting little bits out at a time. (For a handsome consideration, of course.) Now, though, information is losing its value as a commodity, because there is so much of it about and it is so easily accessible. The old guard knows something's up and is looking distinctly anxious, but as yet isn't quite sure exactly what's going on or how to react to it.

Information as a marketable commodity is dying and the people who rely on selling information for their livelihood will have to adapt or watch the world pass them by. *That's* what's meant by the information technology revolution.

The written word: the sequel

The written word has never left us since Tetiphet decided to rationalize his accounting procedures back at the dawn of civilization. Thanks to the industrial action of his scribes, Johannes Gutenberg gave it quite a boost with his remarkable invention of moveable type. Of late, though, it has lost a little of its impact. The invention of the telephone by Alexander Graham Bell and our very own John Logie Baird's contraption to allow him to watch the news in peace have, let's say, knocked it from the pedestal it once occupied in the life of the Western world. These days, you tend to pick up the phone rather than write a letter. You slip in a video rather than read the latest instalment of the *Pickwick Papers* to the family in the parlour. Imagine telling the kids they couldn't watch *Terminator 2* tonight and they were going to have a sing-song around the piano, followed by reading aloud. They'd drop to the floor and hyperventilate to death.

All that is changing. Now people love to write e-mails, which is a little like writing letters, but not entirely and is almost, but not quite entirely, unlike a telephone conversation. We believe that the Internet signals the resurgence of the written word and that characters, words, sentences and paragraphs are a superior medium for teaching and learning than the moving image. It is less easy to savour and digest and reflect on the moving image. It is hard to refer back to, even with a video, and when you do, it seems curiously lacking in depth and context. There's an adrenaline hit there, that's for sure, but something lasting? Uh-uh.

The written word is an ideal medium for learning and when the Internet combines it with the snappiness and dynamism we've come to expect from the moving image, then that's a winning combination.

Which leaves you wondering why we're writing a book. Well spotted, but you didn't seriously think we were going to leave ourselves wide open on this one, did you? It's down to aesthetics. Books are enjoyable things to wield. When was the last time you saw someone lounging for hours on the sofa with a laptop computer flipped open? You can't take a computer to the beach or to bed and there is something pleasing about simply holding a book and knowing that in your hands you have a snug capsule of knowledge. The Internet will never replace the book, it will only complement it. After all, one of the most successful Internet businesses, Amazon.com which we've already discussed, is a book retailer. Books are here to stay and it's a jolly good thing, too.

A final note

One day soon the Internet will probably be delivered to many people via a digital television set, or it may come via the electricity cables and when it does it will be a lot faster and more efficient than it is now. Some people say there's no point wasting money on buying a computer at the moment when it's all changing so quickly; far better to wait until you can see which way things are going.

Ignore these people, for they are dangerous. We say:

One year in Internet time is like seven years in snail time.

Get online!

Now.

Moving On

10

When Not *to Invest*

He that diggeth a pit shall fall into it.
Ecclesiastes 10:8

That graph of the performance of UK shares over the twentieth century is pretty compelling. The value of public business has forged ahead at a rate of over 12 per cent per year and the companies that have fuelled that growth have poured rewards into the widening pockets of their shareholders. It's a story that passes so many people by. Consider that if, in a given year, shares on average rise 11 per cent, they'll actually have turned in an *under par* year. Yet, that 11 per cent return marks the outperformance of the historical average of every other investment vehicle out there, from unit trusts to property, from gold coins to gilts. Slow years on the stock market are fast ones off it. The enduring direction of the stock market is upward; investments in shares this century have doubled on average every six years.

What does all this say? What have we been saying throughout the book so far? We've been saying 'Invest in the stock market, for it will not disappoint'. And that's quite true, it won't, as long as you are ready for the challenge. If you're not ready for it, on the other hand, and you lose faith at the critical moments which will come upon you in years to come, or else you start to invest when you shouldn't even have been considering it, then things could get to look very ugly indeed.

So, when *shouldn't* you invest in shares, Fool?

When you owe money

Harry's in debt. He's already lost a fortune at the Turf Accountant's, but he's got some acquaintances who've made a few bob on the stock market. The light dawns. Why not borrow more money, invest it in shares and pay off the debt in a few months? It's *so* simple!

If the year ahead is like 1993, when shares rose by 28 per cent, then it'll be drinks all round at the Dog and Duck and everyone who wanders into range will be regaled with the share-picking prowess of this Buffett of Ilford. 'Mmm, interesting, Harry. And how are the ferrets these days?' Yawns the hapless citizen, before moving elsewhere.

But, if the market clocks in a year like 1973, always a possibility, those self-same ferrets might just start to look like a succulent substitute for Sunday's roast. In 1973, shares fell by 29 per cent, turning £100,000 into £71,000 in twelve months. Worse, much worse, was to come. 1974 brought a breathtaking 52 per cent decline, shrinking the £71,000 into £34,000. (Excuse us while we pause here for some fresh air and a gallon of hot, strong coffee. *Fifty-two per cent* – did we say that?! Okay, the following year they rose by 152 per cent. That makes us feel a bit better.)

That 1974 was a bad year all right, but while the losses were painful for anyone investing their savings money, they were calamitous for debtors banking on quick profit. Betting against your debt is simply ludicrous *and it doesn't make mathematical sense.*

Fire up your Mark 1 eyeballs, Foolish investor, and spy the numbers with us. Below sits an investor with £2500 in cash and £2500 in credit-card debt, who decides not to pay off that debt, but to put that cash into shares:

What happens with £2500 concomitantly in shares and debt

	Shares (12%)	Debt (22%)	Difference
At Launch	£2,500	£2,500	£0
Year 1	£2,800	£3,050	−£250
Year 5	£4,400	£6,750	−£2,350
Year 10	£7,750	£18,250	−£10,500

A decade later, his debt has grown to over £18,000, while his investments have only grown to just over £7700. Though he started the experiment with enough money to eliminate the debt, he's now in a £10,000 hole and things are looking mighty black down there. 'Loadsamoney', as a well-known comic of the 1980s used to say. In fact, loadsamoney to the tune of five hundred copies of this book, one restricted view seat for the Men's Final at Wimbledon, or a private hip replacement and half a knee thrown in for luck.

Now, had he capped himself in bells and donned motley, he would have paid down the debt first, and later begun a savings and investment plan. Nobody in their right mind lets debt pile up on their credit cards and nobody in their right minds likes to be lectured either. Credit card debt isn't Foolish and long term it will scupper your chances of investing success, sure as too many chip butties are a direct route to the coronary care unit. Anyway (flourish of trumpets, Fool heraldic banner unfurled) . . .

We promise to largely drop that point for the remainder of this book.

Before moving on to the next situation which would cause you not to put new money into the market, let's digress briefly and ask 'What sort of debt can you be carrying as a stock market investor?' There are myriad types of debt, but here's a Foolish rule of thumb: *Any debt at interest rates much greater than 8 per cent will prove enduringly unbeatable.* What kind of debt do we classically carry at around this level? Yup, mortgage debt, Fools, and we will see in Chapter 21 ('Buy Your Own Home, But Do it Foolishly'), how we can get this kind of debt to work in our favour. But those flexible friends, those springy bits of plastic – they will suck your lifeblood if you let them. Oops! We said we'd drop it, but we got carried away, so important is the point. So we're only human, okay? For the last time, the message is: Pay down your non-mortgage debt *before* you start investing. That will bring you one giant step closer to building broad and enduring wealth. There, we're finished.

The first time you shouldn't be investing is when you owe money. The second?

When you'll need to spend your savings

Now that you've bid adieu to the misery of liability, and have squirreled away, say, £2500 to invest, are you ready to get right into shares? There's a stockbroker two doors down from your office. United Kingdom PLC, powerhouse of Europe, is waiting to reward you. You've had a few tips from Uncle Sidney. And Russell Grant says your star is in the ascendant: *Now is the time!*

Just a minute.

Not every penny of your savings is created equal. That's especially true when you may need to use some of them to buy a sandwich for lunch tomorrow, another handful for new clothes, a few thousand for car insurance, thousands more for travel and entertainment, and a half-million or so for the deposit on your dream house. In fact, much of your savings money will be eaten up by immediate concerns. A little preparation and planning: really, no more than a few hours of thought will go a long, long way here. You cannot be investing what you'll need shortly, because over the short term the market can get hammered, devastated, annihilated. Remember 1974? If you lose 50 per cent of the money you will need to live on in the year ahead, you may try and put a brave face on it, look at it as an emotional growth experience perhaps, but cornflakes three times a day for a year? Not pretty.

Sadly, far too many 'investors' have been flattened by a marketplace that has no mercy for those who would chance their savings on a single year. Buying shares with money you'll need next month or next June will have you anxiously pacing a moonlit living-room floor. The miracle of compounding takes time to work its magic. Warren Buffett, the greatest investor of the twentieth century – of all time, probably – has earned more in the past 5 years than in the previous 30. Let's think about that for a second – the 30 years from 1963 to 1992 earned him less than the five years from 1992 to 1997. So how much time can you give to your latest amount of savings? Answer that question honestly and it will help you decide where to put them.

We don't think you should invest in shares any savings you will need within the next four to five years. Why four to five years? Because since 1918 shares have outperformed cash in a bank account in 82 per cent of consecutive four-year periods, rising to 97 per cent of consecutive ten-year periods. This shows that the risk of holding shares long term is very low, lower in fact than gilts (bonds which are guaranteed by the government). For periods less than this, though, as we've seen, you risk a nasty shock if you don't know what you're getting into.

Short-term money, then, should be placed in a high interest bank account. You are aiming to use this as you or your family need it, whether that's for a replacement car, holiday, dental treatment or to pay the rent. Spend it, don't gamble with it.

When else shouldn't you invest?

When you don't yet know enough

You've clawed your way out of debt. You've hived off money you won't need for four or five years. Hi-ho, let's get it into shares!

Brrrrrrrrrrring!

Now just hang on one cotton-pickin' minute. Again. There are two things to think about here; first, do you really, really know what investing in the stock market means and, secondly, does it feel like you're making share selections on the back of a guess and a hope, a wing and a prayer?

You have to be sure you've understood the nature of the stock market beast before you throw money at it. It's a frisky mare and if you're going to take fright every time that it bolts or rears, then you don't yet know enough. Stick outside the market and watch its daily antics a while longer. Similarly, if you're looking at individual companies and can't get over that uneasy feeling that you don't really feel comfortable making a decision about this one or the other one, it's Not Your Time.

Thomas Huxley, described at the time as Charles Darwin's 'Bulldog' and the man who publicized and fought for the theory of evolution against a hostile and sceptical Victorian establishment, had this to say on knowledge: 'If a little knowledge is dangerous, where is the man who has so much as to be out of danger?' Now, none of us can ever be totally out of danger, but we can all achieve a level of knowledge where we feel comfortable with the risks. That level is different for all of us and Foolishness is about finding that level out for ourselves.

Right, so you don't owe anything, you have some money earmarked precisely for stock market investment which you won't have to touch for five years and you know what you know, so when *else* can't you invest, for Pete's sake?

When you are dead

The fourth and final reason not to invest is if the blood has stopped moving through your veins and your lungs are no longer drawing in oxygen. When the background sopranos strike up, and you see that flash of bright light through a tunnel of clouds, and the Giant Hand reaches down to pull you into the next life, that's about as good a time as any to stop flicking Teletext on and off to check your share prices.

Once you're settled at the Gates of Paradise Holiday Inn, you've unpacked your suitcase, tested the bed and the shower and cleared out the mini-bar, we hope you'll spare a thought, just once, for what went before. Raise your Martini and toast yourself as you recall that before your departure, you paid down all your debts, set aside some inheritance for those who would invest after you and even conferred some useful investment principles for your descendants to mimic. The wealth that you have left to trickle down through your family tree – mere earthly riches though they be – will go on to support the scholarship, creativity and daring of your offspring. Certainly, it'll allow a few ne'er-do-wells to flit around the honeypots of Europe, quaffing champagne and cavorting licentiously wherever they go, but your financial gifts will be a big fat positive in the lives of many others and to all your descendants you will be their Most Favoured Ancestor. And while you're in the vicinity, perhaps you'd have an otherworldly whisper in the ear of the management on behalf of all the Fools still toiling down here. We'd all appreciate it.

11

A Share Primer

There is less in this than meets the eye.
Tallulah Bankhead, quoted in Alexander Woollcott's
Shouts and Murmurs

You need never go to the trouble of buying an individual share. If you wish, you can invest directly in the stock market without using a stock-broker by buying into something known as a unit trust. This is essentially a portfolio of shares bought and sold by a management team into which you can buy a stake. If you have good share-pickers in the team, you'll do well; if not, you won't. Mostly, unit trusts don't do very well and the vast majority of them, as we have already seen, fail to beat the average. We do, however, advocate one particular type of unit trust as a first Foolish invest-ment and that is the index-tracking unit trust we talked about in 'A Tale of Two Professions' (see Chapter 7). These worthy animals aim to mimic the movements of the market as exactly as possible and are the first plank in our investing philosophy. If you think you'll be bored by learning just what shares are about and how they are traded, but still want to become a Foolish investor, then skip the rest of this chapter, fly onward to 'How Not to Pay Tax' and that's you sorted out. Don't worry, you're not doing your financial prospects irretrievable damage. In fact, you're still setting yourself up to be in far better shape financially than most of your contemporaries, but you may want to come back at a later date and finish off here. Alternatively, if you know all this stuff already, then purse your lips into a long 'Beeep', as you would if you were beeping over the names in a Russian novel, and we'll see *you* later too.

Overview: shares, the stock market and you

The London Stock Exchange grew out of informal meetings of investors in the coffee houses of seventeenth-century London. Here, bewigged gentle-men with, incidentally, accents far closer to the contemporary American accent than the English one, would haggle with each other to buy and sell portions of likely-looking companies. As the volume of trading grew, they eventually moved to their own premises in Threadneedle Street, renaming it the Stock Exchange in 1773. The Industrial Revolution of the nineteenth century and the need this created for companies to raise large amounts of capital fuelled the growth of the exchange and at one point there were about 20 provincial exchanges dotted around the country. Now they are all concentrated into one – the London Stock Exchange.

In 1995, a smaller, subsidiary market was created, the Alternative Investment Market (AIM). This was to give smaller, more speculative companies the opportunity to be listed on the stock market. The requirements for entry to the AIM are not so stringent and the volumes of shares traded much smaller. We're all for opportunity, but for the most part, we don't advocate investing in shares on the AIM. They can be risky, difficult to trade and often not worth the heartache.

Many of us are intimidated by the City and the Stock Exchange, but really it's just a big market. It's bigger than it was when it was an assembly of gents swapping tall stories and shares in East Indian trading concerns over cups of coffee, but that's all. It's a giant shopping centre, offering shoppers the partial ownership of around 2000 British businesses. Instead of buying a jumper from Marks & Spencer, you buy a portion of M & S itself. Instead of filling your car with £20 of BP's petrol, you buy some of BP itself.

Buying a share makes you into a part-owner of that company. This means that you have a share in the profits and the losses and a vote in major company decisions. If the company does well, then the share price will go up as other people start to look interested in buying into this promising enterprise and earning some profits themselves. Conversely, if the world decides it isn't yet ready for a combined television/microwave/refrigerator ('Never take your eyes off the telly!'), then your shares in MicroWatch PLC are likely to decline in value. The only people who are allowed to carry out these transactions on your behalf are called stock-brokers. As we shall see later in this tome, some charge more and some less for the privilege.

The to-ing and fro-ing of share prices as people value companies differently at different times is what makes up the 'market' and we'll also be talking a little more about this idea of the market later. The major share prices from the previous day can be found in all the major daily newspapers and most of the shares listed on the London Stock Exchange can be found in the *Financial Times*. If you're hooked up to the Internet (and if you've not been convinced to do so by the time you finish this book, we've failed), then you can get the current share prices (delayed by a mere 20 minutes) for free at many places on the World Wide Web.

Specifically, we'll be wondering if it is actually possible to achieve the Holy Grail of investing: 'Beating the Market'; i.e. earning ourselves more than the average amount the market does. By now you will have identified us for the modest, shy and retiring fellows we are and will not, therefore, be surprised to hear that we think the private investor, if he or she be sufficiently Foolish, can succeed where the professionals fail. Strong stuff? You ain't seen nothing yet.

The public company

No, not all businesses have shares for sale. Companies fall into two categories: they are either public or private. Do you own or have you seen advertized a Dyson vacuum cleaner? You might want to buy shares in this company and we couldn't blame you, because it represents one of the most innovative triumphs of British manufacturing industry of recent years (and it's been pretty skilfully marketed too). Here at Fool UK, we'd love to look into grabbing a piece of this action, but this is one business which isn't for sale because it's a privately owned company. At the moment, anyway. Presumably, Mr Dyson is satisfied at the way things are going and he doesn't want thousands of shareholders breathing down his neck, demanding higher profits every six months. Shareholders are just that, part-owners of the business, and often they think they know what's good for the company. In fact, they think they know better than the management and large shareholders have to be listened to. Sometimes this can be admittedly helpful, but if it's not, it'll be distracting or even downright disastrous.

Also, we have to presume he doesn't need the money.

Money?

Yes, companies go public to raise cash. If a company wants to expand its business, it is generally going to need cash to do it and, broadly speaking, there are three routes to new capital. Rent-a-Family – 'Ready-made families by the hour or day to busy business executives' – wants to go national:

1. It can toddle off to the local bank or building society and get a loan, which will demand regular interest payments.
2. As a private company, Rent-a-Family can look for investment from venture capitalists – investors representing large companies, trusts or just wealthy individuals. Venture capitalists make early investments in rapidly growing companies. They aim to strike it rich on start up businesses with big stories but not enough cash to do more than simply tell those stories.
3. Finally, they may decide to divide themselves up into a few million equal-sized bits and flog most of them off to the highest bidder, while keeping a chunk back for themselves. This will give them a huge cash injection, which they won't have to give back, but it will leave them beholden to a crowd of often impatient shareholders.

Just about every public company out there will have gone through these three financing stages. They started by borrowing money, then they brought in some venture capitalists and then they worked with an investment firm to *float* themselves on the market. In Britain this is called a New

Issue and in the US an Initial Public Offering, or IPO. Once it's public, the company must release its accounts to the world (and its competitors) every six months. When a company has gone public, people like you and us can run a simple calculation to see what the company is worth. Why, as if by magic, that would appear to be the very next subject . . .

Market capitalization

The Magic Umbrella Company, Kilmarnock PLC. You haven't heard of them? Never mind, they are listed on the Highland Stock Exchange under the symbol MUCK, and they make umbrellas which will not only keep a Highland downpour at bay, but will retain their shape in anything up to a Force 11. Not surprisingly, sales of this product are going well, with an overseas factory recently opened in Cherrapunji, India, the world's wettest spot. Currently, the shares are trading on the market at 500 pence (that would be £5 to you or us, but in the world of shares, everything happens in pence; just smile and say nothing). There are 100 million shares available to be traded. Are you ready for this? Did you pass 'O' level maths? If not, fire up your calculator, because the answer is . . . £500 million. At current prices, MUCK is valued at £500 million. Another way of saying this is that it has a market capitalization of £500 million, often abbreviated to 'market cap.'

If MUCK PLC corners the heavy duty umbrella industry, boosts its sales, cuts down its costs, and as a result its profits soar, then more and more people are going to want shares in this dynamic enterprise. More, more, more. The share price will go up – supply and demand operating here: if you really want what I've got, you'll have to pay more for it – and so will the market cap. Everyone will be happy, except those prevaricators who foresaw the huge potential of this product but could never find *quite* the right moment to make their investment in it.

Now, market cap. is used in Britain to subdivide shares into 'indexes'. You'll have heard them on the radio and television every morning and evening, sounding like body parts in some strange jig: 'The Footsie's up, the Footsie's down, shake it all around.' What this really refers to is the FTSE indexes. There is the FTSE 100 index, the FTSE 250 index and the FTSE-ASI index. The FTSE 100 index is simply a list of the 100 shares with the highest market cap. (the UK's hundred largest companies), the FTSE 250 is the next 250 and the FTSE-ASI is a list of around the top 900 most important shares on the London Stock Exchange and includes those in the FTSE 100 and the FTSE 250. ('FTSE' stands for '*Financial Times –* Stock Exchange', the two companies which own the rights to the indexes.)

It is useful to subdivide companies according to value in this way because different sizes of companies pose different risks and benefits to the investor. The very largest companies, those in the FTSE 100 and including oil companies like Shell, shops like Marks & Spencer and pharmaceutical companies like Glaxo Wellcome have market caps in many billions of pounds. These companies all own large amounts of what are called fixed assets – buildings, factories, mineral rights, etc. They employ many people, have very large amounts of sales each year and have strong brand names. In themselves they have a lot of 'value'. If you buy part-ownership in one of these companies you are buying part-ownership of bricks and mortar and of a successful enterprise with a proven track record. It's not quite that simple, because you will also be paying a premium above the sheer monetary value of the company based on its earnings and the projected increase in those earnings over the next few years, but still underlying your investment there is the feel of solidity, of a business which is one of the backbones of the economy. In short, you do not lie awake at night worrying that the company may go bust and you will lose all your money. Far more likely is that you will make a comfortable, steady sum from these sorts of investments. Britain without M&S? A country without underpants? Or socks? Unlikely, we feel.

Let's contrast that with a small-cap. biotechnology company, which is far off making it into the FTSE 250 and whose total number of shares on the market is worth just £30 million. This company, Flab-o-Zap PLC, has just one avenue of interest and it's called, yup you've guessed it, Flab-o-Zap. Flab-o-Zap, still in the early stages of development, promises to revolutionize the eating patterns of the developed world. One tablet of F-o-Z will cancel out the flab-building effects of up to twelve Big Macs or fifteen Mars Bars, and the company is aiming to market the tablets in sweetie dispensers and at fast-food outlets around the world ('That'll be four Big Macs, three apple pies, a large Coca-Cola *not* diet and an F-o-Z, please.') If it all comes off, this company is going to be big, but F-o-Z is still very early on in the notoriously fraught drug development process. Anything could happen between now and approval by the drug licensing authorities: tumours in rats, hair in human volunteers turning pink, feet falling off, anything. Flab-o-Zap PLC is probably burning £5 million or more every year as it sinks money into its wonder drug and it has no other income. There is nothing else to this company and if F-o-Z does not make it to the marketplace, then your investment will be worth zilch. The other side of the coin, though, is that if F-o-Z changes the eating patterns of a generation, the share price will double, quintuple, centuple, can you say 'go up a very great deal'?

Mid-way between large-cap. and small-cap., you will find, wait for it, mid-cap. companies, which behave somewhere between the two and which are also a fertile ground for investors. The FTSE 250 is an index of mid-cap. companies.

As a rule, then, small-cap. companies are riskier investments than large-cap. ones, although they may provide much greater returns. These differences in the character and nature of large- and smaller-cap. companies are sufficiently consistent to make it worthwhile separating them out into distinct groups – the indexes we have already heard about.

How to read the share tables

With a cup of coffee on the kitchen table, a piece of bread in the toaster and the children still fast asleep, prop this book up against the cornflakes packet and open up the copy of the *Financial Times* you surreptitiously bought yesterday. We're about to do some work.

As confusing as all those numbers may look, they're quite easy to decipher once you know what to look for. In the *Financial Times*, you'll find the share tables in the 'Companies and Finance' section, nestling inside the main part of the paper. You can find the share prices in other major newspapers too, but since we're used to the *FT*, we'll walk you through the Sporting Pink.

Have you found them? Good. What do you notice first? That it's all looking just a teensie bit dull and not at all the kind of thing you want to be bothered with? Wrong! That's *not* what you notice. Believe it or not, you may be scanning these pages regularly a few months from now and *enjoying* it. Try again. Aha, you've noticed that the companies aren't arranged alphabetically as one might have thought, but by type of business: Alcoholic Beverages; Banks, Retail; Breweries, Pubs & Restaurants, etc. Fool, we knew you had it in you. Splendid work!

It can make it a little trying to find the share you want if you don't know exactly what sector it's classified under, but once you have it figured out, this system actually makes quite a lot of sense, as it makes it simple to compare companies in the same industry. We like this system and are prepared to put up with the minor inconvenience of occasionally having to hunt through a number of industry sectors to find the share we're after. Dare we say this? It's actually a far better system than in the US papers, where US shares are listed alphabetically.

Let's take Glaxo Wellcome as an example. This is one of the biggest pharmaceutical companies in the world and a solid, solid FTSE 100 performer. Where you gonna look, Fool? Under 'Pharmaceuticals', yup, and there it is. No, hang on, there it is. Wait. Grab your glasses. *There it is.* And it looks like this:

Company	Notes	Price	+ or –	52-week high	low	Volume '000s	Yld Gr's	P/E
GlaxoWellcome♣q		1681xd	+1	1983	885.5	5,539	2.1	32.3

Starting from left to right, we have the company name. We're okay with that – we found the company, after all. Then come the notes. If you look at the bottom right-hand side of the page, you will see the notes explained and see that these symbols mean that the Glaxo Wellcome company report can be ordered free from the *Financial Times* report service on 0181 770 0770 (jolly nice of them) and that the earnings used to calculate the P/E ratio (coming up shortly) are based on preliminary and not final company results.

Now comes the price: 1681xd. '1681' is the price in pence at the close of trading on the previous day. This is actually the mid-price of the share and falls between the price at which you could have bought it (the bid price, which will be higher than 1681) and the price at which you could have sold it (the offer price, which will be lower than 1681). It's essentially a fantasy price, used for reference only. Using the mid-price means only one price has to be quoted, saving on time and space. Now, 'xd'. This simply refers to the fact that if you were to buy this share now, you would not be in line for the upcoming dividend payment. This isn't getting any simpler, is it? Remember way back to the introduction of this book: DON'T PANIC. Do, however, ask: 'What's a dividend?'

Dividends are simply payments which companies make directly to their shareholders. Companies like Glaxo Wellcome pull some money out of their flow of earnings and use it to encourage shareholders to hold onto their shares for the longer term. They're like a salary to shareholders. The year's dividend is paid in two halves, six months apart. If you buy Glaxo Wellcome today, though, you won't be eligible to receive the next dividend payment – it's 'xd', remember – and this is to stop people buying in just before the dividend is paid, scooping the cash and then selling just as quickly. Even so, shares do tend to drop in price after their xd date is passed, as their attractiveness to short-term investors declines. Onward!

The next column ('+ or –') shows how many pence higher or lower the share price closed compared to the previous day. In this case, it was a mere penny up, which when compared to a share price of 1681p is almost no change at all.

That's not the case, though, when we look at the 52-week high and low of the share. Over the past year, Glaxo Wellcome has fluctuated between 885.5p and 1983p. Hold on to your hats, pharmo-Fools, this has been an exciting ride! The share price has more than doubled, or halved and then almost doubled again, at some point in the past year. Currently, it is running at almost double its lowest value. It would be interesting to know the story behind this. Did the company run into trouble at some point which was quickly resolved, did they announce a new world-beating product or was market sentiment simply very positive about pharmaceuticals in general in a market which was already rising? We'll see as we move further on that the P/E, the last piece of hieroglyphics we'll be talking about in this section, will give us some idea of how investors are feeling about this share.

It's easy to think that at 1681p, far closer to its 52-week high than its

52-week low, Glaxo Wellcome is looking expensive. Well, fiddlesticks! While many people are leery of buying shares which are near their 52-week highs, you shouldn't make that your instinctive response. You will come to notice that the shares of truly winning companies fairly consistently score new highs, from one decade to the next. Oh yes, they may have a bad three-week run, four-month run or even three-year run, but, if sales and earnings grow, more investors will pile in. Don't be scared off by a share hitting new highs unless you can find something else worrying about the company.

Next, on to the volume of shares traded on the Stock Exchange that day. Five and a half million. A lot, really a lot. This is a popular share. Some companies trade under a thousand shares a day, or even none at all.

'Yld Gr's.' Not illuminating at first sight, is it? This actually stands for 'Yield Gross'. Take the dividend Glaxo Wellcome is paying for the current year, divide it by the current share price and multiply it by 100 to give the percentage. That's the yield, or rather the dividend yield, as it is properly called. If you like formulas, it looks like this:

dividend yield = dividend ÷ share price × 100
or
2.1 = dividend ÷ 1681 × 100

Knowing all the other parts of the equation, we can, if we wish, calculate the dividend to be paid on each share. And after a little mathematical jiggery-pokery, the answer is: 35.3p. This is the value of the dividend without tax taken off, the *gross* dividend. Now, we've shown off and calculated the dividend, but if we'd been patient and waited until the Monday edition of the newspaper, we would have seen that it contains slightly different information to the editions on the other days of the week. It includes the *net* dividend (i.e. the dividend which will be paid after tax has been taken off), the two dates in the year when the dividend will be paid and the next date at which the share will go xd, usually about six weeks before the next dividend payment.

Why do we care what the dividend yield is, anyway? It tells us what percentage growth we may expect from the share if it does not rise or fall at all in the year. In this case, it is only 2.1 per cent, which isn't a great deal, which loses to inflation, loses to a deposit account at the Middle Earth building society and loses to just about anything else you can think of. Clearly, investors are not going to buy Glaxo Wellcome for the dividend alone. They are hoping instead that Glaxo Wellcome is going to increase its earnings by selling more and better drugs next year and that as a result its share price will grow. Okay, here comes a fast-paced, pub-quiz starter for ten. Which company do you think investors are expecting more earnings growth from?

Dividend Yield
GlaxoWellcome   2.1%
Century Inns   7.3%

Yes, you're right. They're counting on more earnings growth from Glaxo Wellcome. If neither share price was to move at all in the next year, Century Inns holders would be happier campers than Glaxo Wellcome holders (assuming Century Inns managed to pay such a high dividend, but that's another story). The market is counting on Glaxo Wellcome to continue to post strong earnings and sales growth.

Unfortunately, in the wake of a column which demanded some basic calculato-fragilistic expertise, we run into a slightly more complicated beast to its right: the P/E ratio. 'P' stands for the company's share price and 'E' stands for the company's earnings per share. Thus, this ratio compares the company's share price to its trailing twelve months of earnings per share. Gasp. What's that? Forget it, you're never, ever going to grasp this. (Just kidding. Take a deep breath and read on.)

Okay, Glaxo Wellcome has a P/E ratio of 32.3 on the day in question. The current price is 1681p, giving us earnings per share over the last twelve months of 52p (32.3 = 1681 ÷ 52). The same numbers for Century Inns are a P/E ratio of 8.4, a price of 126p and earnings of 15p per share. Investors in GlaxoWellcome are prepared to pay *thirty-two* times what each share has earned in the past year for their shares, while in the case of Century Inns they are only prepared to pay just over *eight* times.

The earnings are what the company actually brings home to investors from its forays out into the wide, wild world of commerce. Investors are so pleased to own Glaxo Wellcome, so convinced that it has the potential to boost and enhance and step up its earnings by coming out with ever more wonderful drugs which it will skilfully market, that they have bidded against each other so hard as to drive the share price through the roof. This company is going to have to work hard to live up to its shareholders' high expectations of future growth in earnings, but they believe it has the potential to do just that.

Now look at poor old Century Inns. Its prospects just aren't that good, as assessed by investors, and all they are prepared to pay is eight times earnings. If someone came along and tried to sell his shares in Century Inns at *ten* times earnings, he'd be laughed out of court. This company isn't worth that, he'd be told, it's not going to expand its business quickly enough for us to be prepared to pay that kind of price. Now, begone!

Just how much investors are prepared to pay for a particular company is dependent on a whole range of things. The prime factor is the estimates of potential growth in earnings provided by the analysts who follow the company. These are the people who are paid by the large financial institutions to live, eat, sleep and breathe the company or companies they follow. They assess what the company is likely to earn in the next several years and investors then decide how much of a premium they are prepared to pay for this projected growth.

Other things, of course, figure alongside the projected earnings estimates when investors decide how much they are prepared to pay for a company: namely, the past history and the current performance.

Broadly speaking, then, the higher the P/E ratio, the higher the expectations of the market about that company. There is more, much more, to the P/E ratio and estimates of earnings growth, but that will have to wait until the next book in the Motley Fool UK's investment series: *The Fools' Guide to Growth Shares*. A word of warning, though. Unless you go out now, this very instant, and start hawking this book among your friends, work colleagues, family and all sentient beings within a twelve-mile radius of your home, we will go belly up and there won't *be* a *Fools' Guide to Growth Shares*. Our future is in your hands.

When you get back you can read the next chapter about Obviously Great Investments with confidence, secure in the knowledge that you already know far more about shares than most of your contemporaries ever will.

12

Obviously Great Investments

Greatness knows itself.
William Shakespeare, *Henry IV*

Buying an index-tracker is a sound, Foolish investment and is as far as many people will ever need to go. There are others, though – and we count ourselves amongst this group – who want to be more involved with the growth of their money and who believe that it is possible to actually *beat* the performance of the market as a whole by choosing their own investments. We promised at the beginning of this book that we wouldn't be talking about risky investments here and we're going to keep to that promise. What we're going to consider in this chapter are investments which are so obviously great, so clearly not going to fail you that it is impossible to imagine why in preference anyone would want to invest in an underperforming, overcharging investment scheme such as an endowment policy.

Even so, the jump into investing in individual equities – no matter how much of a 'dead cert' they may be – is a big one and not one you should consider making without ample, Foolish preparation. Go back and read Chapter 10 'When *Not* to Invest'. Particularly go back and read 'When You Don't Yet Know Enough'. If you invest in individual shares before you're ready, what will happen is what happens to anyone who gets out of their depth: they drown. After a few attempts to stay afloat, fairly soon one 'glug' leads to another and they're asking the fishes why the air's so annoyingly thick and wet down here. If you're in shares and the market starts to drop, as it certainly will one day, then you had better have a sound understanding and faith in the *overall* tendency of the market to rise as the years goes by. The shares we are talking about here will lose value, yes, but they won't drop to zero. If, when the time comes, you panic and sell out as your shares start to drop along with everyone else's, then we're very, very sorry you ever bought this book. We hope we're giving you the bare bones here with which to frame the understanding that long-term wealth is assuredly yours if you will but think with a long-term perspective, but only you can know how well you have really digested it.

Whether it's a first-day skier enticed to the top of the hill with a 'The best way to learn is to start at the top and fall all the way down', or a tyro parachutist looking down and reflecting that it's all looking awfully high up here the fact is that any pursuit which requires an appraisal of risks and benefits should be approached with circumspection. Now, if you spend too long circumspecting – or whatever the verb may be – you'll never do anything more positive with your life than switch channels with the remote control and issue dire warnings to all your friends and relations. That's it – just issue dire warnings. As long as you have no other aspirations in life than to spend it ingesting a televisual diet of pap and purveying pessimism to anyone who will listen (there won't be many), then that's all right. But we're presuming that if you have read this far, you're some way towards becoming a Fool and have, let's say, slightly higher aspirations. We're hoping, specifically, that you nurture the aspiration to take hold of your fate with your own two hands and, through your own efforts and endeavours, build a future for yourself.

You do? That's great – read on!

Oh, hang on. You didn't go back and read 'When Not to Invest', did you, you eager beaver Fool? We really think you should. Go back to page 77, read those Foolish guidelines again and we'll see you back here in a few minutes. Don't worry about us, we'll take this opportunity to have a well-earned (well, we think so) cup of tea . . .

Tum tee tum tum . . .

Schlurrrrrp!

(Sorry, you didn't hear that, did you? It was terribly hot. Sorry.)

Now, moving swiftly back to our high-tech, thrilling, 90s investing plot: you've returned and you're thinking of making a positive decision to invest directly in some of the powerful companies which make up the UK market. Excellent! Our hope is that in years to come this decision will bring you market-beating returns, something an index tracker cannot, of course, provide. However, reflect yet again that there is no shame, no shame whatsoever, in never going any further than investing in the index itself. At almost 14 per cent return over the long term, you are setting yourself up perfectly for your life ahead. You will beat most of the professionals, assure yourself the most secure future and all this for next to no input or ongoing hassle at all. By stopping at this point and saying to yourself 'I've sorted my finances, I'm not that interested in all this investment stuff, I'd like to devote more time to my family/quilting circle/tired old MG' then you are being a Fool indeed. You are not letting your initial enthusiasm push you into something you may later regret. Well done. We'll see you Fools towards the end of the book in our eloquent closing dissertations. Now go off and enjoy yourselves.

After what seems to have been a lengthy series of disclaimers on our part (Don't sue, okay?!), the rest of you are finally deemed to have taken the Fool's shilling. We ask you to spend a moment reading this light-hearted, amusing story of an Old Sea Dog from the Second World War. We think it sets the scene for the kind of contrarian, lateral-thinking mindset we like to use in investing. Look on it as a Foolish limbering up exercise and a brief respite from this oh so serious business of investing:

Commodore 'Monkey' Brand had been hauled out of retirement to try and lick the British trawler fleet into shape as a minesweeping and anti-submarine force . . .

> *One of 'Monkey' Brand's favourite tricks was to speed over to a ship in his motorboat, hustle up the ladder on to the assembled quarter-deck, grab off his gold-braided cap and throw it to the deck shouting: 'There's a bomb – what are you going to do about it?' The ruse never failed to create momentary panic. Until one day, when he tried it out on a trawler. As he flung his cap down in front of the startled company and made his challenge, a rating stepped smartly forward and kicked the cap overboard. The surprised Commodore gazed unbelievingly at his cap floating away on the water. But he was not beaten. 'Good work,' he said approvingly, 'splendid.' Then pointing to the cap, he roared: 'Quick, that's a survivor who can't swim – save him!'*
>
> Paul Lund and Harry Ludlam, Trawlers Go To War

You see, we're not going to think like ordinary investors: we're going to try and think a little like Commodore Brand. We are not going to think short-term profit, we are not going to be looking at the market and trading our shares 20 times a day and, perhaps most importantly of all, we shall not believe what the financial press says about the market. We'll talk more about this later, but think of yourself from now on as deeply contrarian. You are going to buck the trend of our short-term, soundbite, 30 second attention span culture and think in years, tens of years. You are going to invest in the easily understandable and recognizable brands which you use in your daily life and with which you have been familiar for many years. You are going to invest in things you can't imagine yourself, Great Britain or the world doing without. In fact, you are going to 'Buy what you know'.

We'd love to take the credit for inventing this natty little investment aphorism and, believe us, if we thought we could get away with it, we would. Sadly, though, we must give the credit to another: Peter Lynch. Peter was a highly successful mutual fund manager (there are some!) in the US through the 80s and penned two excellent books on investing: *One Up on Wall Street* and *Beating the Street.* 'Buy what you know' is a simple idea and it's an excellent route into investing.

Understanding the company in which you are about to become a part-owner is vital to success. Do you know much about drilling for oil around the Caspian Sea? Do you have a detailed knowledge of geophysics and are you equipped to speculate on the potential geopolitical repercussions of a large oil find in this area? Have you been keeping up to date with the progress of organized crime in the republics of the former Soviet Union and are you ready to factor in how much of a cut the Mafia will take of any profits? What are your thoughts on the effect of ongoing wars in the area on the safety of the new oil pipeline from the Caspian to the Black Seas through Armenia and Georgia? We wouldn't be surprised if one or more of these questions drew a blank. What is so much more surprising is how many people are prepared to invest in small companies in these kinds of fields which are so distant from their everyday lives. Can a small company really hope to make a go of it in this dodgy area or is it only the likes of BP, ESSO and Shell which have a chance of turning out a healthy profit at the end of the day? We simply don't know and neither, we are sure, do most of the investors in these companies.

The world is full of investors with tales of woe concerning often small companies they bought into without knowing anything about them, other than hearing from a 'friend' that they had to jump on board quick or else they'd miss the boat! Penny shares, companies you've never heard of, commodities, options, Venezuelan bean futures. If you find yourself thinking that you could make a quick 200 per cent profit in one of these, switch into another, clear 300 per cent with that one, switch around like this for a couple of years, retire, buy a floating gin palace on the Côte d'Azur and spend your remaining years mixing ever more lurid cocktails and swapping '. . . and then this old tub of a *sailing* boat almost rammed me as I pootled out of the harbour at 35 knots, can you believe the cheek of it?' stories, then WHOA! It is possible to clear huge profits on dodgy investments which you don't understand in a short period. You are more likely, much more likely, to lose all your money in one fell swoop. Don't believe you will be the one to beat the odds, because Sod's Law of Investment says you won't. There's a place for people like you. It goes by the name of Las Vegas and sits in the desert sucking up water and fools somewhere between Los Angeles and the Grand Canyon. Buy a cheap airline ticket, take a thousand pounds and no means of procuring any more and return when you're broke or you've made a million. Dealing with your gambling habit in this way will cost you less in the long run than thinking you will make outrageous returns from investments about which you know nothing. It is also less likely to annihilate any long-term relationship you happen to have built up over the years. (For those of you who are nodding in agreement and thirsting for more of this homespun good sense, please rest assured that the Motley Fool Agency of Relationship Guidance and Cooking for One is well on in the development pipeline.)

Consider: the second richest self-made man in the United States and, therefore, the world, is an unassuming Nebraskan called Warren Buffett. (Bill Gates of Microsoft is the first, since you're asking.) The Buffett is worth somewhere between 15 and 20 thousand million dollars. How has he done this? Purely and simply by investing in simple, understandable businesses with favourable long-term prospects and which are already efficient at what they do. Using this somewhat mundane strategy, he has returned 24.1 per cent annually since 1964 for investors in his Berkshire Hathaway investment company. Let's repeat that: Warren Buffett, the world's greatest investor, has returned 24.1 per cent over the last 33 years. It is a phenomenal performance and yet one he calls 'remarkably unremarkable'. By sticking to the basics and investing in companies like Coca-Cola, American Express, Disney and our very own Guinness, he is living proof that the huge investment returns claimed by many investment newsletters and investing schemes are total and utter rubbish, garbage or trash, depending on your linguistic preference. If you buy investing magazines, you will find advertising inserts for investment newsletters falling out all over the place, offering you 20 per cent gains a month or more if you follow their advice (which generally involves stumping up a couple of hundred pounds). These sorts of claims are simply fantastic and we find that the flyers offering them are generally the right size to fit neatly over our corporate Motley Fool dartboard. Buffett has 'only' returned 24 per cent over the long term and this has 'only' made him one of the world's richest men. Fool, if you need a goal, a dream, an aspiration, then 24 per cent every year from easily understandable, reputable companies is sitting slap in front of you. Verily, look ye not to 'Phenomenal profits in just 3 MONTHS!!!!' schemes, lest ye be burned most Horriblie.

Some Monster British Brands and Their Yearly Returns Since 1983

HSBC	35.7% (1992–98)
Abbey National	30.4% (1989–98)
Vodafone	28.6% (1988–98)
National Express	27.2% (1992–98)
Rentokil Initial	26.9%
Lloyds TSB	23.8% (1986–98)
SmithKline Beecham	22.4% (1989–98)
Royal & Sun Alliance Insurance Group	19.1%
Unilever	18.9%
	12.8% (from July 1962 to March 1998)
Barclays	18.23%
Glaxo Wellcome	17.65%
Dixons	17.6%
Guinness	17.1%
NatWest	16.7%
Tate and Lyle	16.3%
Shell	16.2%
Boots	14.8%
Bass	13.7%
British Telecom	13.2%
Marks & Spencer	13.1% (1982–98)
Reckitt & Colman	13.1%
Cadbury Schweppes	12.8%
ICI	12.8%
Midland Bank	12.0% (1983–92)
FTSE 100	12.81% 1984–98

However, we would respectfully like to add a Foolish modification to the 'Buy what you know' credo. As a first venture into the world of Foolish investing, we suggest you don't just buy what you know, but you buy what *everyone* knows. There's a simple reason for this: what *you* happen to know well could just prove to be a rotten investment. Our suggestion, then, is that you invest in the companies *everyone* uses and *everyone* knows are integral to our modern life.

Brands are really the important point here. We are looking for brands which are instantly recognizable, names which give us a little flash, a tingle, of recognition. We're not suggesting you rush out and buy shares in all the companies in the table above, but take a look at how well they have performed over the years. If we had asked you to name a selection of British companies with market-leading brands, chances are you'd have picked many of the ones listed. In the search for good investments, you can't start from a better place than looking at what *everyone knows*.

The percentage changes in the table are the rate at which the share prices of each of these companies have compounded over the years, but they don't take into account the regular dividend payments they make to their shareholders (bless 'em). Since we advocate that the long-term Foolish investor collects up their dividends and reinvests them, you can add another 2 to 4 per cent to the annual returns you see above. *Très* Foolish, *n'est-ce pas?*

The Unilever challenge

Training shoes on, shopping trolley at the ready, you are now ready to take the Unilever challenge. You have two minutes to sweep your local supermarket, *without* picking up any Unilever products. Ready, get set, go!

And they're off! John and Linda Fool are powering down the first aisle, but they're *ignoring the fresh fruit and veg!* Ladies and gentleman, this pair of Fools – he's a municipal waste bin inspector, she's a lecturer in Applied Takeaway Studies at her local college – are *ignoring the fresh fruit and veg!* They could be making a serious mistake. And yes, they've just scooped some Boursin from the cheese display, oh, and there goes some Blue Band margarine! Terrible! And it's getting worse. Have they never played before or is this just some kind of silly joke? Batchelor's Cup-A-Soup – they're shovelling that in – Brooke Bond, PG, Lipton's teas, John West pilchards (ugh!), Pepperami, Bird's Eye peas, piles of Magnums, Wall's vanilla ice cream – four tubs, surely not! Now they've cleaned out the pasta sauces, but why, oh why, did they have to choose Ragu?! Oxo, Colmans, come on, you two, the clock is ticking! And now they've split up, a good tactical move. John's heading down past the detergents, but . . . this is *unbelievable*, ladies and gentleman! He's missed the Ariel and he's scooping in Persil and Omo like there's no tomorrow. And now it's Domestos and Jif. Oh, please!

Let's see how Linda's doing. Not much better there, I'm afraid. What's that in her arms? Bundles of Dove soap?! Oh yes, and she's loaded up with make-up too. I can see Helene Curtis, Elizabeth Arden and what else is there poking out? Ponds, Vaseline, Mentadent, Signal, Sure, Timotei, Close-up . . .

Let's leave this sad scene, Dear Readers. It's obvious that John and Linda Fool don't know this, but the only way they had any hope of getting round the supermarket without picking up any Unilever products was to stick at the fresh fruit and veg section, before moving onto fresh bread and out past the wines and beers. Unilever is *everywhere* in our daily lives.

Clearly, if you have an objection to investing in a multinational company, Unilever is not for you. On the other hand, if you fancy investing in a company with a market capitalization of £45,000 million, sales of £33,000 million and market-beating performance since 1983 and beyond, then Unilever is worth a very Foolish look.

It was in 1885 that William Lever and his brother James formed a company – Lever Brothers – to produce the world's first packaged, branded laundry soap, Sunlight. William saw the importance of mass advertising and the creation of a strong brand and Sunlight was launched with a campaign that asked, 'Why does a woman look old sooner than a man?' The answer was the 'washday evil' of laundering without using Sunlight. It may not be catchy by today's standards, but it hit the spot, and within a few years Sunlight had cornered the market in Britain, before also coming to dominate the scene in Europe, Australia, South Africa and the US. Since they needed vegetable oil to manufacture the soap, Lever established a series of plantations around the world and during the First World War started to use the vegetable oil to make margarine. By the 1920s they were major manufacturers and in 1930 merged with a Dutch organization called the Margarine Union, which effectively had the European margarine market sewn up. For tax reasons, two separate companies were formed, Unilever NV in Holland and Unilever PLC in the UK, and that is how it remains to this day, although the two work seamlessly together.

During the depression and the Second World War, Unilever expanded, despite the best efforts of their arch-rivals, USA company Procter and Gamble, and bought a number of US companies, including Thomas Lipton in 1937 and Pepsodent ('You wonder where the yellow went when you clean your teeth with Pepsodent!') in 1944. Procter and Gamble, however, froze Unilever out of the US detergent market with a massive advertizing campaign backing the first synthetic detergent, Tide. Outside America, though, they have been more successful and a large part of their expansion strategy has hinged around the acquisition of complementary businesses, from Bird's Eye to Ragu, to Calvin Klein and Elizabeth Arden.

Earlier, we said that Unilever was everywhere in our daily lives, but as we've seen it's not just in our daily lives. At the front of the Unilever company annual report for 1997, they have cunningly inserted a map of the world with Unilever's five 'priority regions' in dark blue and, in lighter blue, other countries in which Unilever's brands are sold. All other countries are in white and the sum total of these comprises Myanmar (formerly Burma), Iran, Iraq and Spitzbergen. Since the latter is a group of Arctic islands administered by Norway (coloured light blue) and occupied by just several thousand people, we can't believe that no Unilever brands at all are imported to be sold there. This leaves Myanmar, Iran and Iraq as Unilever-free, although with the flourishing black markets all these countries possess, you probably wouldn't have to be separated from your favourite Unilever products there, either. That's as long as you had sufficient US dollars to pay for them, of course.

So is Unilever likely to disappear any time soon, to pack up, go bankrupt and wheel its filing cabinets down to the local auction house? Is this the kind of investment which is going to have you waking up in a sweat when the market takes a tumble? We don't think so. The world can't do without Unilever, which is just how Unilever plans to keep it.

Here at Fool UK HQ, we've had a team of highly dedicated Fools working night and day on the criteria we see as being essential for a company to be an Obviously Great Investment. Although it's a good start, it's not enough to simply buy what everyone knows. Let's see how Unilever fits those criteria and how we can apply them more generally.

1. Have they built a consumer brand?

No prizes for answering this one correctly. We've already seen that Unilever is a series of worldwide monster brands tripping over each other in their rush to be numbered first. Lux soap sold 3500 million bars in 1997. That's a lot of very clean people.

This is your first filter for an OBVIOUSLY GREAT INVESTMENT. Find the businesses which have built nationwide or, even better, global consumer brands and that almost everyone around you knows. That done, move on to Question 2.

2. Are they the best in their business?

Which business? They're listed in the *Financial Times*'s prices pages as 'Food Producers', and although that is currently the majority of their business, their major growth areas are in detergents and personal care products. We certainly can't think of a British competitor which comes close and the nearest we can think of are mostly in the US: Procter and Gamble, Philip Morris (the huge US tobacco (gasp!) company which owns Kraft Foods, Campbell Soup, Sara Lee) and RJR Nabisco, another tobacco company.

More generally, choosing a best over a second best isn't always terribly easy. However, in any given group you can usually distinguish the superior two or three businesses from the rest. We don't think it's a good idea to invest in businesses trying to turn around or trying to become a top-tier competitor after years of slumber. Once you have the top two or three, decide which is the best of the lot, do a few minutes of research into their financial situation (which we'll consider in a bit) and then buy and hold the strongest amongst them. For decades. Alternatively, if they're good enough, buy the two or three main competitors. The absolute Foolishness of this was brought home to us by a young woman who dropped by Fool HQ in the US. She worked in the software sales department of Oracle, one of the fiercest, strongest competitors of software behemoth Microsoft. Over lunch, she confessed – nay, celebrated – that she held both Oracle and Microsoft shares in her portfolio. With her employer's shares returning her more than 30 per cent per year and Microsoft bringing in more than 50 per cent a year, she was probably making a fortune. She should have bought *us* lunch!

But wait, we only have two qualities pinned down: consumer brand and best of breed. There are more. Read on.

3. Do people buy their stuff regularly?

Once you've smeared, eaten or washed with Unilever's family of products, you have to go back and buy more of them. It's fantastic and not just because it keeps the profits flowing in, but because it means receiving free daily promotion. When selling products through to consumers, marketing is often the greatest expense and thus engenders the greatest risk. In the US, Internet companies are vying with each other for consumer enthusiasm. They are losing money, oodles of it, from their marketing fees, which is exactly how it should be. They're in a high stakes game and if their marketing builds them a global brand, they've won. Companies like Unilever are getting this promotion gratis millions of times a day.

For this reason, we suggest you study most carefully those businesses which are frequent servants of their global base of customers. These companies aren't just getting their promotion free, they're *making* money as they use the daily sales of their products to promote themselves. Contrast that with a car company which pours out tremendous amounts of money to attract buyers for that once-every-few-years purchase.

4. Are they making a lot of money for their efforts?

This varies quite a bit and, of course, companies fight through all sorts of changes. At times, giants have to endure huge short-term costs to get out of grimly declining markets and into hip-hop, happening ones. But in general, what you want to find is companies that make more than seven pence off every pound (after taxes) and you'll generally want those companies to be driving a consistent rise in that rate of profitability.

To be honest, this isn't where Unilever shines. Over the last few years, before tax they've been making around 8 to 9 pence on every pound, but only about 5 pence after taxes. Yikes! Are we going to reject them for this? Lower margins (for that is what the amount of profit is termed) are common in these kinds of bulk consumer businesses. As we'll see shortly, in industries like pharmaceuticals or electronics, margins like this would generally mean the red card, but perhaps with Unilever we can get away with a yellow one for now. They peddle diverse products in practically every market around the world. Their margins have remained steady, while their business has been growing. Coca-Cola, another global consumer brand, has increased its after-tax margins from 10 per cent to 22 per cent over the past decade which might make you think that Unilever is a slouch. But hang on, Coke basically has one single product, allowing it to streamline and standardize production and marketing around the world. Of course its costs are going to be lower. All credit to Coke for cutting those costs, but nevertheless it is a different business. (And, yes, Coke is also an Obviously Great Investment, if not *the* Obviously Great Investment. See Chapter 17 'Where Else to Invest'.)

Okay, Unilever, rules are meant to be broken. We like your brands and your markets (everywhere), you are consistently profitable and well managed. Your kind of diverse, bulk consumer business is never going to have particularly high margins, but you are expanding aggressively into the huge untapped markets of the developing world. We'll let you squeak through, but we'll be watching your margins over the coming years like hawks. Y'hear?

5. Are they up to their eyebrows in debt?

There's good debt and there's bad debt. Credit card debt is bad debt, a home loan is good debt and as we will see in 'Buy Your Own Home' (see Chapter 21) can dramatically enhance the profits to be made from the investment. This is called 'gearing', or 'leverage' in the United States. Take a long-term loan of £50,000 for 20 years at 8 per cent and you'll pay £80,000 in total interest. That's a lot of money, but in the meantime your £50,000 has also been growing at, let's say, 12 per cent. This gives you £482,000 at the end of the time and, after you've paid back the money and accounted for the interest, you've made just over £350,000 on the deal. It's what happens when you buy a house and it's what companies do all the time to enhance their profits. They *choose* to be in debt, because they can borrow at a lower rate than the rate at which their business is earning on the money it is using. In Unilever's case, they are returning about 15 pence on every pound they are using in their business, which is technically known as the 'Return on Capital Employed'.

One of the simplest ways to look at how much a company is in hock is by looking at how many times the income it is making will pay the interest on the loans it is carrying. This is called the 'Interest cover' and for Unilever it runs at almost 15. If you want to express it as a formula, it looks like this:

Interest cover = interest payable / pre-tax profit + interest payable

Interest cover of 15 means that they can pay the interest on their debt fifteen times over, which is plenty. More than plenty, in fact. Interest cover of 5 to 10 is a comfortable norm, so fifteen means that Unilever isn't even blinking at its debt burden and with its assured stream of income (anyone been to India and seen how frequently people wash there?), we don't have to worry about Unilever running into trouble over its debt repayments. Compare this with a householder who has a monthly mortgage bill of £500 and a net monthly income of £1700: only 3.4 times covered. Watch it! Unilever is far less exposed debt-wise than most of the rest of us and is also in fact sitting on a £3000 million cash pile, which it chooses *not* to use to pay off its debt.

Of course, gearing can turn sour, as it did for householders in the negative equity saga which is just finishing in Britain. In the late 80s, people bought houses with massive mortgages (property was booming, right?), only to watch the market crash. They struggled to pay the loan and meanwhile the asset on which it had been taken out was no longer worth that amount. They thought that by buying the most expensive house they could they were cashing in on a 'dead cert' investment. In fact, they were making a highly geared and, as it turned out, highly speculative investment.

The same thing can happen to companies if their profits start to fail and that's why a highly geared company in an industry with highly volatile or cyclical profits like, say, the building industry, could be asking for trouble. None of this applies to Unilever, which has a sensible level of borrowing.

Some people like to make the issue of debt complicated, but really it's quite simple. Think of the interest cover as telling you how comfortable the company is with its debt repayments. That's all.

6. Have they been a success up until now?

Success breeds success. While past success doesn't correlate infallibly with future success, it is an important indicator. It may be pretty Foolish of us to assert this in a world where ubiquitous legal disclaimers reinforce the idea that past performance is no guarantor of future performance, but we're going to do just that.

Any company which comes into consideration as an Obviously Great Investment will have been a success for many years and that success will have carved them dominant industry positions which even further ensure their future success.

How do you find how shares have done over the last five years?

Well, there is only one easy way we know of and that is on the Internet. At the Datastream site (http://www.marketeye.co.uk) you will be able to download, free of charge, price histories on all UK shares for the past five years. Calculating the compound rate of annual growth in share price over the last five years is actually quite easy *if* you've got a scientific calculator. What you have to do is to take the current share price and divide it by the price five years ago, then take the fifth root of that, take away 1 and multiply it by 100 to get the percentage. You've lost us? Okay, here's an example:

Cactus PLC
Share price July 4th 1993 25p
Share price July 4th 1998 75p

Right, fire up daughter Beatrice's scientific calculator and key in:

1998 price (75p) ÷ 1993 price (25p) = 3

Now, press the 'Shift' (or 'Inv') button on your calculator, then the x^y button, then '5' (for five years), then the 'equals' button. And the answer is: 1.2457. Now, take away 1 and multiply by 100 to give you the annual percentage return for Cactus PLC: 24.57%.

Obviously, if it's six years, you'll take the sixth root, if it's four years, you'll take the fourth root, etc.

You can do the same with your savings too. If you were worth £10,000 four years ago and are worth £30,000 today, then the one divided by the other is 3, the fourth root (only four years this time, remember) of 3 is 1.316, which gives us a 31.6 per cent annual compounded rate of return for your savings. What are you doing reading this book? With returns like that you should be writing one of your own!

Before you consider investing in a company, make sure that they have had a rate of compounded annual share price growth of 15 per cent or more and then remember that you may have another 2 to 3 per cent of growth from the dividend coming your way. Taking the dividends into account, Unilever has just about equalled the index over the last five years, although, as we've seen, it has done significantly better in the longer term. It's not going to set the world alight and there are other companies with faster growth out there, but as a core value holding with a proven track record, rock-solid business and good management, we like Unilever and don't believe it will let the long-term investor down.

Show me some more companies, fools

All right, enough already! We were just working ourselves up to it, okay?

Of the 2000 publicly traded companies in the UK, you'll be hard pressed to find more than a few which meet the six criteria outlined above. The businesses which pour operational might into the consumer space, plough their cash into gaining competitive advantages, and work tirelessly to satisfy the needs of their customers are few and far between. There are plenty of pretenders out there who feign a love for the people, but whose products or services eventually lose their lustre. Eventually, consumer demand sheds light on the charade and the business is rent asunder.

Let's study in a bit more depth some outstanding operations, which appear to be engaged in a love-in with the world while roundly boxing the ears of their competitors. They have generated extraordinary growth for investors and provided superior products and services for their customers. They employ thousands of people around the planet and they make an awful lot of money from their daily operations.

Marks & Spencer

It's long been a joke in Britain that out of any gathering of ten people, eight will probably be wearing M&S underwear. George Bernard Shaw said 'When a thing is funny, search it for a hidden truth' and with most of the people reading this likely to be dependent on at least some of the products sold by Marks & Spencer, we'd better have a closer look and run them through our Obviously Great Investments filter.

The consumer brand
This one barely needs answering. Clothes, food, home furnishings and now financial services: M&S stands for quality at a price you can afford. You can *depend* on M&S. With around 550 stores currently being operated around the world and a huge worldwide expansion plan being implemented, this quality brand is going to be brought to an even greater audience. It's a pass on the brand. No argument.

The best in the business
M&S have an uncanny finger on the nation's pulse and, we hope, soon much of the world's, too. They are a well-managed company with a keen appreciation of what will sell and how to sell it. In our opinion, they leave the other British retailers of similar ilk – Debenhams and British Home Stores among them – furlongs behind. M&S has such a powerful brand *because* it's the best in the business. On the food front, no other company produces such quality ready-made food, and for clothes, the value, selection and stylishness is practically impossible to beat.

Profit margins above 7 per cent
After-tax profit margins at M&S are in the region of 10 per cent, excellent for a retail company.

Repeat-purchase business
Clothes wear out and the delicious food keeps you coming back for more.

Traipsing past the clothes to buy his lunchtime sandwich, David B. observes many a person on their lunch break indulging in a little impulse clothes buying. (Hey, he's even done it himself!) M&S's success is firmly founded on repeat-purchase business.

Not over-burdened with debt
Not at all. Marks & Spencer has interest cover of almost 34.

Past performance
Marks & Spencer has returned 13.1 per cent on average every year, excluding dividends, since 1982.

It is hard to imagine how an investor could do herself lasting damage for the long term by investing in this soundly managed, easily understandable, successful company with a terrific brand. In short, it's an Obviously Great Investment, one of the leading companies in Britain today and with a bright future ahead of it.

Microsoft and the two telecoms

The share price of Microsoft has appreciated at 60 per cent per year since its unspectacular flotation in 1986. It currently has margins of over 28 per cent on sales of more than $10 billion and, even after its slow start in the Internet race, it's not just the best in the business, it *is* the business. There's no-one else who can even come close to challenging the global monopoly Microsoft has in providing functional software at a cheap price, something which has resulted in a series of lawsuits from the US government for anti-competitive practices. Why, 'Microsoft' is the only company name which doesn't come up as a mis-spelling on the spellchecker in the word processing program being used to write this, which is – you've guessed it – Microsoft software. Many people don't like Microsoft for what they see as these 'bully boy' tactics against competitors. Whatever you think of them, though, they have a series of sound products and are the Number 1 success story of the last decade, all of which leads us to consider that our next book should have at its core an investment philosophy entitled 'Buy what you hate'. Yes, Microsoft is such an obvious Obviously Great Investment that you can read about them in David and Tom G.'s latest US book *You Have More Than You Think*. (Excuse the self-promotion, but you know by now that capitalism is our creed.) If you take a closer look at Microsoft and decide to invest in this giant, run through 'Where Else to Invest' (Chapter 17) to see how to go about it.

We don't have a Microsoft (http://www.microsoft.com) in Europe but what do we have? Actually, we have two world-beating mobile telecommunications companies, called Vodafone (http://www.vodafone.co.uk) and Ericsson (http://www.ericsson.se). Okay, no prizes for guessing that one of them is Swedish, but we are all supposed to be friends these days.

With the increasing globalization of business, we might have an understandable bias towards investing in our own country, but can we afford not to look elsewhere when impressive opportunities present themselves? After all, when it comes to market stability and regulation, Sweden – and no offence is intended here – isn't exactly Mozambique. In fact, besides being listed in Stockholm, Ericsson shares are listed on the Nasdaq exchange (as are Microsoft's) in the US, which has probably the toughest financial reporting regulations in the world.

The consumer brands
Pop down your local mobile phone shop, which are always staffed by what seem to be twelve-year-olds in suits. Vodafone and Ericsson are two of the major brands you'll see represented there. These companies' activities are entirely dedicated towards the mobile telecommunications industry. Vodafone, with a market cap of around £1900 million at the time of writing is mostly concentrated in the UK market, where it runs the digital GSM call network, although it does have operations in continental Europe and the rest of the world, too. Intensive advertising has meant that Vodafone is a powerful brand in the British mobile phone market and if you were to ask people which company they associated with mobile phones, most would probably answer Vodafone. Ericsson is the name you see on some of the nattiest little mobile phones, of which, incidentally, they sold 87 per cent more in 1997 than in 1996. They are also a worldwide provider of digital mobile phone networks – to over 130 countries, in fact. More than 40 per cent of the world's mobile phones run on an Ericsson system.

The best in the business
Both companies provide quality services. You won't find better.

Profit margins above 7 per cent
Ericsson has post-tax margins of just 7.1 per cent, up from previous years' levels of around 5.5 per cent. These are not exemplary for a high-tech company like this. What are they doing with their profits (for profits there certainly are)? In 1997 Ericsson invested an amount equal to 16 per cent of total sales in new technology and research and development. They also submitted *1200* new applications for patents. This is a company with its face set firmly towards future growth and which isn't afraid to invest today for the markets to come. We're not overly worried by Ericsson's margins at this point, but they're something we'll be keeping a very close eye on.

Vodafone, on the other hand, has operating margins of around 28 per cent. Great. They have been referred to the Monopolies and Mergers Commission for overpricing, along with the other mobile phone network operators in the UK, but it doesn't look likely that they'll be forced into any dramatic lowering of their prices.

Repeat-purchase business

Each customer provided Vodafone with £427 worth of business in 1996/7. The majority of Ericsson's profits come from supplements and upgrades to systems they have already put in place. At the pace at which telecommunications are moving, this doesn't look set to change any time soon.

Vodafone and Ericsson are already daily features in the lives of the customers they serve and they are increasing the numbers of those customers at phenomenal rates each year.

Not over-burdened with debt

Vodafone can cover the interest on its debt almost sixteen times – no worries there. Ericsson has a cash surplus.

Past performance

Since 1987, Ericsson has provided share growth of 36.9 per cent annually to its shareholders. £10,000 in Ericsson back then would be worth over £310,000 now. Vodafone has stormed in with 28.6 per cent since 1988. Can they keep going? Well, that's our next question.

Is the future bright for mobile telecoms?

Do jesters like to poke fun, tease and mildly irritate? Take a look at this 1998 appraisal from Ericsson's outgoing chairman, Lars Ramqvist, who has presided over a 57 per cent annual growth in share price since he took over in 1990:

> *What we can now expect during the years immediately ahead is an even more dynamic market. Despite the fact that we have experienced fantastic growth in telecommunications for a number of years, I still venture to assert that this has been only the beginning. Mobile telephony is continuing to grow. The Internet and intranet systems are growing even faster. And then we have data communications, and multimedia and many other new services that as yet we can only imagine. Deregulation and liberalization are continuing. One important deregulation is the one being implemented within the European Union in 1998. All in all, these are a number of factors, each of which in itself would have been enough to ensure very strong continuing growth in the industry.*

We reckon these easily understandable, well managed, outstanding brand name companies merit consideration as Obviously Great Investments. We like to communicate, we need to communicate, our society is in the process of being revolutionized by communication. One thing we are not going to do is communicate *less* in the coming decades. These companies are ideally placed to capitalize on the communication explosion.

The three pharmo-giants: Glaxo Wellcome, SmithKline Beecham, Zeneca

We are fortunate enough to have three of the world's leading drug companies listed on the London Stock Exchange. If you receive any prescription drugs from your doctor, there's a reasonable chance that the products of at least one of these companies will be included amongst them. Health care is a major industry in the developed world and it's fair to say that our ever increasing obsession to extend the average life expectancy by ever tinier amounts shows no signs of slowing down. We're all obsessed with our health, it's that simple, and investing in companies at the forefront of that drive is likely to be profitable.

Now, we must draw a quick distinction here between biotechnology companies and pharmaceutical companies, because people often confuse the two, sometimes with disastrous consequences. Biotechnology companies are small, often with no products on the market and are frequently dedicated to developing a single, hopeful wonder-drug. Pharmaceutical companies (especially of the sort we're describing here) have legions of products in the development pipeline and established sales of billions of pounds a year. The share price of biotechnology companies often fluctuates wildly, insanely even, on the basis of very little in the way of hard, objective fact. And note that this is in an industry where the countless pitfalls awaiting drugs on the development pathway frequently result in their not making it to market at all and having to be scrapped. British Biotechnology – with two main drugs under development – was nudging membership of the FTSE 100 in 1996, so high was its share price, but has since seen that price cut in four amidst worries about the side-effects and efficacy of those same drugs, and also allegations of a cover-up by the company of poor trial results in relation to one of them. Biotechnology companies are frequently hyped to the heavens and we steer clear of them. Even with one of us masquerading as a medical doctor with a special interest in drugs, we feel unable to adequately assess the prospects of these 'one-hit wonder' companies and prefer the security of a huge drug company with many possibilities up its sleeve and a good track record.

Knowing that it's impossible even for experts to assess the chances of a particular drug under development making it to the market place and being a success, rather surprisingly brings the huge pharmaceutical companies into the realm of Obviously Great Investments. You don't *have* to be a scientist or doctor to recognise success, size and brand name, you just have to be an ordinary person looking at the world around you. The three Pharmo-Giants are Obviously Great Investments. Let's see why . . .

The consumer brand
The three names are widely recognized, as are most of their drugs. Ever heard of any of Zantac, Becotide, Ventolin, Zovirax or Imigran? Or how

about Zestril, Zomig or Zoladex? And then there are Amoxil, Augmentin, Havrix, Panadol, Tagamet and Contac. The first set belongs to Glaxo Wellcome, the second to Zeneca and the third to SmithKline Beecham. We'll say it again: if someone in your family is taking a prescription drug, there's a good chance it's made by one of these three companies. If you ask the man on the Clapham omnibus to name a drug company, he'll come up with one of these three. Strangely, or perhaps not so strangely, medical professionals are just as susceptible to the power of the brand and will feel much more warmly towards a drug if it comes from a stable they already know and respect.

The best in the business
Medicine in the developed world would collapse without these products. There is a strong tendency in pharmaceuticals for companies to bring out 'me too' drugs as they copy other manufacturers' successful products. These companies, on the other hand, produce the very drugs which others attempt to imitate.

Profit margins above 7 per cent
This is too pathetically easy. Well-run pharmaceutical companies have high margins. So high, in fact, that we've been lazy and haven't even both-ered to calculate the post-tax margins: there's no need. Glaxo Wellcome has a profit margin of 35.4 per cent, SmithKline Beecham has a margin of 22.6 per cent and Zeneca runs on margins of 21.1 per cent.

Repeat-purchase business
Clearly, this is the ultimate in repeat purchase businesses. The drug com-panies know this and maximize the repeat purchase potential by spending a great deal of money and effort in developing drugs for chronic diseases and also in extending the indications for existing drugs to other illnesses which require long-term treatment. Patients become very attached to the particular brand name of their drug and often resist attempts to switch them to other, cheaper formulations.

Not overburdened with debt
GlaxoWellcome can cover the interest on its debt 12.8 times from its income, SmithKline Beecham can cover the interest on its debt 13.4 times over and for Zeneca the number is 18.7. The finance directors of these companies are not lying awake at night worrying about their debt. We guarantee it.

Past performance
GlaxoWellcome has returned 17.65 per cent since 1983 (it was previously two companies: Glaxo and Wellcome), SmithKline Beecham has brought in 22.4 per cent since 1989. Zeneca only assumed an independent

existence from parent company ICI in 1993, since when it has returned an average of 36.9 per cent annually.

Sitting on the drug shelves of your local chemist are three Obviously Great Investments. And you thought you were only nipping to the shops for a tube of toothpaste and something for the weekend.

The pizza parlour – on a mission

Remember Pizza Express (http://www.pizzaexpress.co.uk) back in the 70s and 80s? A few half-empty restaurants, pizzas on which they would donate a few pence of the profits to the Venice is Sinking fund (still do, actually) and not much else? Something happened to them about five years ago and now this company can't stop growing. They're opening restaurants across Britain at the rate of around 30 a year and are starting to expand overseas too. These people are seriously successful and if you've ever eaten in one of their restaurants then you're as well placed as any industry analyst to give your opinion on their future prospects. Did you like the atmosphere? Was it a good pizza? How about the service? Ask questions like these about the services you use in your daily life and you're well down the road of successful investing.

We eat at Pizza Express regularly and we love it. In fact, Fool UK top-level management meetings tend to be held in the Bayswater restaurant. And not only do we love the food, but we love the numbers too.

The consumer brand

Pizza Express has managed to forge an almost unique position in the ferociously competitive restaurant world. They offer reasonably fast food which tastes good, authentic and is delivered in a very pleasing atmosphere. They are *the* pizza restaurant in Britain and, we hope, shortly the world.

The best in the business

Speaking here as pizza gurus, we think these pizzas take some beating. Oh yes, if you're strolling down the street in Milan or Naples you might come upon a hundred better establishments, but in Leicester or Newcastle? The restaurant business is fickle but, for the moment at least, Pizza Express seems to have an almost unassailable lead.

Profit Margins above 7 per cent

Did you say 7 per cent?! Somehow, Pizza Express has managed to swell its operating margins from just over 8 per cent in 1993 to over 20 per cent today. For a business of this sort, these margins are phenomenal. Of course, every time Pizza Express opens a new restaurant the costs of their head office and administration are spread that little bit further. It's not only that, though, as they have consistently augmented their 'like-for-like' sales over the last five years – that means more pizzas munched per restaurant, or more profit for the same outlay. No problem with margins here.

Repeat-purchase business
Well, *we* keep going back.

Not overburdened with debt
You would have thought that opening 30 restaurants a year would pretty soon empty the piggy bank and have you surreptitiously sidling up to mum's purse for more, but Pizza Express is not heavily geared and can cover their interest payments more than 50 times over. This is a company which is financing its expansion with its own money – never a bad sign.

Past performance
Since 1992, at the start of its expansion, Pizza Express has rewarded its shareholders with growth of 83 per cent a year: £10,000 invested back then would be worth almost £400,000 today.

But will it keep going?
The retrospectoscope is a powerful instrument. If we were allowed to invest with hindsight, the world would be full of trillionaires. It isn't. However, strong past performance is always going to be a very strong indicator of future success and one we like to follow. We like to invest in companies with a success story to tell and not ones which are – allegedly – about to drag themselves up by the bootstraps from whichever hole they have got themselves into. Look at it another way: you're in the pub and confronted by two people who want you to invest in their businesses. The first is on the verge of bankruptcy, and not for the first time, but the money you're about to invest is going to change his fortune. This *is the turning point!* The second has built up a successful chain of car dealerships and plans to expand to the next town, the next county, the world. Which one are you going to give money to?

Back to Pizza Express. If you look at the back of Pizza Express's annual report, you will see all their restaurants listed and you'll notice that at least half of them are in and around London. It's a big world out there and there looks to be plenty of room for a lot more Pizza Expresses, both here and abroad.

One day, though, the country may become saturated with pizza restaurants, the economy now so dependent on pizza eating that it will become illegal to eat at a pizza parlour less than once a week. Eventually, even these austerity measures will no longer work and the economy will collapse, preceded, of course, by Pizza Express. Alternatively, hard to imagine though it is, perhaps the pizza will go out of fashion, or another competitor will spring up, offering cheaper, friendlier pizzas. In short, Pizza Express is not Unilever, which will *never* go out of fashion. Pizza Express has a market cap of £500 million, not £45,000 million and it has sales of £71 million (growing at 60 per cent a year, mind you) and not £33,000 million. It is a small company (not quite so small now) which has had meteoric growth and is therefore more susceptible to market fluctuations and to factors affecting its single line of business – pizzas. While it has strong fundamentals and good prospects it remains a good investment, but it needs a closer eye kept on it than Unilever, which you could tuck away and forget for ten or twenty years. But then Unilever will never grow at 83 per cent a year, either. There's room for a variety of companies in our burgeoning investment portfolio and Pizza Express merits consideration as one of them.

The six obviously not great qualities

Now let's have a look at some of the pitfalls to steer clear of when selecting companies in which to invest. These are companies in major difficulties which, in our opinion, you'd be crazy to own right now.

Not a consumer brand name: BICC

It goes from bad to worse for poor old BICC. Have you heard of them? Not really surprising if you haven't. They're in the cables and construction business. There are some major barriers to entry in this business, like needing to have a huge industrial infrastructure, and this will always keep competitors from flooding into the market, but equally there isn't much which distinguishes your cables from other people's cables. Once they've been laid, they're, well, just cables. This means that the major deciding factor in purchasing cables from one company over another is always going to be cost, which can lead to ugly price wars and even uglier squeezes on margins. Without a brand name, without people *loving* your products just because they're yours and because they *think* they're the best, you don't have any unique angle and are reduced to competing with the crowd on pennies alone.

You see, it doesn't matter if your products actually *are* the best amongst a group of competitors, as long as people think they are. That's what a brand name's about. (Of course, if your products aren't the best, you won't be able to fool people indefinitely, but that's another story.)

We would venture to suggest that the majority of successful long-term businesses have some kind of consumer brand name attached to them. There are exceptions, but we want to buy easily understandable businesses which really have something going for them.

Today, BICC shares are worth a little over half what they were in 1983 and this in the midst of one of the greatest bull markets in history.

Not the best in the business: John Menzies

It's always been hard to imagine exactly what you go into John Menzies for. You drift in to a large shop with a dazzling array of sweeties, cigarettes, romantic fiction and a few magazines and come away having spent not very much at all. Yes, this is simply our partisan opinion, but some of the most successful investment decisions are subjective. You have to believe that what you're buying is the best in the business, because if you don't believe that, then why should any potential customers believe it and why should they spend their pounds to make the company a success? John Menzies certainly doesn't have the feel of being the best in the business. Its shares have almost halved in value in the last four years. The best of the best is what you're after. John Menzies doesn't even come close.

Not Making Good Money: Acatos and Hutcheson

Margins dropping from 6 per cent to under 2 per cent over the last five years and heavy depreciation in earnings have not made this company a happy investment. Something, somewhere seems to have gone severely awry in edible oils and fats, the company's sphere of activity. There are always plenty of excuses for failure and in this case one of the main ones is delays in opening a new factory.

One of the two brokers following the company rates them a buy as of early 1998, presumably on the basis that the long-awaited opening of their new facility will signal a turnaround. We prefer to let Acatos and Hutcheson's record speak for itself: today the shares are worth less than half what they were in 1987 and all this, if you remember, in the midst of one of the greatest bull markets in history. Whatever unfortunate blend of circumstances is cited for a company's poor performance, remember that nothing compels you to buy shares in that misfortune in the hope that shortly its luck will change. There are plenty of successful, market-beating companies out there – go buy them!

Not a repeat-purchase business: Hepworth

Among other things, this company manufactures and sells heating and pipeline systems for the housing market. They have seen their share price halve in the last six years. How many times do you have to renew your heating and piping? We really don't like to invest in this kind of business which is so dependent on one-off, long-term products and which is critically sensitive to the overall state of the economy. That's not to say that you *can't* make money by investing in these sorts of companies, just that we prefer not to try and to invest instead in something which we can understand and in whose repeat type of business we have more confidence.

Heavily laden with debt: Eurotunnel

It took 150 years for them to get around to building the Channel Tunnel. It will probably take another 150 for it to get out of debt. Currently, Eurotunnel's debt has been rescheduled to be paid off around 2050, but whether this will happen is anybody's guess. Eurotunnel owes almost eighteen times as much as it's worth and its income is sufficient to pay around one-*twentieth* of the annual interest charges. From February 1993 to February 1998, Eurotunnel shares lost 51 per cent of their value on average every year. Put it another way: they've dropped in value almost eight times in the last five years and all this in the midst of one of the greatest bull markets in history.

Someone out there must be buying Eurotunnel shares, as otherwise it wouldn't be possible to sell them. Who are you? The person who stops by one of our online areas and gives us a sensible explanation for why they have bought Eurotunnel shares will win their choice of a Motley Fool T-shirt, cap or book. (You'll have realized by now, we wouldn't make this challenge if we thought there was a serious chance of us having to part with any merchandise.)

Not performing very well: Laura Ashley

Oh, where have all the flower-y skirts gone? Once the darling of the darlings, Laura Ashley is in trouble. They have a brand all right, but what's happened to it? High levels of costs and an imprudently rapid expansion into the US market, where many another British retailer has come a cropper, that's what. In 1997 they posted a loss of almost £50 million, compared to a bare profit of £10 million the previous year, and at the time of writing they have already had to renegotiate banking facilities three times in the last six months and are looking at total sales down 14 per cent even on 1997. A large Malaysian group has just stepped in to buy 40 per cent of the company and probably saved them from going to the wall – who says there are no optimists left in the world? Maybe they'll make something of the brand and turn the company round. You might know by the time you read this.

In the meantime, Laura Ashley has lost over 80 per cent of its value in the last eighteen months and all this in the midst of one of the . . . (you get the idea, now?). As with Acatos and Hutcheson, we don't invest in turn-around stories and don't suggest that you do either. Success breeds success: stick with it. What's interesting about Laura Ashley is that a few years ago it may have been a company we'd have considered investing in. This shows once more that smaller capitalization companies need a closer eye kept on them than large capitalization giants like Unilever, the drug companies, or Marks & Spencer.

Buy what you are

So, where do you look for your investments? We've already talked about buying what everyone knows and it's hard to imagine getting more Foolish than that. Buying shares in companies whose products and services you and everyone else knows to be worthwhile is an excellent start. As you become more engaged in the growth of your future wealth, however, you're going to find yourself looking more and more deeply at the way in which your own individual life is supported by the products around you. Look at what you use in your job, what your company produces, what your competitors produce, what you use in your leisure hours (you do have some, we hope), what your family uses. If you're anything like us, you'll soon be saying to yourself: 'Hmm, this is a good product, but how would I market/manufacture/advertise it better?' Say that to yourself about most of the products you use and you'll often come up with a great idea for how to do it better because you – the end-user – are just the person to see the openings and opportunities which the company's management has overlooked. All you then have to do is send your idea off to the company, offering to enter negotiations for a licensing fee for your brainwave, sit back and let the royalties flood in. (Dream on.)

Occasionally, however, you'll find a product or service which you don't think can be bettered, one which is so expertly marketed and correctly targeted that you are speechless, dumbstruck with admiration. Congratulations! You have possibly just found a great investment. What you must do now is find out all you can about the company and crucially, whether it's publicly or privately owned. If it's privately owned, then tough luck: this company is going to have to go on your wish list, just in case it does one day decide to go public. (Unless, that is, you're a venture capitalist with a few million burning a hole in your back pocket and just itching for somewhere snappy, snazzy and right on to invest it. An Internet startup company, perhaps? In which case, e-mail us *right* now: FoolUKBook@fool.com.)

If it's a public company, then that's marvellous, but hold your horses, put the padlock back on your wallet, you have some *work* to do. First, you need their annual report and from there you want to know its history, what other products it produces, what future plans it has, its numbers (Is it growing? Is it profitable? Tiny market cap?) and what other people think of it. Look up recent articles about it in the press and ask the company themselves to send you copies of any recent analysts' reports: these can be illuminating. Finally, or perhaps firstly, stop by the Motley Fool's online resource – the people of Fooldom – and post a message about the company on one of our message boards.

If you're convinced that this company is the best thing since Mother's

Pride, you believe its product fills a unique niche, it is expertly managed and it satisfies all the financial criteria you will have by now developed for a company you're prepared to invest in, then go ahead – put your money where your mouth is!

A(nother) word of warning, however. If you're looking at a small capitalization company, you're going to have to be much more canny and you'll have to keep a much closer eye on your investment than if you're simply choosing consumer giants of the type we've mostly been talking about here. Pizza Express is the closest to the smaller, 'growth'-type shares we're alluding to in this section. That said, there are real profits to be made in using the specialist knowledge you use in your daily life to invest in companies which reflect what you **are**, whether those are small growth companies or multinational conglomerates.

For more on choosing smaller, more volatile companies in which to invest, you'll have to wait for our next book *The Fool's Guide to Growth Shares*. As you know, though, this depends on your hawking this book to death amongst friends, acquaintances, total strangers and the occasional passing Alsatian.

When you're back from your next tour of the neighbourhood, selling our book, you can read the next chapter, 'A Less Obvious Obviously Great Investment'. See you there!

13

A Less Obvious Obviously Good Investment

Cleanliness is, indeed, next to godliness.
John Wesley, *Sermons on Several Occasions*

Been to see your favourite band of ageing rockers, the Dead Pet Police,[1] recently? No? You should do. They're starting to look a little tired and may not be touring much longer: 30 years of relentless rocking has a price, you know. If you have been a faithful groupie, though – and we hope you have, because these guys need your support – you may have noticed the badges some of the security guards and marshals were wearing. The days when the Grateful Dead used the local Hells Angels chapter to keep order at concerts are now, thankfully, long past. In the late 90s it's the local pest control people who patrol the crowd lines. Which, if you think about it, makes a lot more sense.

If you'd been attentive, you could have learned much more at that concert than that you didn't much relish hairy rockers fixing you with bewildered, bloodshot eyes before stumbling off in the direction of the Gents. Right in front of your nose as you swayed with misty-eyed nostalgia was a Less Obvious Obviously Good Investment strutting its stuff along with the band. As we shall shortly see, there are no flies on Rentokil, or rather, Rentokil Initial, as they have called themselves since they took over another company called BET in 1996.

Rentokil Initial – the company

Rentokil is a name like 'Hoover'. It doesn't matter if you think the stock market is a place where they sell different types of bouillon, because if you have had even the briefest spell of animate life in the last 20 years you *will* have heard of Rentokil. For this, ladies and gentlemen, is a **brand**! If you

---

1 David B.'s been itching to use this name for years. It has all the elements needed for a successful group and we will therefore license it out to suitable candidates for a share of the royalties, to be agreed, but not less than 10 per cent. Contact the Motley Fool UK for more details.

have a pest to get rid of – rats, cockroaches, unwanted lodger – who you gonna call? PestBusters? No, Rentokil, dummy!

There's no competition. We challenge you to name another pest control company (and you're not allowed to look in the Yellow Pages). Difficult, isn't it? Would you fancy trying to compete with this company? No, neither would we. Why, though, if we've all heard of Rentokil, is it a *Less Obvious* Obviously Good Investment? Because we take pest control and wiping our hands for granted. They're not something you think about until you start to see little tooth marks in the cheese or there's no clean towel left in the dispenser. The funny thing about this is that even though they are the largest commercial pest control company in the world, pest control is now the *smallest* of the company's six divisions. Things have changed greatly since their acquisition of BET PLC in 1996 and the company now has the following divisions, listed in order of the size of each of their businesses:

- Hygiene and Cleaning Services
- Plant and Distribution Services
- Security Services
- Property Services
- Personnel Services
- Pest Control

Notice anything about this list? How about the word 'Services' which crops up in five of the six divisions? The new Rentokil Initial is dedicated to serving others. Ain't that sweet? Definitely, because 'Service' means repeat business and repeat business means the repeated chance to make a profit. Rentokil is not dealing in one-off contracts to build dams in the Far East, or sporadic orders for freight trains, which may roll in every couple of years. Or may not. Rentokil deals in millions of ways every day with millions of things which we take for granted, as long as they're there. But if any of those things start to break down or become unavailable, watch people yell. Take a look at what these divisions actually do and some of the other brand names they encompass. It makes thought-provoking reading:

Hygiene and Cleaning Services

This is one of the most recognizable parts of the business. The ten times you wash your hands on a Friday night in the pub (you *do* wash them, don't you?), you contribute ten times to the profits of Rentokil Initial who provide the hot air dryers and towel dispensers on which you dry yourself. Hygiene may be uninspiring, but you'd miss it if it wasn't there. It's also an area which hasn't changed much since a nineteenth century Austrian physician called Semmelweiss discovered he could halve the infection rate – and thus the death rate – among his gynaecology patients by washing his hands when he came from the post-mortem room to the ward. (Ugh!) Since hygiene is unlikely to change much in the future either, this means that Rentokil Initial is unlikely to have to pour large sums of money into keeping up with technological advances. They'll just go on steadily servicing public and office loos into the next millennium, while keeping nice and quiet as they work on cutting down their costs and expanding their empire further. And who, we put it to you, could blame them?

Elsewhere in this division are various hospital and textile services, along with specialized cleaning services to the catering industry. It gets better and better, but it's time to wipe our hands and move on . . .

Plant and distribution services

Not toilets, but still tough, dirty work. This is another inheritance from the BET takeover. Initial Plant Services supplies and hires equipment like scaffolding, aerial work platforms, cranes and lifting equipment, accommodation units and offshore cranes. This division also includes City Link and A to Z couriers, Rentokil's own express parcels delivery service. It's not quite the same as Hygiene and Cleaning, as it requires much more capital investment (in the form of expensive equipment) and is much more sensitive to the state of the economy (people will never stop using the loo, but they might stop building new office blocks). Traditionally, it is also more competitive and thus there is more of a squeeze on profit margins, but Rentokil's magic has always been in being able to cut costs (and therefore increase profit margins). Their results for 1997, published in March 1998, showed that the old magic was still working for Rentokil Initial. Profit margins in this group went up.

Security services

These were the people who stopped you mobbing the Dead Pet Police. They also provide electronic security in the form of alarms and closed circuit TV.

Property services

This division encompasses just about everything Rentokil does to look after properties, which can be offices, schools, factories or holiday resorts. Have you noticed the tropical plants every time you go into an office building? It's likely they've been provided by Rentokil.

Personnel services

Initial Personnel Services provides temporary, contract and permanent staff to a wide range of businesses.

Pest control

Finally, the one you thought would be the biggest. This part of the business is phenomenally profitable, but probably quite 'mature' in terms of how much room it has to expand.

Rentokil rules the world in pest control. If you rule the world and you want to get bigger, you have to find new worlds to conquer, which was why Rentokil took over BET, effectively doubling the size of the company. BET provided the opportunity to turn around a series of new businesses with quite low profitability by using Rentokil's sleek management techniques. So far, it's working.

The Rentokil Initial bottom line

Rentokil Initial, this company whose stock in trade is now wiping your hands, has provided year-on-year growth of 20 per cent or more for the last fifteen years, all the while characterized by an excellent management and emphasis on cutting costs to the minimum. If you had invested £1000 in Rentokil back in 1983, you would be worth £35,600 today, an increase of 3560 per cent. The stock market index during that period would have turned that same £1000 into £7700, a healthy sum but just under a fifth of the amount you could have made out of the pest people. Is it going to do the same again over the next fifteen years? Well, if not quite that rate of growth, why not something close to it?

You've wiped your hands on their towels, ditched your chewing gum in their tropical plants and called them in to clear your house of cockroaches. In all three cases the company has provided a quality service, but it is still a big step to go out and invest in them. How do you go from using or being familiar with this company's products to becoming a part-owner? Is it enough to say: 'Hey, I've got a great investment idea! I don't like cockroaches, neither does anyone else I know, so I'll buy Rentokil!'? Well, let's see how Rentokil fits the finely crafted criteria we applied earlier to some of our Obviously Great Investments:

1. Have they built a consumer brand?

No doubt about that. From their traditional territory of pest control to Initial towel services, Rentokil property care, A to Z couriers and well beyond, this company has brands coming out its ears. We've seen how we all need to use Rentokil's services regularly in our daily lives and how they provide the infrastructure for a whole lot more besides. Rentokil's management realized the importance of branding when they decided to add the name Initial after taking over the parent company BET in 1996. Rentokil likes branding, we like branding, the world likes branding. You can't underestimate the power of a good brand to sell products and Rentokil Initial is in no danger of doing that. Yup, pass on the brand issue.

2. Are they the best in their business?

Definitely. At least in some of their businesses – the old Rentokil core businesses and Initial hygiene services. For the rest of the businesses which they have taken over from BET, we'll have to give Rentokil's outstanding management the chance to prove themselves. They've done it before, they'll probably do it again.

3. Do people buy their products regularly?

Yes, again. (Is this starting to get monotonous? Did you really think we'd have started writing about Rentokil as our benchmark Less Obvious Obviously Great Investment if we didn't have a shrewd idea it was going to make the cut? Shame on you!)

4. Are they making a lot of money for their efforts?

This is where Rentokil has always shone. Margins of 34 per cent in the cockroach side of the business prove that. Margins across the whole of the business in 1995 were a storming 24.5 per cent, but then came the BET takeover in 1996 and the margins fell that year to 13.6 per cent. Ouch! Or rather, what an exciting challenge and certainly one which Rentokil has risen to. In 1997, the first full year after taking over BET, the margins increased to 14.5 per cent. The highlight of the year was in the Personnel Services division where margins increased from 6.1 per cent to 8.4 per cent. This capacity to improve margins is going to fuel Rentokil's growth over the next few years.
So, margins? ✓

5. Are they funding new growth with their own money?

You'll remember what this means: Are they in debt up to their eyebrows? 'No' is the answer. In fact, up to the BET takeover, they carried no debt at all. In 1996, they had a debt of £510 million and in 1997 this had been reduced to £410 million and with interest cover of 8.4, there's no problem with debt here. Expect Rentokil to whittle this down further in years to come, despite an ongoing series of commercial acquisitions.

6. Have they been a success up to now?

We know the answer to this: 20 per cent per year compounded earnings growth every year since 1983, compounded share price growth since then of 26.9 per cent. It generally pays to back a winning horse. 'Nuff said.

Here Endeth the Lesson

You tell your children that if they don't clean their rooms you'll have to get Rentokil to fumigate them, you use a towel dispenser in a public loo, you go to a rock concert: every time you carry out one of these Great British Activities, one of the Great British Investments of the last 20 years stares you in the face. The lesson is that beyond every Obviously Great Investment, a whole series of Less Obviously Obvious Great Investments lies waiting to be discovered. It simply remains to go out and find them.

14

The Foolish Operating Manual for Obviously Great Investments

A Company for carrying on an undertaking of
Great Advantage, but no one to know what it is.
Anonymous. Company prospectus at the time of the South Sea
Bubble in 1711, the greatest market crash there ever was

By now, our approach to selecting Obviously Great Investments is so deeply integrated into your soul that it is the work of just a few seconds to spot that the company quoted above doesn't quite fit the criteria. But before you go on to consider opening a brokerage account and actually *buying* some shares in your Obviously Great Investments, we'd like to run through what some of the advantages are to you of your Obviously Great Investment portfolio.

No exhaustive research

The most common reason people give for not investing their own money intelligently on their own behalf is lack of time. Everyone has enough time to invest in an index tracker and we would say that pretty well everyone has enough time to invest in Obviously Great Investments. Twelve hours a year, one hour a month. How much time did you spend watching television last week? One hour a month is easily within your grasp. We're not counting here, of course, the fact that you are doing your most basic company research every day as you toddle through the activities of daily life. As you become more attuned to this way of thinking, you'll find that every new product you use or pick up will raise a question mark in your mind. Is this a good product? Could I live without it? Who else provides it and do they do it better? *Does* anyone else provide it? And the crucial one: Might it be a good investment? One question we like to ask ourselves is, if *we* ran this company, how would *we* do it better? This can make a nice game for those long, tedious car journeys with the family. Either that, or they'll get so sick of you banging on about shares all the time that they'll murder you and leave your body in a lay-by. On second thoughts, be careful with this one.

The challenge for Obviously Great investors, and in fact any investor, is to sort out just which activities are crucial to your success, which aren't and then modify your actions accordingly. If you assemble the right model for choosing your investments, then you're not going to be flicking Teletext on every five minutes to catch the latest price, wading through reams of investment information and living, eating and breathing shares. What the FTSE does from one day to the next is totally irrelevant to you. You can be the anti-investor, the investor who doesn't watch the market slavishly. In fact, as long as the underlying business is good, you don't need to check on your companies more than once every six months, perhaps even once a year. One of the posters at the Motley Fool's US site, a chap who signs himself Doubting Thomas, summed it up nicely when he wrote: 'In the end, I doubt that I'll look back on my life and remember the good times I had monitoring the price of a particular stock.' True enough. Investing is meant to support your ideals and dreams, not distract you from them. Despite what we've said about every minute of your life being a share research opportunity – we're tuned in to this stuff fifteen hours a day, so you'll have to excuse us – it will become clear to you that your challenge isn't actually to find hordes of new companies to research, or to scour the financial pages of the newspaper for investment opportunities. You won't need to subscribe to expensive newsletters, consider ten different industries and forty shares a year and try to make sense of it all. Instead, your successes will be determined by how well you can save money and how strong are the few businesses you've selected. If £1000 invested in Unilever shares 35 years ago is worth £75,000 today, what lessons can we learn from that? Perhaps that finding just a few great companies and adding money to them each year will make for a smashingly successful investment career.

No anxiety

Some people do genuinely believe that if they don't monitor the price of their shares 20 times every day, the company might go bust. It isn't so. A friend of one of us also believes that if she doesn't concentrate every moment her flight is in the air or if she presses down too hard with her knife and fork, it will immediately drop out of the sky. That isn't so either. The result? She takes a lot of trains and this despite the fact that trains carry *twice* the risk of aircraft, while getting there much less than half as quickly.

Obsessive checking of the share price is one thing, but what are we really, really worried about? Losing it all, of course. Everything. The lot.

'I'm sorry, darling, it's, it's . . . all gone! GONE! GONE!'

'Well, Quentin, it's your own fault and I'm afraid I shall have to leave you forthwith. I shall be taking the children and any remaining assets you have. I believe they make quite a fair wage selling the Big Issue these days. Farewell.'

You'll sob and tug at their coat-tails, but you'll be pushed aside, the children will be bundled into the car and the last you'll see of the little blighters is a pair of small, sad faces pressed up against the window. And all because you invested in the **Stock Market!** (For the full effect, you have to say this in a deep, Ben Elton style voice, laden with dread. Try it and look around wide-eyed at the audience as you do so.)

Okay, okay, this really is *not* going to happen. Well, all right, it *might* happen if you select terrible companies. What we hope to have pointed out here is that there are a lot of large, highly successful companies whose products you are likely familiar with from your everyday life and in whom you can easily invest. By sticking to things you know and understand as a consumer and picking large, quality companies, you are unlikely to get into serious trouble.

Finally, take a deep breath and go back to the Bible of the Long-distance Investor (see Chapter 4). The trend of shares is from the bottom left to the top right of the graph. There are blips and dips along the way, but if you selected quality companies or bought the whole market via an index tracker, a couple of sour market years are not going to hinder the long-term growth of your savings. There's no cause for stress if you take the market on your own terms. Let the short-term fluctuations horrify the rest of the investment world. You're in for the long haul.

No foreign languages

Here's a simple notion that works whenever you have your wallet, credit card, Switch card or brokerage account number and password handy: If you don't understand what you're hearing, walk away. In any big money transaction – from car buying to insurance to share purchases – if you can't explain entirely what you're doing, why you're doing it, and what to expect from it, don't make the investment.

So much in the traditional money world has been designed to confuse you. Before the birth of the Internet and the advent of Folly, investors using advisory brokers operated alone against corporate armies designed to extract the maximum amount of pounds from their wallet each year. For years now, your average financial salesman has known that you are all alone, uneducated on financial matters and keen to just Get The Thing Signed. Many people we know have been so worn down by financial sales-men and so intimidated by the seeming complexity of the whole thing, that they've signed just to get rid of them and so they don't have to think about it all anymore: 'Look, Alan, it seems like a good idea. We'll sign, just as long as we don't lose and it's the right thing, we'll sign.' Then they often say, with a laugh: 'We trust you. We haven't got any choice, after all!' Wrong on both counts. They didn't really trust him because they didn't understand a word he said, and they did have a choice, but couldn't face going through the whole thing again.

Until you understand what you're doing, your money should be in the bank or building society walking in step with inflation. Speaking foreign languages to make money is not a fruitful long-term investment approach.

No buy points

There are really no buy points with these models – no magic moment when you *must* purchase your picks. The aim is to find a small group of the most financially sturdy, most profitable, best performing, best of breed, strongest brand, most professionally managed companies. When you find them, you can buy them and turn your eyes away from the stock market. There are other things in life and you have years, if not decades, to let the power of compounded returns work for you.

Now, if you buy and hold great shares, you will have successfully tiptoed through an industry buoyed by overpriced information and conveniently supportive jargon. Many Foolish investors believe that the most valuable financial resources out there are the ones that are free: the guides and books that sit in our public libraries, the rapidly increasing amount of information available on the Internet. With a dash of cogent research, a sprinkling of basic business principles and a heavy load of patience, investors needn't worry about what the present prices are of the shares in their portfolio.

In fact, the idea of buying 'low' and selling 'high' is essentially absurd for investors looking to make money over the next 30 years. For them, the better line is: Buy intelligently, buy when you can and buy again when you have more cash you can put away for at least three to five years. Invest it into these cash-strong, well managed, rapidly growing, strong brand companies. And when a decade has passed, look for the next ten great companies – you'll probably find many of the same ten among them.

There are hundreds of varied and wonderful financial resources out there – expensive newsletters, hot tips in investing magazines, whisper columns in the daily newspapers, expensive computer software – all designed to tell you when precisely to BUY! and when to SELL! shares. These may be just the resources which will help you get *beaten* by the market. Once more, engage the market on your own terms and, in doing so, worry far less about the timing of your entry than the quality of your selections. Don't put off investing in a popular and successful company which looks overvalued. It will have been so many times in the last ten years and would always have been a good investment.

No great expense

Think back to the Miracle of Compound Interest. There we saw that costs of any kind can seriously eat into our returns. One of the easiest kinds of costs to accrue is that of frequent trading, with the consequent hits in terms of trading charges and tax which that implies. Unless you have a couple of hundred million pounds or more, we don't think it's a good idea to furiously trade your selected investments. Leave active trading to the unit trust managers, more than 90 per cent of whom actively *under*perform the market over the long-term. Buying Obviously Great Investments is a play on market outperformance *and* minimizing associated costs.

It is fundamental to our investment methodology that you do not spend a great deal of money on research materials (The Motley Fool Online and many other resources on the Net are free), that you do not pay out large sums of money in commissions or taxes and that you do not end up paying significant opportunity costs – like missing a walk on the beach with your family next Saturday in order to stem the flow of losses from your options trading.

It's time now for a multiple choice question. As is usually the case, marks are deducted for a wrong answer, but this time a wrong answer will also cause the book to burst into flames. Good luck!

The investment philosophy of the Motley Fool may best be encapsulated by the following motto:

1 Win at all costs!
2 Kill or be killed!
3 No guts, no glory!
4 No work without enduring profit.

The answer, of course, is '4'. Unless you can show markedly improved returns by spending more time on investment, and unless you enjoy spending that additional time, a good blend of Obvious Greats and an index tracker are enough for the whole of your life.

A Caveat

In our urge to simplify matters, we are perhaps guilty of lumping together too many categories of investment under one roof. While we consider the above operating manual to be an excellent starting point, use it Foolishly, especially when investing in smaller capitalization companies. A Pizza Express, a Games Workshop, or a JJB Sports – three growth shares of the last couple of years – simply will have to have a closer eye kept on it than a Unilever or a Marks & Spencer. If you do wish to tuck away your investments and not look at them for a prolonged period, do not buy a smaller capitalization company, however tempting it may look. Settle instead for a humongous, successful consumer giant. You won't be disappointed. And you won't lie awake at night worrying either.

And finally . . .

If you're not psychologically prepared for the business of investing in shares, if you haven't rehearsed it in your mind for some time and even on paper, you may be setting yourself up for a long and painful fall. Investing profitably for the long term – a neat encapsulation of Foolishness, we think – is all about adopting an approach which is deeply contrary to the sentiments of most of us. Increasingly in our age, we have come to expect instant results and instant gratification. If something's boring us, then 'Zap!' goes the remote control again and we're onto something else. Don't like your kids/husband/wife/car? Trade 'em in! Don't like it here? Go there! Don't like it there? Come back! Doing that in the stock market will seriously damage your wealth. In 'A Foray Into Some Very foolish Futures' we saw how that kind of short-term approach to wealth accumulation can turn very sour very quickly.

Long-termism is a profitable investing creed, so read on for more of it in the next chapter.

15

Beating the Footsie

'The game,' said he, 'is never lost till won.'
George Crabbe, *Tales of the Hall*

Different people have different temperaments. Some will wish to stick with an index tracker for the whole of their lives, others will look for Obviously Great Investments, yet others will invest in more speculative small-cap. shares and some will always feel safest and happiest handing their money over to someone else to manage. There are also some people who are fascinated with odds, people who like to stake their money on the winning side, even if that winning side doesn't win every time. They know that you don't have to win *every* time to win over the long term, simply more of the time than you lose. These people probably appreciate the elegant simplicity of the index tracker; they smile ruefully as they reflect that this philosophy is exactly how casinos turn in huge profits over the long term and they are almost certainly not regular players of the National Lottery, for such an activity would be an intolerable affront to their sensibilities. Even if you're not one of these people, read on. You might be by the time you finish this chapter.

In the early 90s, a US money manager by the name of Michael O'Higgins published a landmark book entitled *Beating the Dow*. In it he outlined a mechanical investment strategy which involved buying those five of the thirty members of the Dow-Jones Industrial Average which had been 'excessively' penalized by the market, holding them for a year and then at the end of that time rebalancing the portfolio into the next five laggards, or 'Dogs' as they are often referred to. During the course of that year, the Dogs tended to move up as the market's 'excessive' marking-down of these shares bled away and they came closer to what might be termed a fairer valuation. Over the years, this strategy brought in astonishing market-beating returns and required no share-picking skill at all to follow. It was also totally and utterly objective, not allowing for any subjectivity in which shares to buy, which shares to sell and when to do it. It depended on the fact that *often enough* the market over-reacted to bad news about particular companies, only to change its mind later. Buy the companies when they're feeling the full heat of their market disgrace, hold them until tempers have cooled, sell them at a profit and, hey presto, you have a market-beating strategy.

Let's take a couple of graphic and rather distasteful examples to make the point. Union Carbide poisoned the entire Indian city of Bhopal in 1984 with clouds of poison gas, killing thousands. Union Carbide is a massive industrial conglomerate and was never going to go out of business as a result of this. It was going to be expensive, yes, but the company was always going to recover. The public, however, and the market were so shocked that the shares dived sharply at the time, to recover later when all the *brouhaha* had died down. The same thing happened when the Exxon Valdez oil tanker was driven onto a reef and polluted hundreds of miles of pristine Alaskan coastline. Again, Exxon, a massive oil company, garnered adverse publicity from this, but the cost was never going to be paralyzing. The market, however, marked the shares down, making them a potential bargain. Happily, O'Higgins's strategy isn't for the most part founded on such tragedies as these, but more commonplace ones such as temporary interruptions in profit flow, or adverse trading conditions. The thing to remember, though, is that this only works for huge companies which have the might to withstand what are essentially gnat bites on their elephant hides and come back fighting a little later.

That's all fine, but how do you identify these companies? The answer is in the dividend yield. Remember this? It is the relationship between the dividend and the share price which we talked about in 'A Share Primer' (Chapter 11). Now, are you ready for the clever bit? Share price fluctuates according to the whims of the market. Dividends, however, are set by the companies themselves twice a year and there is a tremendous pressure on them not to cut them. Firstly, it looks very, very bad indeed and the implication it brings that the company is in real trouble is only going to hammer the share price even more. Secondly, shareholders, both private and institutional, reckon on the dividend for at least part of their income. Cutting it is going to make a lot of people very angry. So, as the share price drops and the dividend stays the same, the yield (the dividend divided by the share price and expressed as a percentage) goes . . .

Can you see which way it goes? Yes, it goes *up*. So, high yielders are more likely to be shares in trouble, or at least shares currently in disfavour for whatever reason. O'Higgins evolved a system of taking the ten highest yielders from the thirty shares of the Dow-Jones Industrial Average – some of the largest companies in the US – taking the five *cheapest* of those, buying them in equal dollar amounts and holding them for a year, before reallocating to the next 'Dow Dividend Five', or 'DD5'. At the Motley Fool, we did some of our own backtesting calculations on this strategy, from 1961 to 1997. Here's the result:

	Yearly average	Total Return
Dow 30	12.07%	6778.13%
DD5	15.96%	23991.25%

Isn't it interesting that with less than four percentage points between the index and the DD5 strategy, the total return over the 36 years should be so different? It is, of course, the power of compound interest once more laying its gentle hand upon our shoulders. And the thing to remember is that these world-beating returns are being obtained by investing, once a year, in some of the largest, most successful companies in the world, companies such as Coca-Cola, General Motors, IBM and Procter and Gamble. It's also worth noting that this period includes the 60s, which was not a particularly good decade for shares as a whole.

So that's Beating the Dow, asks you, but what about Beating the *Footsie*, which is what we're supposed to be talking about here? Well spotted. Back in 1935, the FT 30 index was invented as an equivalent to the Dow-Jones Industrial Average index in the United States and most of the backtesting of the high-yielding strategy in the UK has been done on this index. From 1970–96, anyway, Johnson Fry, a unit trust company, has done some backtesting and the results look like this:

	Yearly average	Total Return
FT-All Share Index	15.6%	5,028%
Footsie 5	20.5%	15,370%

Pretty impressive numbers for a strategy which requires no thought and no skill to implement. An investment of £10,000 in the Footsie Five back in 1970 would have been worth £1,537,000 by 1996. But what exactly is in the FT 30? Here's what:

ASDA Group	Granada
Allied Domecq	GKN
BOC	ICI
BTR	Lloyds / TSB
Blue Circle Ind.	Lucas Varity
Boots Co.	Marks & Spencer
British Airways	National Westminster Bank
British Gas	P & O
British Petroleum	Prudential
British Telecom	Reuters
Cadbury Schweppes	Royal & Sun Alliance Insurance Group
Diageo	Scottish Power
EMI group	SmithKline Beecham
General Electric	Tate & Lyle
Glaxo Wellcome	Vodafone

We bet you recognize most of these great British brand names and it's from amongst this stable that you buy and hold your Footsie Five for a year at a time. As in the US, the unloved high-yielders come good if you give them sufficient time. What follows is some backtesting we did on our own account. Unfortunately, we've only been able to accumulate the required data – dividend yield, share price, etc. – going back to 1983 and even then we've had to make a couple of assumptions. For various reasons it's very hard indeed to get hold of information from before that date and although we did ask Johnson Fry to let us use their data, d'ye know what? They didn't even answer us! Anyway, here's what we've got and it's pretty interesting. Here's what would have happened had you simply chosen to buy and hold for one year the ten highest-yielding companies in the FT 30 on the last Friday in January, every year from 1983 to 1997:

Year	Percentage Return
1983	60.75
1984	28.48
1985	27.30
1986	29.65
1987	17.45
1988	25.27
1989	22.50
1990	**–4.02**
1991	20.26
1992	38.05
1993	42.53
1994	**–8.07**
1995	12.54
1996	0.43
1997	26.52
Average	21.40%

Ignoring tax and share trading charges, £10,000 invested into this strategy in 1983 would have been worth £183,350 in January 1998.

Now look what would have happened had you simply bought the five *cheapest* of those ten highest yielders, a combination we call the Footsie Five:

Year	Percentage Return
1983	56.22
1984	38.97
1985	45.61
1986	31.05
1987	8.42
1988	26.74
1989	31.96

1990	2.43
1991	28.09
1992	42.75
1993	36.26
1994	− 11.83
1995	16.96
1996	− 2.89
1997	17.67
Average	**23.7%**

Invested in the Footsie Five, £10,000 in 1983 would have been worth £243,000 in January 1998.

These rates of return are truly extraordinary and require precisely no skill whatsoever to achieve. What they do require, however, is a sound understanding of the strategy and its contrarian nature. In the last four years, it has had two down years, and the return from 1993 to 1997 of the Footsie Five strategy has been a 'meagre' 9.9 per cent per year, while for the high yielding ten it has been higher at 13.4 per cent every year. Occasional reports about the strategy in the press have reported its 'failure' in the raging bull market of recent years, but we consider reports of its death to have been grossly exaggerated. At the time of writing (June 1998), a Footsie Five portfolio started in January 1998 is up over 20 per cent, as compared to the FTSE 100 which is up 14 per cent and the FT30 which is up 18 per cent.

One question which may have been forming on your lips is: 'Why the five cheapest of the ten highest yielders?' Good point. In fact, there is reason to believe that the strategy might work even better by simply choosing the five highest yielders. The reason we choose the five cheapest is that's the way O'Higgins did it, citing as grounds that a low share price made it more likely – from a psychological point of view – that the share price would climb. This depends on investors thinking they're getting a bargain by buying a share at 200p instead of 500p and, although we know this is ludicrous, this is often what happens in the market. We'll be looking at this issue in months and years to come as we refine the Beating the Footsie strategy.

There are no guarantees that the strategy will continue to bring in market-thrashing returns over the next 30 years, as it has over the last 30, but, as we have pointed out in previous chapters, we are firm believers in past performance. Combine that with a strong theoretical basis as to why the strategy works, which depends on market over-reaction to company news and the ultimate tendency for that over-reaction to be corrected,[1] and there is a sound intellectual heart to this strategy. Remember, though, it is as a long-term approach that this strategy must be tackled. If you're a short-term, 'day-trading' investor, this approach is not for you, in fact the Motley Fool is not for you. Danger! Do not approach any closer! Just put down the gun nice and gently and back off the way you came. No sudden movements. There you go. Easy, easy, boy . . .

Another question which is likely to be coursing through your minds: Why use the FT 30 index as a starting point? It's the first time this index has been mentioned in this book, it's rarely quoted elsewhere and seems to have been superseded by the FTSE 100 and FTSE-All Share Index. Further, you say – warming to your theme now – there are some members of the FT 30 whose market capitalization has slipped so far they are no longer even included in the FTSE 100, Tate & Lyle being a case in point. This index is ridiculous, you say. We admit it. You're spot-on: all this is true. However, it makes for a circumscribed group of well-known, large capitalization shares and, importantly, it contains representatives from all the main industrial sectors. The 900 shares of the FT-All Share Index are clearly too many to sort by yield and, in any case, this strategy depends for its success on using very large capitalization shares which have the resilience to withstand a touch of market disfavour. A company with a market capitalization of only £100 million which disappoints the market will get *killed* and may never rise again. One which has a market capitalization of £5,000 million, on the other hand, has the momentum to surge through the other side and emerge victorious once more. As for the FTSE 100, yes, that would be a possibility, but again 100 shares is rather a lot to sort through, although limited backtesting has been done on the FTSE 100 which reveals the strategy works pretty well. One argument against using the FTSE 100 is that it may be possible to end up with a selection of high yielders in which several may all be from the same sector – banking, say. This potential lack of diversity in share selections from year to year makes the FTSE 100 less appealing as an index and isn't an issue with the FT 30. One reader at the Motley Fool UK who goes by the screen name of 'Pyad' has created his own index of leading British shares which he called the 'Pyad 26'. This looks to have some interesting qualities, but work is ongoing on it. Stop by the Fool UK online for the latest thoughts on this and the Beating the Footsie approach as a whole.

For now, the FT 30, unloved and unquoted index that it is, is proving more than adequate as a universe of shares from which to start and the next question on your lips is likely to be: 'Just suppose, right, just suppose, I was Foolish enough to want to give this Footsie Beater thingy a try, how *exactly* would I, er, do it?'

This is how. In fact there are two ways. Here's Method 1:

---

1 Buffett calls the market a voting machine in the short term and a weighing machine in the long term.

1. Choose a day of the year which will be your day for changing your portfolio every year. (Let's say you've chosen the first Friday of a particular month, which will allow you to do the calculations over the weekend and buy the shares first thing Monday morning.)
2. Buy Saturday's *Financial Times.*
3. Obtain the current list of the constituents of the FT 30 from the *Financial Times*'s faxback number (0891 437 014). Do this after the market closes on Friday to gain the closing prices. (It is important to get this up-to-date list, as the index's constituents vary slightly from time to time.)
4. Using the faxed list, write in the dividend yield next to the 30 companies, using the information from the prices page in the Saturday *FT.* (You'll find it under the 'Yld' column next to the share price.)
5. On a separate piece of paper write down the ten companies with the highest yields and write in Friday's closing prices next to them.
6. If you're following the High Yielding Ten: Buy these ten in equal pound amounts. (This is important. The strategy has only been tested – and probably only works – with the shares equally weighted at the start in terms of monetary value, not numbers of shares.)
7. If you're following the Footsie Five: Pick the five cheapest of these and buy equal pound amounts of them. (This is important. The strategy has only been tested – and probably only works – with the shares equally weighted at the start in terms of monetary value, not numbers of shares.)
8. Keep a record of what you have done, either on paper or in financial software designed for the task, like Quicken or Microsoft Money.
9. Bide your time patiently and with Foolish sang-froid for one year.
10. One year later, revisit steps 1–7, reinvest the sum earned from dividends and make sure again that the total investment in each share is equal.
11. Keep doing this year on year.

The above process should not take much more than 20 minutes and if you allow another 10 minutes for setting up the share purchases, that adds up to 30 minutes' effort per year.

Now take a look at method two, which takes even less time.

How to construct a Beating the Footsie portfolio, Method 2:

1. Choose a day of the year which will be your day for changing your portfolio every year.
2. Download the current High Yielding Ten or Footsie Five rankings at the Fool UK (AOL Keyword: FOOLUK or website http://www.fool.co.uk).
3. Buy them in equal pound amounts.
4. Keep a record of what you have done, either on paper or in financial software designed for the task, like Quicken or Microsoft Money.

5. Bide your time patiently and with Foolish sang-froid for one year.
6. One year later, revisit steps 1–3, reinvest the sum earned from dividends and make sure again that the total investment in each share is equal.
7. Keep doing this year on year.

Why Beating the Footsie works

If you've paid attention this far, first, well done and, secondly, you might be wondering why, if this is such a super strategy involving investment in the *crème-de-la-crème* of British industry, doesn't everyone do it? Obviously, it is a market-beater, therefore you'd think that word would get around, large numbers of investors would start to follow it and, as they did so, this would drive the prices of these supposedly 'out of favour' shares upwards immediately, thus scuppering the whole thing. Aha! You sound suspiciously like a proponent of the Efficient Markets Theory. But no! *Donner und Blitzen!* Tell us it isn't true!

The Efficient Markets Theory is taught in economics classes around the world. It says something like this. In our world in which information is so freely distributed, it is impossible for one group of people to be at an advantage in terms of the information they hold; thus, once information gets around about a company, the price of those shares will come to reflect this information. In other words, there can never be any 'inefficiency' in pricing and the price of a share will always reflect everything which is known about that share at that particular time. By this argument, it is impossible for anyone to ever consistently beat the market. We say two things in response to this:

First, we say 'Warren Buffett'.

Secondly, we say that although information may be evenly distributed, the capacity to process that information most definitely is not. Anyone who has watched share prices fluctuate from hour to hour on the basis of no news or insignificant long-term news about a company will testify to this.

So, there are a number of reasons why this strategy works. Firstly, it is deeply, deeply contrary. Yes, it involves investing in some of the most well-known companies, but they are also currently the dogs which no-one else wants to buy. And, once these mangy canines have been bought, they quite commonly slip even farther south, before starting the slow crawl north again. This is why holding periods of at least a year are necessary to allow these out-of-favour shares to finally come good. (In fact in the US, the holding period for the Motley Fool's Beating the Dow variant has been increased to eighteen months for Capital Gains Tax purposes and works even better.) It can take some strength of character, a belief in and an understanding of the strategy to sit out what can be an occasionally uncomfortable ride in shares everyone else steers clear of.

Another reason why this will never be a popular strategy is that not only does it require a contrary spirit, but it is dull, dull, dull, oh, so deathly dull! Many people want a more hands-on approach to stock-picking and in between once-yearly bursts of activity lasting precisely one half hour, there is nothing for a restless investor to do, not even keep an eye on the market. The tendency for even seasoned Foolish investors is to want to tinker and try and 'improve' the returns because we know that this particular share really is not going to do well this year, so if we just sell it and buy the next one on the list and don't tell anyone we're bucking the strategy, just this once . . . But no, this is fatal to Foolish investment hopes! Read on to see how important it is to be a cool, calm Foolish player of the long-term odds.

If you look back to the second paragraph of this chapter, you will see the words 'often enough' highlighted in italics, referring to the frequency with which high dividend yields are predictive of an undervalued share price. This is important, because it is not always the case that shares with a high dividend yield are relatively undervalued by the market, merely that they are so *often enough* for us to profit. This puts the high-yield investor in a similar situation to the casino boss, who is betting that 51 times out of 100 he will win at the blackjack table. The punter, meanwhile, knows the long-term odds are against him, but hopes for a bit of luck on the day. Of the two, the casino boss will indubitably win in the long term, but will miss out on the short-term excitement, while the punter will ultimately lose if he keeps coming back, but will have certainly had an exciting time. The casino boss has no emotion invested in his sensible, long-term approach, while the punter's approach involves nothing but emotion.

If we now take an unemotional look at the high dividend yield strategy, we will see that the odds in our favour are far, far better than 51 per cent; in fact they are probably at least 65 per cent. This is the percentage by which high dividend yield stocks beat large stocks in general in James O'Shaughnessy's ground-breaking book *What Works on Wall Street* (detailed in Appendix 4 'Publications You Should Like'). In it he back-tested a number of investment strategies in the United States over a period of 43 years and came up with the high dividend yield as being the best of the lot. The 65 per cent refers to the 28 out of 43 years in which high yielding shares beat large stocks in general (i.e. the equivalent of the index or market average); *but* over every rolling five-year period in the 43 years, they won 85 per cent of the time and over every ten-year rolling period they won all but once.

We like these numbers because they support our case that the well-informed, unemotional, Foolish investor will consistently be able to handsomely outperform the market and that there is infinitesimal risk of this strategy ever becoming so popular that it will strangle itself. The other thing they confirm is that its success is indeed critically dependent on a commitment and a faith in the fact that the strategy will deliver over the long term. Attempting to 'juice up' the returns by eliminating this or that share which you 'know' is actually a real disaster, introduces the *subjective* into a strategy whose entire *raison d'être* is based on an *objective*, mechanical approach to the markets. And that, of course, is a no-no.

Where does 'Beating the Footsie' fit?

Knowing all that you now do, you might well be wondering how and whether to integrate Beating the Footsie into your investment portfolio. As with much in life, it is down to temperament. Some people will swear that this method of investing – in which a knowledge of the fundamentals of the company is not only irrelevant, but can be counter-productive – is strictly for the insane. Others will be charmed by its apparent elegance and simplicity. We would suggest, however, that if you do decide to follow it, that you do some more background reading than is found here. Perhaps you might like to buy O'Higgins' book itself, or else O'Shaughnessy's, although to be honest this one is a little bit of a heavy read. You might even like to buy the Motley Fool's US book on the subject, *The Unemotional Investor* by Robert Sheard. Stop by the Motley Fool UK's Beating the Footsie area and while you're at it, stop by the Dow area at the US site, too. Peruse the regular reports and message boards at both sites and you'll get a fair idea of what it's like following the strategy on a regular basis. If you have questions, of course you can post them.

History tells us that buying the high yielders has been a highly lucrative strategy, and in large part this is because it is a deeply contrary one. Make sure you understand what it's all about before you start and your investing career will be both happy and lucrative.

16

The Ten Most Common
Investing Mistakes

The man who makes no mistakes does not usually make anything.
Edward John Phelps, Mansion House speech, 1889.

If you're the type who likes helpful restatements and summaries of the major portions of a book, read on. We are going to wind our way gently towards the close of this part with the ten most common investing mistakes we see people making as we wander through the online and offline worlds. There are other common ones besides these ten, but if we could all just prevent ourselves from making these, the world would be a much safer place to invest.

No. 1: Buying what you don't understand

Baptisms of fire are common in the stock market. Poll the investing public and you'll likely find that most of them didn't have a clue what they were buying when they made their first investments and many of them still don't. Cousin Dennis, the chap who can't programme his video, he's starting a Web publishing business. 'Five thousand, that's all I need from start-up investors. It's a dead cert. No-one's done this before. I'll double your money in six months.' And you what? You gave it to him?!

Or maybe a colleague at work has a hot tip on a biotechnology company which he whispers to you over the coffee dispenser. 'Psst! Thunder-Box Biomedical. Hot new products. A new oscillo-proteinase inhibitor, goes like the clappers,' he says, talking in biotech-speak. 'Ripe to be bought out by one of the big pharmaceuticals, too. Get in now before the price hits the roof!' Uh-oh – you don't really know, do you?

The pathway to superior investing is unfortunately littered with speculations in low-grade, cash-burning outfits, hyped to the heavens and with operations that are largely unfamiliar to their shareholders. But any investment which you don't understand is a mistake, even if it does beat the market for you. Allow us to make our point by going to an extreme. Would you buy Unilever or Rentokil solely on the basis of what you have read here? Oh, you know the basis for our thoughts on these businesses and their great prospects for the next few decades. But hang on. We're just a triad of Fools. Would it be particularly intelligent to rely solely on our ramblings when:

- you can come and discuss them with thousands of other investors at the Motley Fool Online *right* now
- you can phone them directly, ask for their latest company reports and any analysts' reports they happen to be giving out (for free), and run them past your investment club, mother or work colleagues for further insights
- you can tap instantly and for free into the growing amount of information available about them over the Internet?

The salient point here is that the story of your epic journey into the world of savings and investing has as its antagonist anyone who tries to rush you. If you've found any useful investment principles in this book, read them again. Soak them up slow-w-w-ly. Get hold of one or two of the other books in Appendix 4 'Publications You Should Like'. Read them. Slow-w-w-ly. Becoming accustomed to this sort of approach and deliberation will benefit you as an investor; it's the direct opposite of what most people do, which is to rush to act quickly on the recommendations of others. And by 'others' we mean anybody or anything: an advisory stockbroker, an online investor, your lucky rabbit's foot, great-aunt Cicely in the middle of one of her winning streaks, or even the Chief Executive of the company in which you are about to invest.

You're responsible for your investments and so you had better verify any information or analysis you are presented with. Be canny, not gullible.

No. 2: Focusing on your short-term performance

It's unfortunate that no matter how frequently the Miracle of Compound Interest is evoked, with the mightiest profits appearing at the far end of an investment life, some investors continue to believe that profits at the front, profits *today*, are meaningful. Which is a shame. Because, in many cases, that impatience results in flawed logic, poor investments, frightful indigestion and pacing the floor after midnight.

It isn't worth it.

Consider, once more, the Buffett. In a section in his 1997 Letter to Shareholders entitled, 'How We Think About Market Fluctuations' (see Appendix 4), he had this to say:

> *A short quiz: If you plan to eat hamburgers throughout your life and are not a cattle producer, should you wish for higher or lower prices for beef? Likewise, if you are going to buy a car from time to time but are not an auto manufacturer, should you prefer higher or lower car prices? These questions, of course, answer themselves.*

> *But now for the final exam: If you expect to be a net saver during the next five years, should you hope for a higher or lower stock market during that period? Many investors get this one wrong. Even though they are going to be net buyers of stocks for many years to come, they are elated when stock prices rise and depressed when they fall. In effect, they rejoice because prices have risen for the 'hamburgers' they will soon be buying. This reaction makes no sense. Only those who will be sellers of equities in the near future should be happy at seeing stocks rise. Prospective purchasers should much prefer sinking prices.*

Most of us, for at least the five years to come, are going to be net purchasers of hamburgers, er, sorry, shares. So, if our investments fall in value, then that is a good thing, because it will allow us to purchase more shares which we value as long-term buys for lower prices. Our existing long-term holds may have fallen slightly in value, but it doesn't matter.

Remember that 20 per cent of £1000 is £200. And 20 per cent of £100,000 is £20,000. As time expands your base of capital, each later year of growth will provide substantially more profits. Let's hark back to Anne Scheiber, the American lawyer who started with $5000 in 1944. Back then she earned less than $1000 per year. By the time she died in the mid-nineties, she was earning more than $500,000 in dividends alone and an average market year brought in more than $2 million in paper gains.

It's the tomorrows which build wealth, not the frenetic activity of the todays. What your portfolio does in the coming week is several orders of magnitude less important than what it does between the years 2005 and 2010, or better yet, 2015 and 2020. To buy and sell your shares on the back of short-term market fluctuations will mortally wound your wallet as you try to predict which way the dice is going to roll next. The trading commissions will eat into your profits and you'll become one of those sad, skeletal souls who dances to the tune of a share pager which bleeps whenever your chosen shares move more than a specified amount. Can you afford to let yourself exist on this level, a level which can only be sustained by frequent injections of caffeine, adrenaline and whisky? We say: '*Nyet!*'

Truly, Fools: 'Lift thine eyes from the dust of the short-term, up, up unto the Heavens and regard the glory that is the long-term panorama!'

---

3. Finding yourself becoming enduringly bearish

Bears, bulls – do you know them? Bears think the glass is half-empty, bulls think it's half-full. Bears think the sky is perpetually poised to fall on their investing heads, bulls fall headlong over their own two feet in their rush to invest *NOW* in this amazing market that is going to be climbing to the skies for ever. Don't miss it!

Moderation, the Middle Way. Whatever you want to call it, a long-term investor can't live without it. Excessive bearishness, though, as much as excessive bullishness, will injure your investment returns. Possibly, it will injure them mortally. There is, you see, no 'right' time to invest, no point at which the economic signs, the market sentiment and the pattern of goose entrails all come together to give you the green light. In a rising market, well, things are looking overvalued and the market may just be on the point of crashing. You'd look pretty stupid, wouldn't you, if you invested now? Best just to wait a bit. In a falling market, you're never quite sure how far it's going to fall. I mean, it might just keep going down and there's no sense in buying something which is *decreasing* in value. That would just be stupid! Then the trough comes and you're a whisker too late and the market's climbing again. You missed it, but maybe this is only a temporary rally. A friend of yours who likes to look at charts of share prices has said that this is a classical 'Double nelly, triple falco' appearance in the star – oops, FTSE 100 – chart and signifies another impending downturn. And then you decide he's wrong and that the market is on the way back up, but now you're aching at having missed your chance earlier on and . . .

And so it goes on. It's a disease. You can never be a perfect parent, only a 'good enough' parent, and so it is with investing. No-one, even Warren Buffett, can invest without regrets. They are part of the game and trying to invest without incurring any will not move you forward. Repeat to yourself your Foolish mantra: since 1918 the London stock market has returned 12.2 per cent on average *every year*. It has, on average, doubled investors' returns every six years. Why now, at a time when our economy is growing ever faster and being propelled forward by the wonderful new technologies of our Age, should this precedent suddenly be shattered? There's no real reason why it should be. Just have faith that you don't need to get it perfectly right or perfectly timed to come out the other end clutching a profit.

Remember that you are now a card-carrying contrarian. In fact, you won't be disappointed if you buy and six months later things start tumbling down, because you're a regular saver and you *like* bear markets. They give you the opportunity to pick up even more great businesses at bargain prices, or even to buy the whole market at a bargain price by sinking your funds into an index tracker. If you happen to be making a regular investment into an index tracker and you then increase your payments as the market turns down, then you make your purchase even more cheaply. What a terrific business this all is!

Don't be a bear. Instead, be a 'good enough' investor, a long-term, patient bull, for this, history tells us, is the true nature of the market.

No. 4: Believing the financial press is expert

Do financial advisers have *your* best interests at heart? Is every fibre of their being dedicated towards *your* long-term enrichment? The answer, by now, is obvious. So, what sells newspapers and gains television viewers? Is it a dedication to your long-term enrichment? Do financial journalists go to bed at night wondering if they have done the best they can by investors that day? If you said 'Alarm, despondency, froth, short-termism', you wouldn't be far off the mark. It isn't often that you see the true power of Brother Time and Sister Logic played up in the financial press. To date, the media has shown little interest in speaking to the patient private investors who tuck money away into shares and hold them for decades. Not that there is much to say to them and that is partly the point. In the media's race to present (or design) the latest controversy and in its obsession with *today*, the business press largely ignores the variable of time. The great self-sufficient investors haven't created their wealth over the last 40 years by buying on the rumour and selling on the news. They buy on the research, their own research, and often don't sell. At an investor's conference in 1997, an elderly gentleman talked with us about his decades of investing, chuckling that it seemed like everyone from investment firm to financial newspaper had tried to rock him out of his position in Schering-Plough, one of the leading US drug companies over the past 40 years. 'And, thank God, I ignored them all and held straight through.'

Thank God, indeed. He made $7 million out of that investment.

It's controversy and disaster which sell in the media business. Train crashes and terrorist bombs, estranged celebrity couples and ethnic cleansing, and . . . the collapse of the stock market. The editing process at most newspapers is heavily biased in favour of matters catastrophic.

When we return once more to Warren Buffett, who claims not to read financial papers, we're reminded of what matters. Private investors have quietly and methodically grown their savings for decades. No, they aren't half as exciting as the collapse of Barings Bank or (*sigh*) the next market collapse, so they don't often gain coverage from the press. But they do seem to be making a good deal of money this century.

Now, none of this is to imply that the market won't lean this way and that, that it won't crumble again, perhaps even soon. At some point, it will. But the average investor (median age of 34) has four decades ahead in which to invest. Whether the market drops by 30 per cent tomorrow is of supreme *inconsequence* to most individuals. Regrettably, that decline is of supreme *consequence* to the financial media, on the look-out for casualties and collision. And therein lies the inversion of interests, pitting patient reader against desperate writer. In a world where learning was prized over controversy, those financial papers whose currency is hype might become worth reading. We're not quite there yet.

No. 5: Concentrating your attention on share price

One of the frequent mistakes of the novice investor is a preoccupation with share prices. Our first inclination as investors is to believe that a share trading for 150p is less expensive and holds greater potential for reward than one trading at 1500p a share. Seems reasonable, doesn't it? After all, we've been buying products all our lives and things which have a lower price are cheaper. Simple.

Unfortunately, this principle doesn't hold on the stock market. A share price in and of itself is meaningless. Oscar Wilde is, as so often, on the side of the Fools: 'Nowadays people know the price of everything and the value of nothing.'

What is the total value of a business? Let us hark back to Chapter 11 'A Share Primer' and reiterate that the total value of a company equals the number of shares times the price of those shares. Thus, if Alan's Aardvark Adventures PLC has one hundred million shares, each priced at 150p, the company is valued at £150 million (150p × 100 million = £150 million). And Ethelred's Elephant Enterprises PLC, with 5 million shares trading at 1500p a share, is priced at £75 million. In this case, the 1500p share represents a lower-priced company than the 150p share. The fair-pricedness of a share depends on the highness or lowness of the total value of a company, not whether it is trading at 150p or 1500p.

To combat the tendency to focus on share price, imagine that all of the shares in your portfolio were trading at 1000p a share. Further, imagine that every share on the market were trading at that price. Now, which companies would you invest in? Would you buy that tin-cup-waving, self-promotional Caspian Sea oil driller, or would you buy Marks & Spencer? Would you become an owner of debt-crippled Eurotunnel or would you buy an ownership position in debt-light Rentokil Initial?

Shield from view the daily to-ing and fro-ing of share pricing and you will naturally bear down more rigorously on the businesses you are buying. In doing so, you will have avoided our fifth giant investing miscue. Now, on to number six.

No. 6: Buying penny shares

'The exception proves the rule.'

It would be so appropriate to quote this pithy saying now, as we move swiftly from telling you that share price doesn't matter to telling you that in some ways it matters a great deal. We'd love to quote it, but the fact is it's a nonsense. 'Proves' in this context has the same meaning as 'tests', as in 'proving ground'. The exception 'tests' the rule. Doesn't make sense, does it? How did this happen? How did the meaning of this ubiquitous phrase become so distorted over the years? All will be revealed in the forthcoming *Motley Fool Guide to Life, Loving and Comparative Etymology*. Until then, tingle at the mystery that is the English language and reflect that the following statement is indeed true:

Penny shares *will* seriously damage your wealth.

Penny shares refers to shares whose price can be measured in multiples of just a few pence and whose market capitalization can usually be measured in just a few million pounds. When companies go public, they often don't do so with an initial share price measured in multiples of just a few pence. Companies whose shares trade in pennies have often *earned* their way to the bottom of the heap.

If a share trades at 8p, then an increase in price to just 10p is a 25 per cent gain, a far easier move for a share to make than, say, from 1000p to 1250p. 'Penny shares offer quick and easy profits.' Newsletters exist and prosper on this principle and purport to guide the naïve investor into stunning profits by offering tips on which penny shares to buy. Fellow Fools, if it were so simple, we wouldn't be writing this book and if you wanted to contact us, you'd be dialling the country code for the Seychelles first. Briefly, the rub is:

- Since the number of shares in the market place is so small and the amount of solid news so scanty, hype and rumour are likely to be the biggest motivators of penny share movements.
- The small number of available shares can make them exceedingly difficult to buy or sell – remember every purchase or sale requires another party to complete the transaction. The technical term is that these shares are *illiquid.*
- The spread between buying and selling prices (the 'bid-offer spread') can be so large as to rub out any potential profits.
- Whereas the share price of Glaxo Wellcome or Unilever will never fall to zero and is highly unlikely ever to be cut in four, this kind of thing is not just possible, it is *likely* with penny shares.

There are no consistent, long-term profits to be made in penny shares. If you like to throw away money on the roulette wheel, then penny shares are for you. Our bet, though, is that if you've invested weeks of unrelenting misery to get thus far through the book, you're not the Johnny-Go-Lightly, betting type.

So, what exactly *is* a penny share? Where is the cut-off? How do you decide by price alone what is a volatile, unpredictable investment, more likely to end in tears than not and, importantly, how do you make sure you don't also end up excluding some great, up-and-coming companies with a novel product or an original idea? It's a tricky question to which there is no right answer and in the early days of the Fool UK, we had quite a long discussion on this topic on our online message boards. We use the following criteria when deciding whether we are prepared to consider a company as an investment prospect:

> *Share price greater than 50p*
> *Market capitalization greater than £30 million*

Some will think this too high, perhaps others will think it too low, but it's a level at which we feel comfortable. Don't worry if you don't agree with us precisely. As long as you're discussing just where the cut-off point should be set and not the whiz-bang investment opportunities which penny shares offer, you've got the right attitude.

Having avoided six potentially fatal errors, you're in pretty good shape, but look what else is waiting to drag you down into investment hell . . .

No. 7: Not tracking your investment returns

With the Internet and with a variety of software packages available, tracking the performance of your investments is easier than ever before. By typing in your positions and updating them each week, month or quarter, you can distinguish between market-beating, market-meeting and market-losing performance. Is your financial adviser beating the market, after the deduction of all management fees? Has your strategy to buy ownership positions in predominantly small-technology companies proven fruitful? How have your 'Obviously Greats' performed over the past two years?

Not knowing whether your investments are thriving or barely surviving from year to year is somewhat akin to not knowing how your favourite football team is doing, or worse: how your children are doing at school, or how old you are. The process of maintaining and updating your portfolio's performance relative to the stock market should be painless . . . nay, joyous.

Too many investors don't know how their savings did in 1996 or in 1997 or over the past decade. There are entire investment clubs that perform wonderful research, do a top-notch job with analysis and yet, at year-end, don't know how their investments have performed relative to the Footsie. Much as we enjoy the process of researching businesses and investing, measuring performance is critical. And in too many instances, our lack of attentiveness to the numbers brings good humour to the financial services industry. Not just a few unit trusts have run advertisements that read, '1995 was a great year. Our fund rose 26 per cent!' This in a year that the market climbed 35 per cent. The investor tracking returns knew to sell off that unit trust for promoting its own mediocrity.

No. 8: Not diversifying your portfolio

At various times along the way, some of your individual holdings will heat up and swell into overlarge positions in your portfolio. At one time, the online Fool Portfolio at our US site was sporting two shares which had appreciated so substantially that they accounted for over 70 per cent of the value of our portfolio.

We were excited. Prospects looked great for both companies. Research analysts on Wall Street that we respect were championing both enterprises. Everything was right at The Motley Fool Online. It doesn't take a cynic to note that when absolutely everything seems right with the world, it must not be so. It was at that time, in our fury of glee, that we should have been paring back our positions in both stocks. To have over 70 per cent of value tied up in two positions is to beg for a come-uppance – one that we did get.

Our recommendation is that portfolios of greater than £10,000 never have more than 15 per cent of their capital initially invested in any one share. From there, we recommend that you think about lightening any positions that grow to become more than 25 per cent of your total portfolio. Let's walk through a brief example, with a £20,000 portfolio. First, you would never invest more than £3000, or 15 per cent, into any one position. Then imagine that your portfolio took this shape two years hence:

Purchased	No. of shares	Security	In At	Now	Value
May 1998	3370	Alfie's Chip Shops	89.00	402.00	£13,547.40
Nov. 1997	450	Soup and Snails	578.00	848.00	£3816.00
May 1997	850	Rentokil	220.00	401.00	£3408.50
Jan. 1997	900	Eileen's	278.00	343.00	£3087.00
May 1995	450	M&S	330.00	555.00	£2497.50
Aug. 1998	550	Shaving Kits	490.00	318.00	£1749.00
Aug. 1997	2900	Laura Ashley	100.00	49.00	£1421.00
April 1998	1200	Motley Fool UK	250.00	68.00	£816.00

TOTAL: £30,342.40

In this scenario, you'll see that although no initial investment exceeded 15 per cent, one of our holdings has exploded. Alfie's Chip Shops has more than quadrupled; our holding in Alfie's has swollen to over 40 per cent of the total value of our account. Red lights should flash here. The account has become overweighted in one direction. It's time to slack off on Alfie's, even though it's been our top performer. Before leaving this section, did you notice the shaggiest, smelliest, wettest dog in our portfolio? Yikes!

No. 9: Not being online

The financial story of the past two years has most certainly been the growth in activity on the Internet. Investors from across the planet are tapping into a network of resources that dramatically outdoes the amount of information available via any other medium.

The Motley Fool UK Online (www.fool.co.uk and Keyword: FOOL UK on America Online) services conversations between stockbrokers, analysts, consumers and private investors far removed from the City. In three short years, we have gone from a world where only the wealthiest individuals and the largest institutional investors could gain access to valuable information and research. Today, the beginning investor with a personal computer and a modem can click into ongoing conversations about personal finance, business and investing that are educational and inclusive.

It is a profound mistake for anyone with access to the Internet – either at home, school, or via a local library – not to take advantage of the resources and the opportunities to have your individual questions answered online. A mass conversation about savings and investing is occurring even as you flip through these pages. And it's a discussion that is changing the way the money world works, an ongoing transformation that greatly works in favour of the individual.

As consumers band together and negotiate with the big boys on a far more level playing field, the balance of financial power is shifting. If you can access the Internet, you should give Fooldom a whirl, as well as a number of other financial sites which we have detailed in Appendix 2 'A Fool's (Brief) Guide to the Internet'. Rather than learning by passively reading, you can, with your networked computer, learn through co-operative endeavour.

No. 10: Spending far too much time on investing

It seems only right that we close down our investing don'ts with a recognition that many of us fall into the trap of dedicating too much time to money management. If this notion seems ludicrous to you today, don't be surprised if in three years you systematically check your shares each morning and find yourself in regular conversations about the prospects of JJB Sports and the future market for Manchester United football shirts with your athletically challenged third cousin Rupert.

Studying businesses, becoming a part owner of enterprises, and talking about your smartest and dumbest investments is actually a great deal of fun. The very brightest among us find ways to involve themselves just enough to wallop the market's average returns, to learn much from the ongoing investigation, but never (or rarely) to compromise the other joys of life – your grandchildren, a picnic lunch, handling the wheel of a 60-year old MG, sleeping until lunchtime one Tuesday in April.

Very few investors altogether avoid at least one period in their life when they spend too much time thinking about their money, when they become consumed by their savings growth. In the very dreariest of scenarios, some even take to trading shares each day, while passing the daylight hours in torn pyjamas, bathed in the unearthly glow of a computer monitor, blindly reaching to their left and unknowingly eating a two-week old tuna sandwich off the wrong plate. Although we find it hard to imagine a scenario where this sort of trader makes money and beats the market, even so, can you imagine this sort of living? Can you imagine eating that sandwich? Can you imagine that taste going unnoticed?

As captivating as the market can be, as much fun as the whole process of saving and investing is, verily it does not take the place of living. The blend of online services, the study of business and market-beating investing has proved nearly irresistible for some. Take heed, though, at the words of W. H. Davies in his poem 'Leisure' of 1911:

What is this life if, full of care,
We have no time to stand and stare.

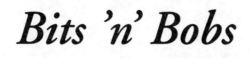

Bits 'n' Bobs

17

Where Else to Invest

They change their clime, not their frame of mind,
who rush across the sea.
Horace, *Epistles*

In his excellent book *Mother Tongue – The English Language* Bill Bryson reveals that in the 1920s, a US novel published in Britain required a glossary to apprise readers of the meaning of words like *grapevine, fan* (in the sense of a sports enthusiast), *gimmick* and *phoney*. In the 1940s an article in the *Daily Mail* proposed that British readers would be confounded by the use of words such as *commuter, seafood, rare* (as applied to meat), *mean* (in the sense of nasty), *dumb* (in the sense of stupid), *dirt road* and *living room*. As Bryson points out, it does seem an unjustified slight on *Daily Mail* readers that they would not be able to deduce the meaning of at least some of these words, but it does show just how close our countries have become in the last 50 years. There are still major, major differences, as both sides would admit, but in investment terms – and let's pinch ourselves to remind us that we are meant to be talking about investing here – there are many more similarities than differences.

The fact is that what happens on the US markets, on Wall Street, is very shortly mirrored on the UK market and others around the world. We don't believe in monitoring short-term market hiccups as a route to successful investing, but it is extraordinary the way the UK market will hang on news of the decision of the US Federal Reserve Board (their equivalent of the Bank of England) chairman on US interest rates, or be propelled upwards by confidence in US stocks. The one does not move without the other. Or rather, the UK market mirrors its transatlantic partner.

In researching this book and looking at the topic of great consumer brands, we came across a table in the *Hoover's Handbook of World Business* listing the world's top 50 brands in order of financial value. Of those, 39 were associated with American companies and – you've guessed it – zero were associated with UK companies. That's not to say we don't have some terrific brands and terrific companies in Britain – we've seen a few of those in Chapter 12 'Obviously Great Investments' – but it makes it less surprising that in a book about investing in the UK our investment horizons should wander across the ocean, especially since that is where the Fool was born. Take a look at this graph, which shows the progress of the Dow-Jones Industrial Average (a US index of 30 of the most important industrial stocks) since 1896:

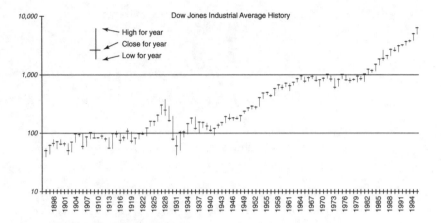

Looks suspiciously familiar, doesn't it? That's because you saw almost exactly the same thing when you looked at the performance graph of shares on the London Stock Exchange earlier in this Foolish tome. Where they dip, we dip, where they peak, we peak and just as ours does, their graph zigs more than it zags and soars more than it sags. Since 1918 the Dow-Jones has returned an average of 10.8 per cent every year, slightly lower than our 12.2 per cent, but no slouch none the less and in terms of *real* return, actually fairly similar, as US inflation rates have tended to be slightly lower than ours.

What's more, many, many of the companies over there are just as familiar to us, or more so, than our own. Ever heard of Microsoft, Nike, Gillette, Wrigley, Pepsi, Coca-Cola, Johnson & Johnson, Disney? It's hard to imagine that British consumers are much less familiar with the products of these worldwide giants than are their US cousins. What Brits may be less familiar with are the incredible returns that some of these mega-corporations have produced over the years:

All these companies have beaten the S&P 500 (another US index of major companies) handsomely over the years. $10,000 invested into Microsoft in 1987 would be worth $2 *million* today. There are huge investment opportunities in the US. As the Internet opens up global markets to the investor it seems foolish not to take advantage of the immense possibilities, and just as Foolish to seize that chance with both hands.

Starting from the Motley Fool's US site (AOL Keyword: FOOL or website http://www.fool.com), it is in fact easier for a UK-based investor to research US companies than it is to research UK companies. The resources at the Fool make a great start, of course, and there are people available 24 hours a day to give you a helping hand, but beyond that US companies have far more informative and wide-ranging websites than their UK counterparts; they also have to file an official report on how they're doing to the investment authorities every *three* months. In the UK, this is required only every six months and there is no requirement to file

Ten-year Performance of Some US Consumer Giants

	1987	1997	Return
Microsoft	$2	$130	6,400%
Nike	$2	$59	2,850%
Gillette	$7	$98	1,300%
Wrigley	$8	$70	775%
Pepsi	$6	$37	520%
Johnson & Johnson	$11	$63	473%
Disney	$16	$76	375%
S&P 500	$290	$917	216%

These numbers span the ten-year period up to July 1997.
Share prices are adjusted for splits. (Please see STOCK SPLIT in the glossary.)

it online, unlike in the US where every financial report from every listed company is available on the Net, in its entirety, for everyone to see (http://www.edgar-online.com). Now *that* we like. One day it will be the norm here, too, and the Motley Fool UK won't stop pushing until that happens. Other facilities you will find easily accessible and far more comprehensive than on the UK Internet are share quotes, graphs, earnings estimates and company news.

Buying and selling US shares over the Internet from the UK is also easier and cheaper than buying and selling UK shares. Using a US-based, Internet 'deep discount' brokerage, you can expect to be able to buy and sell shares for as little as a flat rate charge of £6, no matter how large the transaction. And you can expect the trade to be carried through within under a minute, too. Much less sophisticated computerization on the London Exchange means that even if you do send your transaction in by e-mail, then it will still have to be carried out manually. Things may improve towards the end of 1998, but even then it will be but a shadow of the US systems.

Some people get a little anxious at the thought of sending their money across the world and then trading it via the Internet. Just a few years ago this was science fiction and so it's not surprising that we feel wary. However, the Internet really has shrunk the world and with the opportunities that exist on the US market it seems perverse not to take advantage of them just because you're dealing with something new.

As we've just seen, the financial regulations concerning public companies are stricter than any in the UK – including four times a year company reporting – and any broker you choose should be indemnified up to at least $500,000 by the Securities Investor Protection Corporation (SIPC). Many carry far higher indemnity provisions than this (this is the US, land of litigation, remember) and one we know of carries provision as high as $57 *million*. Your friends and neighbours might look at you a little strangely because you're now buying a stake in some of the world's greatest businesses via your computer, but let them! You're a Fool now, you're making use of the communication revolution to invest sensibly and profitably for your long-term future and nothing's going to stop you.

The first step is often the most difficult. We suggest that you buy our US books *The Motley Fool Investment Guide, You Have More than You Think* and the *Motley Fool Investment Workbook* (well, we would, wouldn't we?). Actually, what we really suggest is that you don't go out and start spending more money right away. Spend some time at the Motley Fool US site before you make any decisions about whether or not you want to invest in the US. There are some terrific investment ideas over there and first-time investors might want to pay particular attention to the Cash-King and DRiP portfolios, each of which focuses on investments in great American companies. Then there is the market-beating Foolish Four portfolio with its disciplined approach to investment in certain of the Dow-Jones heavies. The possibilities are limitless, links to resources for further research are easily accessible and help is readily at hand on the message boards.

If you do make the decision that you want to invest in the United States, then you have a number of options, including:

1. Doing so via a UK-based stockbroker. Simple, but expensive. Although if you're just going to be doing so to buy and hold Obviously Great Investments, then this shouldn't be too much of an issue and in fact some major US companies can be bought and sold on the London Stock Exchange.
2. Doing so via your Individual Savings Account. The details of how this works will vary and although there will be an obvious tax advantage, transaction charges may be hefty.
3. Setting up a US Internet 'deep discount' brokerage account. Simply stop by the Fool's deep discount brokerage centre (http://www.fool.com /media/DiscountBrokerageCenter/DiscountBrokerageCenter.htm), then:
   • Fire off a series of e-mails to likely candidates asking about whether it's possible to open an account from the UK
   • Ask your selected broker to snail-mail (that's what we Internet jockeys call the normal post) an application form and US W8 tax form. They use the normal post to send you the forms to make sure you're who you say you are, living where you say you do
   • Count off the days until they arrive and then fill out the forms and send them back
   • Await e-mail confirmation that your account is open
   • Transfer your pile of Foolishly saved cash by bank transfer to your new brokerage account
   • Await the e-mail saying that your money has arrived
   • Reflect that you are now an international Internet tycoon and investor, surfing the crest of the global investment wave. Feel good? You should!
   By logging into the site using your username and password, you will be able to access the details of your portfolio, updated in real time

according to the latest share prices, as well as buying and selling shares with the utmost ease. Of course, you're not going to let the ease and cheapness of the service tempt you into becoming a day trader, are you? As you do with your UK investments, you buy and hold quality companies on the basis of their fundamental performance, not on the whims of the marketplace or the hype of a hypester.

One useful place for those with an interest in the US to visit is the Nasdaq website specially dedicated to UK investors: http://www.nasdaq. co.uk. The Nasdaq is a US stock exchange which tends to cater for high-tech companies and which has a large number of foreign companies listed on it. Microsoft, Intel and Ericsson are all listed on the Nasdaq.

What about currency fluctuations over the years? Currently, the pound is very strong, meaning it will buy a lot of US dollars. What if it gets even stronger in 30 years' time when you want to bring your dollars back to live in the UK? It might happen that way, yes, or the pound may be weaker then than it is now. In our opinion, there is risk inherent in any enterprise, but there's idiotic risk and there's Foolish risk. At the kinds of returns which great American companies have provided over decades (Coca-Cola: 17 per cent every year since 1918) and with the general strength of both our economies, this is a Foolish risk and not one which we think will figure hugely in your financial equations a few decades from now.

Where *else* to invest: EuroFool

So that's it, is it? America and Britain. There are no other countries in the world worth investing in. The 300 million or so people on the other side of the English Channel are all living in an economic and investment wasteland where mangy dogs roam the streets and the occasional burst of gunfire breaks the tense silence of a sultry afternoon.

Er, no. Keen-eyed readers of this book will have noticed that one of our Obviously Great Investments is in fact Ericsson, a Swedish mobile telecommunications company, although it is listed both in Stockholm and on the Nasdaq exchange in the US. There are many great investment opportunities in Europe, but to be honest most of us don't know a huge amount about them. We don't like to speak foreign languages when it comes to investing and we mean that in the nicest possible way. Actually, we *love* to speak foreign languages, but like to know what we're investing in. If we don't understand an investment, or don't feel comfortable with it, we don't invest. However, our lack of familiarity with Europe and the European markets is something which is going to change rapidly with European Monetary Union and the Internet. You don't have to be interested in the financial news these days to pick up the vibes that something momentous is happening across the water. Love the idea, or loathe it, there's one almighty currency shaping up for business over there, one which may come to challenge the dollar as the world's most sought-after currency.

The ease with which the new currency, the Euro, will allow trading across borders is likely to open up the stock markets of Europe to such an extent that this book, largely confined as it is to dealing with investment in the UK, will seem like a laughable anachronism in just a few years. Whereas today we talk about the FTSE 100, tomorrow we'll be talking about the FTSE Eurotop or Dow-Jones Stoxx indices, two new pan-European indices. If what we're primarily worried about in investment is total return on our money, then we wish to invest in the best businesses we can, whether they're French, Dutch, British, American or Italian, and as long as there's no potential currency hit to be reckoned with, it seems ludicrous not to invest in a company simply because it's foreign. In a very few years, you will likely be able to trade almost instantaneously via the Internet on any of the exchanges of Europe, using your single pan-European stockbroker and frankly we think this is going to be one hell of a market. Currently the US – the largest market in the world – has companies adding up to a market capitalization of $9,250,000 million. The Euromarket, including countries such as Switzerland and Norway (which are outside the EU) and the UK (in the EU, but not proceeding with monetary union at the moment) is currently worth $5,700,000 million.

Of course, if the standards of financial regulation aren't up to scratch in the country in which a company is listed, then that isn't much good, no matter what you think of the company itself. That's why we're so attracted to the soon-to-be-united countries of Western Europe with their high standards of financial reporting and some very well known brand name companies. What would make us drown our grandmothers before investing in some of the other countries of Europe is precisely the lack of any of those things. Entry into some of the emerging markets of Eastern Europe, or indeed emerging economies anywhere else in the world, is to lay yourself open to precisely the kinds of currency fluctuations which could prove disastrous to your investments and to the possibility of outrageous scams or accounting 'irregularities' over which neither you nor anyone else has any control. There is real money to be made in the stable economies of the Western world. Don't spoil your investment returns by throwing money into a cauldron of economic turmoil.

If you do have special knowledge of a particular European market or some European companies, please come and tell us about it at the Fool online. And if you're impressive enough, you could be penning the *EuroFool Investment Guide* in a year or two. If you do decide to invest in any foreign companies, please be sure that the market you are investing in has stringent financial reporting standards. If you decide to open a brokerage account overseas, then follow the checklist to be found in Appendix 5 and provided by Motley Fool UK reader Yvonne Ravenhall in Portugal. If you can't find a broker which will satisfy these exacting criteria, then chances are you shouldn't be investing in that country anyway.

The Ethical Fool

A custom loathsome to the eye, hateful to the nose, harmful to the brain, dangerous to the lungs, and in the black, stinking fume thereof, nearest resembling the horrible Stygian smoke of the pit that is bottomless.
James I (James VI of Scotland), *A Counterblast to Tobacco*

Agree or disagree with him, King James certainly had one or two strong thoughts on the smoking weed which had so recently been introduced from the Americas. So, certainly, will many of the people reading this. Whether you're pro or anti the free marketing of tobacco, there is no escaping the issue that there is an issue here, as there is with many other activities in the business world. What about arms manufacturing, or mining, or paper manufacturing and its consequent effect on deforestation? Depending on your outlook, this stuff can be tricky.

So what are we going to call this subject where the passions run so high? 'Socially responsible investing'? 'Ethical investing'? 'Green investing', even? The choice, ultimately, is yours, but what we're trying to get at is a self-imposed, selective approach to investing, one which has ultimately kept millions of potential investors around the globe from buying into certain public companies, whose corporate activities they deem immoral, damaging or exploitative.

In Utopia (from the Greek *ou topos* meaning 'no place'), we could simply tell you to invest without concern. You'd be living in a perfect society with perfect laws and no need for regulatory bodies. You would know, in every moment that you invested, that your company was maximizing the growth of well-being for every constituency: customers, employees, shareholders, management and society. If ever one group was temporarily over- or under-compensated, the whole structure would tilt immediately to correct it (probably slightly too far in the other direction, briefly, to create total equity). Doesn't it sound great?

Look at the name again. *Ou topos* – no place.

No such world has ever yet existed, unless Thomas More's legendary traveller was telling the truth. And most importantly, no single life has ever been continually, uncompromisingly painless. With no Utopia in our personal or professional lives, we certainly shouldn't expect one in our investing life. At the most basic level, we all just have to do our best, make the best of things.

The whole concept of ethics in investing has had much ink spilled over it, with many zealots beating each other around the head with their own moral codes and a number of very bad and highly charging unit trusts springing up to meet the need for people to feel wholesome about their investing endeavours. It's a deadly serious issue and that's why we're touching on it here. Our approach is very simple, so simple in fact that we're in danger of being called naive:

Buy what you are; buy **only** *what you are.*

If you don't like British American Tobacco, don't invest in it. If you think companies which manufacture and export arms are immoral, don't invest in them. Never lose sleep over an investment that you made tentatively in an enterprise you don't wholeheartedly support. Flog it. Buy something else.

Buying what you are, what informs your daily life, what sits snugly with your beliefs and values about the world is the only way to feel comfortable with the investments you hold. No-one else can tell you what you are and especially not the fund manager of an 'ethical' unit trust. When you buy one of these – and why would you, because their returns are so abysmal – are you buying what you are or what someone else is? When you buy a unit trust, you're consigning the destiny of your money to a stranger you'll most likely never meet. Social responsibility? If you take ethics in investing at all seriously, then we fervently argue that you're being most *irresponsible* by saying, 'I'll buy that pleasingly named unit trust.'

Let's go a little further. You don't like British American Tobacco, but you hold an insurance policy with Eagle Star. Whoops! Which is going to help BAT more, the shares you hold in the company and on which they pay *you* a dividend, or the profits they are making out of the insurance policy you hold with their wholly owned subsidiary? Let's say you avoid investing in SmithKline Beecham because you don't like animal testing. Then you fall ill and are prescribed a medicine by your doctor. Three days later, you look at the name on the packet . . .

If you're going to avoid investing in a particular company, then make sure you're not helping them more directly by buying their products. Make your investment pounds work in harmony with your consumption pounds and you'll feel right about what you're doing. You'll be in sync. You'll be a Fool.

The active shareholder

There's no way we can dictate the moral choices which you alone can decide for yourself. The history of the world is full to bursting of people moralizing to others and we have no intention of adding to their ranks. Decide for yourself what is acceptable, decide if your investing philosophy sits easily with your life philosophy and if it does, then that's fine. There may well come a time, though, when a company you bought into, and which you thought you knew well, goes off on a tangent with which you don't feel comfortable. Alternatively, perhaps you disapprove only mildly of the activities of a company and would like to invest in it, but at the same time would like to do what you can to modify their behaviour. The answer is to become an active shareholder.

Quite apart from the purely financial reasons not to own more than ten to fifteen companies at a time, there are good reasons from an ethical point of view not to hold more than this number. Not only can you not follow the details of their business if you own many more than this, but you can't follow their ethical activities either. As an active shareholder – a part-owner, remember – of whatever business you're invested in, you are uniquely placed to make your views heard. You can attend shareholder meetings, bombard who you like with letters, faxes and e-mails and generally make a nuisance of yourself (polite or otherwise) and at all times your views will have to be heard and answered courteously. Working from the inside to change the face of business is likely to be much more effective than standing on the outside knocking on a large, smoked glass door.

Investing in this way in a company whose business you essentially deem worthy of respect, but which has one or two practices of which you disapprove, can be very positive. What about the business, though, which you think is an absolute shocker? How can you justify to yourself making money out of that company and using it for your own personal gain? That, we're afraid, is an issue between you and your bathroom mirror. However, one rather elegant line of approach which you might want to consider is to only invest money in Evil Activities PLC which you would otherwise donate to charity. Then, as an active shareholder you keep up your barrage from the side of morality and probity, but channel the profits from your investment – it's a sad fact that 'nasty' companies often are very profitable – into activities or charities which seek to counteract the damaging effects of the actions of your evil company. It's quite a neat way of changing the world, but won't do anything for your investment returns. Don't, therefore, take this money from the funds you are allocating for your retirement nest egg. This is strictly hobby money, but using part of your investment life to try and put things right can be an attractive idea for many people who are turned off the very idea of stock market investing by the dirty corporate world they feel they're buying into.

One thing to note is that it is worth asking your stockbroker just what shareholder rights you are entitled to if you are holding your shares in a nominee account. (These are the types of accounts which many execution-only stockbrokers use to hold clients' shares communally, thus making dealing easier.) It's no good planning to be an active shareholder if you then find you don't have an easily exercisable voting right at meetings. A useful resource for the active shareholder is *The Shareholder Action Handbook*, which is crammed full of information and published online at: http://www.bath.ac.uk/centres/ethical/share/0home.htm. Alternatively the paperback version is cheap and can be ordered from your local book-shop, quoting ISBN number: 1897806000.

Conclusion

We live in a dirty world. (You didn't need us to tell you that.) As an investor – if you wish to use this opportunity – you have much scope to shape that world for the better. Do debate and discuss this issue with others, for down that path lies greater understanding and tolerance. Don't, however, let others bully you into a course of action with which you feel uncomfortable: you won't stick with it and the sum of resentment and ill-feeling will have been increased in the world, surely the very opposite of what we all hope will occur.

19

How to Open a Brokerage Account

Many a time in the past, when an active operator on Wall Street,
he had done things to the Small Investor which would have caused raised
eyebrows in the fo'c'sle of a pirate ship and done them without a blush.
P. G. Wodehouse in *Heart of a Coof*, describing Bradbury Fisher,
a stockbroker and 'one of America's most prominent tainted millionaires'.

You've decided you want to do your own research and invest in some shares for the long term, but how do you go about it? In our experience it's this kind of mundane detail which puts people off investing in shares most of all. Don't worry, it can be simple, unlike the experience Neil Fletcher from Liverpool described when he wrote to us at our online site in early 1998:

> *I've always had a somewhat ambivalent attitude to the stocks and shares scene, slightly in awe of it but at the same time secretly wishing to be involved.*
>
> *Until November 1997 I had never bought a share in my life. But having just received the proceeds of an endowment policy, I decided more or less on the spur of the moment to have a go. The only drawback was I knew absolutely nothing about how to do it. So on a wet Monday morning I went to my bank, one of the larger branches of NatWest in Liverpool city centre, eager to shell out £2000 on some shares I'd seen tipped by Paul Kavanagh in the* Sunday Times *and which were in a field I knew something about – education. I was told that I'd have to go to an even larger branch, one that did all the share dealing.*
>
> *I traipsed through the rain to the branch in question where I was informed the dealing charge would be 1.5 per cent. I asked the girl to arrange it for me, but she couldn't find the company listed anywhere on her monitor (and we're not talking AIM or penny shares here, by the way). I would have to return to my own branch where they would buy the shares for me over the phone but with somewhat higher charges. Another trudge through wet Liverpool back to my own branch where I had to explain the whole rigmarole all over again – by which time I just wanted to buy the damn things and go home. The deal was finally done. I had become a shareholder, but only by paying a hefty 1.75 per cent for the privilege.*
>
> *Because I was even greener then than I am now, I paid up without hesitation. I just wanted to buy them, for heaven's sake, before they went up in price (they've subsequently done quite well, incidentally). It's only since reading the various Fool UK postings that I've discovered there are easier and cheaper ways of buying shares. So I hope this anecdote will be helpful to those*

entering the share buying jungle for the first time and prevent exhausting and expensive safaris through wet streets.

Neil, we won't let you down.

Shares can only be bought and sold on your behalf by stockbrokers, who naturally charge for the privilege. Those are the rules. How much they charge depends on a number of things, but primarily whether they provide an advisory service or are 'execution-only' brokers. Advisory brokers do just that – they advise you what to buy and sell, often with a fairly short-term perspective. They'll say things like: 'Zelda's Zips is looking good at the moment and it's ripe for a takeover bid.' Or: 'The market's bearish on pharmaceuticals at the moment. Let's move out of Glaxo Wellcome for a while.' The thing is they are getting paid by commission for *each* trade. That's how they make money. How they make *more* money is to induce you to trade more frequently. It's against the rules for them to trade on your account simply to make themselves money but, as so often in the murky world of finance, there is a storming, stonking conflict of interest here. While Independent Financial Advisers (salespeople) have strong incentives to sell you high-commission investments, advisory brokers have a similar incentive to trade you in and out of shares on a regular basis.

Here's a salutary tale of advisory broking from a Motley Fool reader posted on a message board the very day this manuscript was submitted to our publisher at the end of May 1998:

> *My wife and I have experienced stockbrokers. They persuaded us to sell good stock to buy not so good, netting huge commissions in the process. We were advised to sell 3500 Prudential shares at £3.03 and buy BTR at £3.34. Weeks later, the Pru was at £5.00 and BTR at £3.00. They then advised us to buy more of the Pru at £5.00 and sell Unilever for consolidation purposes.*
>
> *Another time, we were advised to buy De la Rue at £9.60. They fell and fell, but we thought, 'Well, the professional knows what he's doing,' and waited for a rise. At £3.70 they wrote and said we ought to consider selling them. These are 'active fund managers'.*
>
> *Professional advice? Never again.*
>
> *I have in the past worked for an insurance company, and seen some of the dirty tricks they play on customers, but that's another story.*
>
> *Best wishes,*
>
> *Adrian Gill*
>
> *PS We eventually sacked them two months ago and sold BTR at £1.60, while the Pru were over £9.00. The only ones to make money in all this were the brokers who received our commission. We are now invested in a Legal and General index tracker and to my mind these so called fund managers are in the main not competent.*

As long as everyone believes the fiction that this kind of frequent trading is beneficial to your financial health, then it looks like everyone is having their cake and eating it. However, introduce a subversive into the equation (sorry, we meant 'Fool') and pretty soon things start to fall apart. It's especially undermining when that subversive threatens the very foundations of the belief system they are challenging. Remember that chap Galileo we mentioned earlier in the book? The one who said that the Earth moved around the sun? His revolutionary ideas, which fitted the observable facts so neatly, caused consternation in his era and he was lucky not to have his head neatly disengaged at the neck and served up to him on a platter.

Times have moved on, but as a Fool you're going to come up against similar antagonism as you strike at the roots of a rotten system and challenge not only a set of deeply held beliefs, but – let's face it – the means of earning a livelihood for very many people. Does that make you feel bad or guilty? Do you feel that you must continue to support a flawed system which has provided the daily bread for so many people for so many years? You do? That's lovely and so thoughtful. Why, you Fool! We didn't know you had it in you! In which case, you need an advisory stockbroker, charging the highest fees per transaction possible, the fattest yearly portfolio management fee and pursuing a policy of 'active management, based on the most up-to-date stock market trends, of a client's portfolio'. And while you're at it, enlist your favourite group of rock stars to put on a benefits concert: BrokerAid. And don't forget the website: http://www. brokeraid. co.uk. Or the adoption programme: 'Adopt a broker today. It could make all the difference to one child's private school education.'

The rest of you hard-hearted fiends should avoid these people as if they carried the Black Death. Which, in financial terms, they do. What you need to find is an execution-only broker who will buy and sell shares on your behalf when you ask them to. Nothing more, nor less.

Unfortunately for us in Britain, it is still not as simple as the situation in the US where an execution-only broker will be able to effect a transaction in seconds via the computerized trading systems which exist on all the American exchanges. This means that trading over the Internet in the United States is cheap, reliable and very, very fast. Let's look at what the situation is on the London Stock Exchange.

For there to be a trade in something, there have to be buyers and sellers and the stock market provides the physical setting for the trade in company shares to take place. If you think of the stock market as a not-so-glorified Indian bazaar, you won't go far wrong. Before the autumn of 1997, if you wanted to sell or buy a share, your stockbroker would get hold of someone called a 'market maker'. Market makers are the people who match up sellers with buyers. If you like, they are brokers to the brokers and their cut comes in the form of offering a lower price to the seller and a higher price to the buyer. Jonathan Swift must have had something like this in mind back in 1733:

So, naturalists observe, a flea
Hath smaller fleas that on him prey;
And these have smaller fleas to bite 'em,
And so proceed *ad infinitum.*
Thus every poet in his kind,
Is bit by him that comes behind.

The market maker, then, would buy the shares from you at the seller's price and sell them on at the buyer's price, pocketing the difference.

Since 1997, however, things have been different for trades on the FTSE 100 shares (the hundred largest shares by market capitalization) and those of the FTSE 250 shares which are on the 'reserve list' for the FTSE 100. These shares are now traded by means of a computerized system known as SETS. This fixes the buy and sell prices automatically according to what buyers and sellers in the market are prepared to pay. When it finds a match between a buyer and a seller, the deal is carried out. The idea is that this will narrow down some of the very high spreads between buying and selling prices. It hasn't worked out quite like that, but that's another story. Of course, for transactions of any other share in the UK, the market maker system still holds. Different market makers offer different prices, but your broker should always select the best of these and if they have a good relationship with the market maker, they may even be able to negotiate you a better deal.

Phew!

So, to summarize:

- Trades of FTSE 100 shares and FTSE 250 shares on the FTSE 100 reserve list – the computerized SETS system
- Trades on all other shares – market maker system

Why do you have to know all this somewhat tedious guff about the ins and outs of share dealing when you're only going to deal with the execution-only broker anyway? 'You don't really have to' is the short answer (and if you have skimmed through all this with your mind on dinner tonight, then don't worry) but we think it can be worth having at least a sketchy idea of how the trading system works. If nothing else, this will explain to you why it is so much more expensive to buy and sell shares here than in the US: (There are more people in line to take a cut and since the process is not fully computerized, it is less rapid and less slick to do so over the Internet.) It will also allow you to better understand some anomalies of the system, like why there can be a very large difference between buyers' and sellers' prices on small, thinly traded shares. (Only one or two market makers actually cover the share and, having a monopoly, they can therefore charge whatever they like.) If you're really interested in this business – and some people are – then fire up your browser and pop over to the London Stock Exchange website (http://www.londonstockex. co.uk), which is quite a good place to start.

One more thing about brokerage accounts is that execution-only brokers tend to keep your shares in what is called a 'nominee account'. That means they are actually holding the shares and share certificates on your behalf. This makes it easier for them and the market makers to settle the bills and will not affect you at all, unless you want to vote in your companies' Annual General Meetings or make use of any perks which come along with share ownership, like cheaper travel through the Channel tunnel if – God forbid! – you were an owner of Eurotunnel shares.

That's the background, but how do you find an execution-only broker? Well, we have a handy little list in Appendix 8. Otherwise, you can look for advertisements in the back of investment magazines such as *Investor's Chronicle*, or else stop by a website such as Moneyworld (http:// www.moneyworld.co.uk), which has listings of brokers with a presence on and off the Internet. What you are looking for is good value in terms of charges and a prompt, efficient service. As with any purchase, shop around for what you think is the best deal. Ask friends, neighbours, acquaintances. If you are online, stop by one of our message boards and make use of the co-operative endeavour of Fooldom: ask others for advice.

When you have found one whose telephone (or e-mail) manner you like and whose charges you can live with, you ask them to send you the forms to open an account. You then fill these in, send them back with a cheque to open the account (it works a bit like a bank account) and you're in business. When you receive your account number, you are ready to trade. Simply ring up your broker, quote the account number and start trading: 'Sell Rentokil! Buy low! Sell high! Short Vodafone! Get me BP! I wanna kick some ass and I wanna kick it now, goddammit!'

We're kidding.

The Fools Propose . . .

The Fools propose that French be adopted as the national language of the United Kingdom . . .

The Fools propose to set this book to music and take it to the West End . . .

The Fools propose a fair and equitable way for stockbrokers and other investment advisers to be compensated . . .

Of the three proposals above, one is utterly beyond the pail and the other two, although unlikely to be successful, are not totally beyond the bounds of possibility. Predictable, isn't it, which one we're going to deem entirely fanciful? Yes, it's the third all right.

Imagine a world in which brokers and financial advisers were not paid by how big a lemon they had sold you or by how frequently they traded you in and out of shares. It would be a wonderful world, a world of hope and peace and prosperity. Picture the following scenario:

You present your stockbroker, Simon Cyclepath, with your accrued monies. Let's be fair and say you give him five years. If, at the end of that time, your investments have underperformed – taking into account trading charges – what you might reasonably have expected from an index tracker, then he gets zilch. On the other hand, if they have surpassed the average performance of shares on the exchange, then he receives a sliding scale of compensation, depending on how much he beat it by each year. If he beat the average by 1 per cent each year, give him a certain amount. If he beat it by 2 per cent, give him more. If he beat it by 5 per cent, give him a lot more and if he beat it by *10* per cent, he won't be needing any contributions from you, as he'll be doing very nicely on his own account, thank you very much.

The question is, if you don't get performance, why should you pay for it? Ninety per cent of fund managers underperform the market average. Why pay them exorbitant charges to do so? Our system would rapidly sort out the wheat from the chaff and bring some much needed focus to the whole issue of investment charges.

Likely to happen this side of 3000AD? You decide.

A caveat: not all brokers are bad brokers

Reading this chapter, and indeed much of this book, you might start to form the opinion that we consider stockbrokers and indeed anyone involved in the sales side of the financial services industry to be competing with the *Paramecium* in the lowest form of life stakes. This is not entirely true. The fact is that, as we've shown, we believe the system as a whole mitigates against a fair deal for the customer. Within that system you will always be able to find many outstanding examples of humanity who do a good job for their clients and you will even find some of those posting on our boards; people you would be proud to let your son or daughter marry, people you might even let manage your money.

Enough, now, is enough. We call, for a short while, a truce. To prove at the end of this chapter that we are not irretrievably 'broker-ist', we urge you to:

Hug a broker today!

20

How Not to Pay Tax

Only the little people pay taxes.
Leona Helmsley, US millionairess. Addressed to her
housekeeper in 1983 and reported at her trial for
tax evasion in the *New York Times*, july 12th 1989.

Leona Helmsley got caught. You don't have to because you're not about to do anything illegal. Britain has some of the most remarkably liberal provisions for tax free investing to be found in the Western world and this chapter is all about how best to make use of those tax breaks in building for your Foolish future. As you're about to see, it's an exciting story and one with great scope. We'd even go so far as to say you're very lucky: investors in the US would sell their grandmothers to have the kind of tax freedoms we enjoy in the UK. Let's see just how lucky you are.

Until April 5th 1999, every British resident over the age of eighteen is allowed to make tax-sheltered yearly investments into shares of £9000 per year in PEPs (see below). After April 5th 1999, this will decrease to £5000 per year into an ISA (see below) and PEPs will be abolished. Now, this is something totally separate to the tax *relief* you get on personal pension plans (PPPs). With PPPs every £100 you put in is made up by the government to £130 if you're a basic rate taxpayer or £167 if you're a top rate taxpayer.

With PPPs, you will eventually have to pay Income Tax on the income they provide, but exactly the opposite is the case with PEPs and the new ISAs. With these two, the money you put in comes out of your *taxed* income and the government adds not one whit, not one crumb to them. However, down the line, whatever income you take from them, whatever profits you make, will be tax-free. Also, you can do with those profits whatever you like – buy a yacht, start a rock band, put it all on number 36 at the casino in Monte Carlo – and don't have to deal with the irksome restrictions which come along with PPPs and their cousins, AVCs. We'll talk about them in Chapter 22.

Even with the drop in allowance as PEPs are phased out and ISAs phased in, from £9000 per year to £5000 per year, these remain phenomenally generous tax-sheltered entitlements and should bring joy to the heart of any investor.

We have chosen to talk about PEPs and ISAs only in this chapter and to leave the rest of the book largely free of references to them. This is not because we don't believe they have a central role to play in the planning of the Foolish investor, or that they're not the greatest invention since the home delivery pizza. It's just that wherever you look in the financial press, you see advertisements like this: 'Buy our Growth PEP now!' After April 1999, it will be: 'Open our Growth ISA now!' For many people, the term 'PEP' has become synonymous with investment and that's largely the way the industry would like to keep it. As long as people simply think they're buying a 'PEP' or an 'ISA', they're unlikely to question precisely what is in it, how well it is performing and how much they are paying for it. Unbelievable as it sounds, some people don't even know that their 'PEP' is actually invested in the stock market.

Further, to buy an investment solely for the tax advantages it provides is a fundamental mistake and one which many, many people have been lured into over the years. Sort out your investments first and *then* go about planning how to make them tax-efficient. A poor investment in a tax-sheltered environment will serve you much less well than an excellent one which is nevertheless exposed to tax. By keeping your mind clear in this way, you are able to sort the wheat from the chaff and the pattern of your approach should look like this:

1. Which is the best investment for me to make at this point?
2. How best can I shelter that investment from tax?
3. How best can I minimize the charges associated with both the investment and the tax shelter?

Now it's time to take a closer look at exactly what PEPs, ISAs and those other strange beasts, TESSAs, are. We'll also have a quick skirt through Capital Gains Tax (CGT).

PEPs (Personal Equity Plans)

They're on the way out, so we're not actually going to spend too much time on them. Let's reserve our brainpower for what's really important. Too much information in the world today means we need to clearly set our priorities.

PEPs were started in 1986 and in recent years have given investors the chance to salt £9000 per year away into the stock market. Shares or unit trusts held within a PEP grow tax-free. You won't ever have to pay Income Tax or Capital Gains Tax on the investment profits you make. Compared with the provisions for tax-free investments to be found in other countries, PEPs, Messieurs et Mesdames Fools, are 'ze bees' knees'. Six thousand pounds can go into what is called a general PEP, in which can be held unit trusts, investment trusts or individual shares. The majority of PEPs contain unit trusts and generally the two are bought together as a unit trust already incorporated into a PEP. It's the owners of these kinds of PEPs who will sometimes express surprise that they are invested in the stock market at all. If you buy an animal known as a 'self-select general PEP' on the other hand, you will be able to buy and sell individual UK and European shares as and when you want, and contribute, of course, the same £6000 per year. This is a good way to buy Obviously Great Investments or follow a Beating the Footsie strategy.

The other £3000 can go into a single company PEP, in which, not surprisingly, you are allowed to hold only the shares of a single company. Dividends on holdings in PEPs are also paid with tax relief, although the amount of this decreased in 1997, following the Labour election victory.

PEPs have been a huge draw into investing for thousands over the last thirteen years and some people have accumulated hundreds of thousands of pounds in PEPs.

The important thing to remember is that all they are is a tax-free wrapping enclosing whatever investment happens to be nestling inside. If the investment isn't performing, all the tax freedom in the world isn't going to bring you out with a profit at the other end. Since the majority of PEPs shelter unit trusts and we've already seen that unit trusts mostly under-perform the market, while charging excessively for the privilege, we can conclude that most people haven't been getting the best they could out of their tax shelter allowances.

Coming up to April 5th, 1999, any UK resident over the age of eighteen can open one single-company PEP for a maximum of £3000 and one PEP for a maximum of £6000, for the tax year 1998/99.

When April 5th, 1999 does finally roll around and this book is already on its fifth reprint (we can dream, we can dream), any existing PEPs will be allowed to continue indefinitely in their current form with all their tax freedoms intact. However, you won't be able to open any new ones and the baton will have passed over to the ISA for all future investments.

ISAs (Individual Savings Accounts)

ISAs are going to replace PEPs and TESSAs from April 5th 1999. Here's a brief rundown of what they're all about:

- The initial life of the ISA is planned at ten years, with a review of what happens next after seven years.
- Contributions of up to £5000 per year for every adult British resident will be permitted.
- Up to £1000 of this will be allowed to be in cash and another £1000 will be allowed to be in single premium life insurance policies.

- In the first year (1999/2000), though, you will be allowed to put in £7000, of which up to £3000 may be in cash.
- You'll be able to invest in: UK or some overseas shares; Unit trusts and investment trusts; Banks and building society accounts; Money market unit trusts; National Savings products which aren't already tax-free.
- As with PEPs and TESSAs, all funds in ISAs will be free of Income Tax and Capital Gains Tax.
- Investors in both ISAs and PEPs will receive a 10 per cent tax credit on dividends until 2004, when the credit will stop.
- ISAs will be run by authorized managers, like PEPs.
- You'll be able to open one ISA per year.
- You'll be able to transfer ISAs from one ISA manager to another.
- No-one's quite sure what the charges are going to be. If they are hefty, then it will make short-term holdings in ISAs pointless, especially for people who are basic rate taxpayers. But you're not a short-term holder, are you?
- The government will introduce a so-called 'CAT' benchmark (this stands for 'Charges, Access, Terms') for ISAs. The only share-based investments which will likely qualify for this stamp of quality are index-tracking unit trusts.

When it comes time to open an ISA for the shares or index tracker you'd like to buy, look in the *Financial Times*, one of the financial magazines such as *Investors' Chronicle* or on the Internet (http://www.moneyworld.co.uk is a good place to start) for advertisements. Alternatively, your current stockbroker will likely have a selection on offer. If you want to find out what other Fools like you are doing, you'll stop by, well, you know where.

The opportunities which PEPs and now ISAs present us with in the UK for tax-sheltered investment are formidable. Take hold of them and use them for all they are worth, but don't lose sight of the fact that it's the investments inside them which count far more than the tax efficiency they provide.

Capital Gains Tax

Let's suppose that you've been a successful Foolish investor for many a year now and have built up a huge pile outside the shelter of PEPs and ISAs. You're exposed to (horror!) Capital Gains Tax. Okay, what does this mean? It means very simply that if you sell any of your investments and make a profit above a certain amount (currently £6800) in any given tax year – and remember these run from April to April – you will have to pay part of the proceeds to the Inland Revenue in tax. As of March 1998, the Chancellor has changed a few things when it comes to 'CGT', as we invest-o-nerds like to call it.

First, it has changed from being a flat rate (40 per cent for higher rate taxpayers and 23 per cent for lower rate taxpayers) to a sliding scale, where the longer you hold an investment, the less the tax rate is. As long-term investors, we have to applaud this. Heartily. The rates start to drop if you have held an investment for three complete years and by the time you've held for ten or more years, they're down to 24 per cent and 13.8 per cent for higher and lower rate taxpayers, respectively.

So what's the catch? (Hey, you *are* suspicious, aren't you? Didn't your mum ever tell you it's better to take life at face value?)

Right, since you asked for it, here's the catch (three of them, actually):

First, the Chancellor abolished **indexation**. In the past, you used to be able to calculate how much your investment would have increased in value anyway due to inflation and then these gains were discounted for tax purposes, which was jolly nice. No longer.

Secondly, he abolished **bed and breakfasting**. As you read this, vanloads full of Bobbies are descending on your town and raiding the houses of anyone offering a bed for the night and full English breakfast. Such miscreants will be liable to a fine not exceeding £5000 or a prison term not exceeding two years in a cell with a teasmaid timed to go off at 6 a.m. every morning. (No, no, we're kidding and, as you can see, 173 pages into the book are starting to run out of jokes.) Bed and breakfasting really refers to selling your investments one day, thus realizing your profits, before buying them back the next day, when hopefully the price will hardly have changed. If you wanted to do this now, you'd have to wait 30 days to buy them back, when of course the price may have changed a great deal, adding a high degree of uncertainty to the whole process. B&B-ing was a common practice, allowing investors to use up their CGT allowance every year, leaving them with less to pay down the line, but it's gone now.

Thirdly, he introduced a 'last in, first out' rule. This one is a right royal swizzle for index-tracking Fools. Remember we talked about paying less CGT the longer you have held an investment? This rule means that if you've been saving regularly into an index tracker for ten years and decide to harvest the fruits of your investment, instead of getting the ten-year tax rate, you get the tax rate applying to the most recent contribution – i.e. you get no tax break at all.

So what do you do about CGT? First, you make the maximum investment possible into PEPs and ISAs. Relatively few of us need ever be liable for CGT, as many of us probably can't save enough to fill our PEP and ISA allowances. Remember, we can save £9000 in a PEP up to April 1999, then £7000 for the first year of the ISA and £5000 per year thereafter. Double those annual contributions up for co-habitees and you're looking at a lot of money in 25 years.

Suppose you do find yourself exposed to CGT, what can you do about it? The major way around CGT used to be to use B&B-ing to mop up the yearly allowance, as we've just seen. Well, you can still do this, as long as your partner or very good friend (and we mean *very* good friend) immediately buys the shares which you sell, instead of your doing it yourself, as used to be the case. Say you hold 3000 shares in Marks & Spencer and your partner holds 3000 shares in Tesco on which you want to realize gains, thus using up your CGT allowance. All you have to do is each sell your shares and the other buy them back straight away. Since you're in it for the long term – together, as well as investing – it doesn't really matter which of you holds which shares. Simple. If you're swapping shares with a very good friend, you just swap them back after 30 days. It may cost you two sets of dealing charges and stamp duty, but it may be worth it – you probably use a relatively inexpensive execution-only broker, after all.

A final word on TESSAs (Tax Exempt Special Savings Accounts)

Don't get too excited here. Not only are TESSAs on the way out along with PEPs, they weren't too spectacular to begin with. TESSAs are essentially bank deposit accounts in which the minimum holding period is five years. If you keep funds in the account for that long, you will then be able to collect the interest gross – i.e. tax free.

Why are we so underwhelmed? Because if you hark back to the Barclays Capital Gilt-Equity Study, you will recall that in 83 per cent of consecutive five-year periods since 1918, shares have outperformed cash in a deposit account. If you can leave your money where it is for five years, why would you *not* want to have it in shares? On the other hand, if you need money on short-term deposit for periods of less than five years, there'd be no point to a TESSA anyway, as you wouldn't get the tax advantages.

Still, if you're holding a TESSA on April 5th, 1999, you will be able to keep it going until it matures and then, if you wish, transfer the money into an ISA.

Conclusion

There is great scope in this country to build up large sums of money in tax-sheltered investments. The new ISAs will have a lower annual contribution limit than their predecessors, PEPs, but will allow a wider range of investments, including overseas shares. Be Foolish – use your tax-free allowances to the full!

21

Buy Your Own Home, But Do It Foolishly

The best thing we can do is to make wherever we're
lost in look as much like home as we can.
Christopher Fry, *The Lady's not for Burning*

They do things differently in Belgium. Take Monsieur et Madame Albert
Chips-Cooked-In-Lard-Why-*Do*-They-Do-That-It-Really-Spoils-Them
as an example. Monsieur Albert is a branch manager at a small bank in
Brussels. Madame is a clerical officer at the country's (and therefore the
world's) leading Cream Cake Development Institute. With sensitive
documents such as '*L'éclair: crème où chocolat?*' and '*La Patisserie: l'avenir*'
passing across her desk on a daily basis, we can see that both Monsieur et
Madame occupy jobs of the greatest responsibility. Their teenage twin
boys, Philippe and René, have broad interests ranging from '*le football*' to
'*le football*' and back again, and there is nothing to mark this family out
from the vast majority of the Belgian bourgeoisie, including the fact that
they do not own their dwelling place.

The four-bedroomed apartment in a respectable part of town which
they've inhabited for years is rented. Like many so-called respectable
people on the Continent, they have never felt the need or inclination to
buy their own place to live. Why is this? We have no idea, but doubtless
PhD theses have been written on the subject and universities are even now
offering courses on 'Comparative Home Ownership: Europe and Britain
1945–98'. You'll tell us we should enrol for one of these and, yeah, maybe
we will (read: 'When Hell freezes over').

In the mean time, though, let's do some brainstorming about property
as an investment. Is it a good one? In Britain, we seem pretty convinced
that it is, but clearly in Belgium – and in much of Europe – many people
are convinced that it is not. Purely in terms of the return on your investment, and you won't be surprised to hear this coming from us, property is
not as lucrative as the stock market. '*Mais non! Sacre bleu!*' you might well
retort. And yes, people who bought houses 30 years ago have indeed done
exceedingly well out of them. They have watched rampant inflation in the
70s and 80s shrink their mortgage repayments today to negligible
amounts, while rapidly rising house prices have given them a warm glow
of satisfaction. The facts, though, tell us that houses appreciate at only
8.5 per cent per year (average rate from 1945 to 1994, according to the

Anglia House Price Survey). Compare this with the average amount the stock market has returned over the comparable period of 1945–97 of 13.54 per cent. In *pure* investment terms, property in general isn't as good as the stock market.

However, the problem, as so often, is the British climate. You *need* a roof over your head. Also, of course, none of us likes to have to ask the landlord before we bash in nails, fit mirrors to the bedroom ceiling or tear down the living room wall. Further, we don't much like paying the landlord rent either – it feels a little like money down the drain. But is it? Yes, often it is. As a general rule, it's probably fair to say that unless the rents in your area are *much* lower than you'd pay for a mortgage, you'll probably do better financially by buying a place to live in rather than renting. After all, the money you are paying to buy your house is purchasing you an asset which appreciates at 8.5 per cent every year. However, if the rents *are* much lower, then you can do better by investing in the stock market the money you save by not paying into a mortgage, where you'll get a higher return on your money than you would have got for the property – we've just seen those numbers. Still, though, your landlord can chuck you out of your rented place more or less at will and you don't feel as if the place is your own. For most of us, buying a place to live probably does make financial sense, is something we'd do anyway even if it didn't, and is the single biggest purchase of our lives.

One point to make in all this, however, is that it's not a good idea to buy *too much* house purely as an investment. If part of your purchasing decision sounds like this – 'Well, we can afford more, so let's go for something a bit bigger as an investment' – then stop and think. Property is a decent investment, but the stock market is better.

Enough. We're going to almost certainly buy a place to live. Let's look at how to do it Foolishly.

What's a mortgage?

Referred to in everyday language as the 'bloody mortgage' and most commonly incorporated into the phrase, 'Well, it pays the bloody mortgage, I suppose' when referring to one's job of work, the mortgage is the cheapest form of long-term loan there is. Lending money to house buyers is a good business to be in, because a house is unable to change its name and leave the country. If the loan stops being repaid, you simply step in, take possession of the property, sell it and move on. Most people, however, *do* repay their loans over many years, filling your coffers with lots of cash in the process. You obtain the money which you lend out from people depositing their savings in your deposit accounts. You pay these savers a bit less in interest than you charge the people to whom you are lending out the money and you pocket the difference. In short, you're a broker and that's why you, the money lender, can afford to offer such cheap mortgage rates. It's a system which keeps the lenders exceedingly profitable, allows people to buy houses for seemingly astronomical prices and in fact keeps most people happy, most of the time.

The simplest kind of mortgage is a repayment mortgage. In this type of mortgage, most of your monthly contribution goes towards paying the interest on the loan and some towards paying off the actual sum you have been loaned. At the end of 25 or 30 years, you have paid back all the money you have been lent, along with all the interest over the intervening period. The house is now yours and that's it. Simple.

The other type of mortgage is an interest-only mortgage. You borrow the money and you don't repay any of it at all until the end of the mortgage term. Over the 25 or 30 years of the mortgage term, you end up paying a fair bit more interest than with a repayment mortgage, because you owe all of the money for the whole period. (With a repayment mortgage, remember, you pay off some of the money you owe every month, so the amount you actually owe gets less and less and as a result the amount of interest you have to pay goes steadily down.) Finally, you get to the end, you've paid all that interest for all that time and then you realize you've forgotten that you still have to pay off the original amount you borrowed. Whoops! Now you have to start again, but you're in your sixties, no-one wants to lend you any money because they don't think you'll live long enough, your retirement income isn't as much as your salary was, eventually the house gets repossessed and you take proud possession of two Sony 17" cardboard boxes just off Waterloo Bridge, on a patch next to 'Whizzy' Pete, the speed freak. It's ugly, it doesn't look good when the grandchildren come to visit and it's a situation well worth avoiding. Which, by a fluke of happenstance, is the subject of the very next section . . .

Foolishness starts here: interest-only mortgages and paying off the original loan

---

How *do* you arrange to repay the original loan at the end of the time if you have an interest-only mortgage? By paying into a regular investment scheme of some sort, which will grow your money and, 25 years on, leave you with a pot of money to hand over to the mortgage lender who will then hand you the deeds of your house in return. Traditionally, interest-only mortgages have been backed up by an investment in the form of an endowment policy. We examine these in some detail in the next chapter, or rather we tear them limb from limb before feeding the remains to a flock of hungry vultures and exorcizing their dark spirit with a series of ancient Druidic incantations. Suffice to say here that these are an expensive, inefficient means of paying off your mortgage, whose major pay-off is to the person who sells you the policy. Back in the Dark Days of the late 80s, well over two-thirds of British mortgages were backed by endowment policies. Now the number is down to a third or so, which is better, but still lamentable.

(NB If you are reading this and already have an endowment policy, as many will have, don't panic and certainly don't rush out and cancel it without going into the matter in some detail. That may be the worst thing you could do and would probably benefit no-one but the company which sold you the policy. Probably your endowment *will* pay off your mortgage and leave you a little over. Perhaps you could have done better, but you weren't to know. Anyway, skip to our final diatribe, er, sorry, Chapter 22, on endowments and pensions if you're still thirsting for information.)

With interest-only mortgages backed by endowments not even making it past the regional heats for Miss Mortgage Fool 1998, who is going to win the cruise to Barbados, the modelling contract and the free year's liposuction? (You're going to think it's fixed, we know you are, but it honestly isn't.) And the winner is . . .

> *'Oh, Ladies and Gentlemen, the tension here at Fool Central is unbearable and I just can't seem to get this envelope open . . . Ah, here we are! . . . I can't believe it! It's so wonderful! It's so marvellous! She's so beautiful! Step up onto the podium, Miss Mortgage Fool of 1998, Miss Agnes Index-Tra-a-a-acker!'*
>
> *'Well, Agnes,'* (sotto voce: *'That's right, stand here, luv, and flash yer gnashers into the camera with the light on'*) *'It's a great honour. You've done so well and against such strong competition. What does winning here tonight mean to you?'*
>
> *'I weell use my poseeshun as Meess Mortgage Fool to work for world peace, spread ze Folliculitis and I love all children and ze animals. I love you all so much! Mwwoooh, my darleengs!'*
>
> *'Thank you, Agnes! I think you meant "Folly" there. "Folliculitis" is a nasty skin infection, as we all know! Har! Har! Isn't she wonderful, Ladies 'n Gennulmen?'*

And there we must leave this happy scene, but not, we are pleased to say, the index tracker.

Now, suppose you had taken out a repayment mortgage for £100,000 for 25 years – no index tracker, no fancy stuff, you just pay off the interest and a little bit of the capital each month. This would cost you £815 per month at the average mortgage rate from 1945 to 1996 of 8.65 per cent (according to the Compendium of Housing Finance Statistics 1997). At the end of that time, you've paid £144,608 in interest and have also paid off the original loan of £100,000, meaning you've shelled out a total of £244,608 for your £100,000 house. Youch! That's a lot of readies, but at least now you own the house. And that's the important thing, right?

Suppose instead, though, you take out an interest-only mortgage for

£100,000 for 25 years. That means that over the time you pay £216,250 in interest. (Maths dudes will realize that it's worked out like this: £100,000 × 0.0865 × 25 = £216,250.) £216,250 in interest over all that time and you still haven't paid off any of the original loan: frightening, hey? And still £100,000 to pay off. Oh my gosh, what now?!

Hey, relax, because your interest has only been costing you a cool £721 each month, again which is worked out like this for the mathematics-heads amongst you: (£100,000 × 0.0865) ÷ 12. Now, take that away from the £815 you would have been paying with the repayment mortgage and you have £94 every month which you can invest in an index tracker. (Hey, index trackers again!) We're going to be conservative here and reckon that you can expect the index to bring you around 12.2 per cent every year. That's the average yearly amount it has returned since 1918, which includes the downtimes of the Crash of 1929, the Depression of the 1930s, the war years and the 1973/74 bear market. In the last decade or two it has returned over 14 per cent, but we're being very low-key, so as not to get over-excited. In fact, we're going to be even more low-key (we'll be flat on our backs soon) and say that the index tracking unit trust you are going to use will charge you around 0.5 per cent per year and will have a tracking error of around 0.3 per cent (the amount by which it is inaccurate in following the index). Subtract these from the 12.2 per cent average return and we're left with 11.4 per cent expected annual return. Getting lower, but don't worry. Look at this:

£94 per month invested in an index tracker for 25 years at 11.4% = £160,387

That's right, we can still pay off the hundred grand and have a £60,000 surplus as compared to the repayment mortgage, yet the monthly cost has been exactly the same over the 25 years (£721 + £94 = £815). Not bad at all, but what about tax? As we've already seen in Chapter 20 'How Not To Pay Tax', an individual can squirrel away and invest at least £5000 per year into an Individual Savings Account without it being liable for any tax, ever, and a lifetime team of two (Aren't we politically correct?!) can double that. Since the investment you've been making in this case is only £1128 (£94 × 12) per year, you're well inside your limit; you can invest almost another four grand a year as an individual – nine grand in combination with your partner – and you'll still never have to pay any tax on it. Tax isn't a problem if you're using your index tracker to pay off mortgages of the kind most of us will have.

Now, you decide to be clever. 'Aha!' You say to yourself, 'I could just pay off the mortgage early when the amount in the index tracker reaches £100,000 and save myself several years of interest payments.' Smart, very smart.

But not smart enough.

In this case, your index tracker investment reaches £100,000 around three years before the mortgage term finishes, i.e. at 22 years. What if you pay off the mortgage now and then invest the *combined* money which would otherwise have gone into the interest payments and the index tracker (i.e. £815) into the index tracker? Now, instead of putting just £94 into the index tracker every month, a massive £815 is going in. ('We're in the money! We're in the money!') How much does that give you after the three years which it would have taken you to reach the end of the mortgage term? Just £36,500 is the miserly answer. And remember, you *would* have had a surplus of over £60,000 if you'd simply plodded on as you were. So, we can conclude that it's often not worth paying down your mortgage debt as long as you're investing at a higher rate elsewhere. At various sites on the Internet you can find calculators which allow you to input the size of the debt you owe and the interest you are being charged on it, along with the monthly amount you have available to either pay down that debt or contribute to a savings plan elsewhere and the rate of return you expect that savings plan to bring you. Then, when you hit the calculate button, they calculate whether you are better off paying down the debt or investing the money you have available elsewhere and by how much. Nifty, we think, and you'll find the website addresses of a couple of them in Appendix 2 'A Fool's (Brief) Guide to the Internet'.

One argument which is occasionally advanced against this way of paying off your mortgage is what happens when the stock market plummets just as it comes time to pay off the lump sum? Well, there are a couple of points here. First, as we've seen, this is a highly efficient way to pay off the loan and you'd be unlucky if your investments dropped from £160,000 to below £100,000 overnight. It could happen, it has happened, but you'd be pretty unlucky. One thing to do if it *did* happen would be to extend the mortgage term, of course. Just keep paying and wait for the market to recover. In the end that is likely to be a profitable solution. Alternatively, you could pay a little more into the index tracker right from the start, so you would be in a position to pay off your mortgage even more quickly than the example we've just seen where you paid it off three years early. A five-year leeway is plenty. Although it might hit your profits slightly (remember, investing the contributions you *would* have paid in interest doesn't net you quite as much as if you'd left the whole lump sum growing where it was), if you're the worrying type, you'll sleep soundly at night and *still* do better than a repayment mortgage. Overall though, playing these kinds of odds – savvy, Foolish odds – is likely to bring you great reward and unlikely to bring you disaster. Think back to the Bible of the Long Distance Investor (Chapter 4): in the long term the stock market is a very safe place to invest.

If, despite all this Foolish consideration, you're going to worry about paying for your house via the stock market ('This is where I *live*, for Heaven's sake!'), then get a repayment mortgage. It'll save you a lot of heartache and *Angst* and doesn't mean that you can't invest in the market with other portions of your savings. There's no shame in it.

One piece of advice, though, if you are considering getting a repayment mortgage: look around for an 'Australian-type' mortgage. Remember that in a repayment mortgage, you are paying off some of the capital all the time and so the amount outstanding is getting lower. With an Australian-type mortgage, this is taken into account and the amount of interest you owe is calculated every month, or even every day, as opposed to every year for most mortgages and the repayments adjusted accordingly. This works far more in your favour and means you pay much less interest over the period of the mortgage. *Moneyfacts* magazine has calculated that this could be worth almost £4500 on a repayment mortgage of £50,000 over 25 years at 8.5 per cent interest. Obviously, in an interest-only mortgage where the capital is paid off in a single swoop at the end, whether the interest is calculated daily or yearly makes no difference. Two companies offering this type of mortgage at the time of writing are the Royal Bank of Scotland and the Yorkshire Bank. The disadvantage to this system comes only if you end up falling behind on your payments, in which case the amount you owe will build up far more quickly than with a conventional repayment mortgage where the interest is calculated yearly. But you're not planning to do that, are you?!

Maybe it's time to sum up what we've said so far:

- Mortgages are the cheapest form of long-term loan.
- Don't pay back that cheap loan for as long as you can.
- Instead, use the money which this frees up to invest elsewhere (the stock market) at higher rates of interest.
- Meanwhile, the house, into which you have sunk almost nothing (just a minimum deposit) also increases steadily in value.
- Continue for 25 or 30 years.
- Come out far richer than you would otherwise have done.

In other words:

- Maybe you *should* just buy a house, but use someone else's money to do it and don't pay that loan back for as long as you possibly can.

The five steps to a successful mortgage

It's always been our personal experience, and people have been telling us over the last few years, that there is a yawning chasm between knowing the theory and feeling able and confident enough to put that theory into practice. That's why here we'd like to include some practical steps on how to get the mortgage you want. Your mortgage is going to be with you for a long time and it's worth putting just a little effort into getting it right.

Step One: Do not buy a mortgage from anyone who spontaneously offers to sell you a mortgage

These people should be approached with the greatest caution, as they can be very convincing. They are, however, looking at you as a potential gold mine and will almost certainly try to sell you an endowment mortgage. On no account let them get between you and the exit: instead speak soothing, polite words, avoid eye contact (this can be dangerous) and back slowly out of the door. If you do this skilfully enough, they will still be talking to an empty room as you turn the key in the door of No. 1 Fleapit Mansions, your current, luxury residence.

Step Two: Also do not buy a mortgage during a face-to-face encounter

You know what you want. You do not have to be 'sold' to. Agreeing to a face-to-face encounter with a mortgage salesperson is agreeing to the possibility that the salesperson may be able to change your mind and sell you what he/she wants. If this is the case, then you are not ready to buy a mortgage.

Step Three: You're the customer, so act like one. Go out and shop!

It's easy to think that the people who lend you the money to buy your house are being kind to you, that they are doing you a favour. This is wrong. You are doing them a favour by gracing them with your custom. Try not to forget this, as it helps in the game of psychological one-upmanship on which you are about to embark. *They* have to earn *your* business; you do not have to prove yourself worthy to them. Be upfront, pushy even. If the person on the other end of the line is starting to sound exasperated or is even putting on mock offence, then go elsewhere. The likelihood of your causing real offence with your polite questions is small and remember this Foolish law of personal finance:

It's your life and it's only their job.

Step Four: Pop down the newsagents

And buy a copy of *What Mortgage* or *Your Mortgage* or anything with 'mortgage' in the title. We promise you this is not going to become your regular reading, supplanting *Dishwasher Illustrated* or *Turnip Life* in your affections. You will only ever have to buy one or two copies of these magazines and never again have to walk furtively up to the cash register, hoping no-one you know has seen you.

It's interesting that at the time of writing this book, a frequently shown advertisement on television is for a mortgage lender. A well-known comedian is shown scratching his head over a copy of one of these mortgage magazines and getting his knickers in a twist over all the options on offer. Finally, he gives up, leaves it all up to the mortgage leader and in the next shot is seen happily thumbing through a copy of *What Pub* instead. A heart-warming tale, no doubt, but does the financial services industry really think it's going to be able to spend the next 30 years in the way it has spent the last – by patronizing the public and encouraging them to remain ignorant so that just about any abomination can be sold to them without their realizing? It seems as if they do, but, in our opinion, they have severely misread the signs of an increasingly aware population, with exploding access to information. Watch out, dinosaurs – the last great upheaval on Earth saw you entirely wiped out. Don't make the same mistake twice.

We'd love to be able to say to you that you can do all the shopping you need for a mortgage on the Internet, but at the time of writing (although perhaps not the time of publication), it just isn't true. You might be able to do some preliminary research out there, but you'll end up falling back on the telephone and that's where the magazines come in. They have listings of all the mortgages and mortgage companies and also large glossy advertisements with telephone numbers and, occasionally, website addresses.

Step Five: The telephone

Park yourself by it with the Foolish mortgage-hunter's survival kit: pen, reams of paper, cup of tea and one box of Jaffa Cakes, comfort-eating for the use of. By now you've decided what you want. Let's assume you've decided on the Foolish combination of an interest-only mortgage, backed by an index tracker. You start phoning likely-looking organizations on your list. Here's how it might go:

DIRECT MORTGAGES FOR FOOLS. Hello, Direct Mortgages for Fools, how can I be of Foolish assistance today?

YOU. Hello. I'm interested in an interest-only mortgage, which I will back with an index tracker. I'm wondering what you've got to offer me.
(This is a good start. You're confident and you've shown you know a little bit about the subject. The person on the other end is already saying to themselves: 'For this is a Fool!')

DIRECT MORTGAGES FOR FOOLS. Certainly, we have the blah, blah . . .
(If you're lucky at this point, they will indeed give you the information you ask for. If you're not, you may find yourself giving away a load of demographic information designed to ensure that you and your family unto the seventh generation shall receive direct mail from these people. If that is the case, then you may want to ask them to cut through the malarkey and get to the point.)

DIRECT MORTGAGES FOR FOOLS. . . . and then we have the ValuePlan

Five Year Fixed Rate Mortgage.

(You're going to be faced with a bewildering array of superficially enticing schemes designed to make you buy one of DMF's mortgages. We go into some of the permutations below – you'll figure them out pretty quickly and it doesn't make for the most exciting of reading – but just remember that there ain't no free lunches. If it looks too good to be true, it definitely is.)

YOU. Sounds interesting. I wonder if you'd send me some details?

(You're for it now. They really are going to ask you a whole lot of questions about your income, spouse's income, other debts, etc. They need this to make up a proposal for you which they will then send out. Despite the rigour of this interrogation and the professional, personalized nature of the proposal when it arrives, be reassured that this commits you to nothing.)

DIRECT MORTGAGES FOR FOOLS. No problem. May I just ask how you are planning to pay off the amount of the loan at the end of the mortgage term?

(At this point, you say either that you're going to link it to an index tracker as you pointed out at the beginning and you already have one in mind, thank you very much (see Chapter 7 'A Tale of Two Professions and Basic Foolish Investment'), or else that you will be making regular contributions into a self-select PEP/ISA and building up an equity portfolio. If you plump for the latter, sound very confident and knowledgeable. To be honest, we feel that to back your house purchase it is probably best to stick with a simple index tracker into which you make a regular monthly contribution.)

DIRECT MORTGAGES FOR FOOLS. That sounds interesting, sir/madam. I wonder if you've considered one of our endowment policies? They have quite impressive bonuses at the end of the policy, they provide life assurance as well and they are portable.

(You didn't sound confident enough, did you? DMF thought there was just the minutest chance that they could flog you an endowment policy. Remember, it means a lot to them and they're going to try very hard. They always use the life assurance thing, because you need to have life assurance to cover your mortgage and they always plug the fact that you can keep the same endowment policy if you move house – i.e. they're 'portable'. Luckily, you were ahead of them and you reply:)

YOU. Thanks very much, but I'm not all that impressed with endowments in general. I'll be shopping around for the best deal I can find in level term life assurance and the index tracker's portable in any case.

(Way to go, Fool! [Sorry, that was the Americans in this writing team getting a little out of hand. Normal service will now be resumed.] Yes, you've done really well. Level term life assurance is what you will need and unless DMF is willing to offer you the best deal, don't buy it from them. Level term simply means that you will be insured for the whole sum of the

loan for the whole *period. If the credits start to roll before your time – or what you thought ought to be your time – then the insurance company pays out on the policy. If you survive until the end of the policy and pay off the mortgage as planned, the insurance cover finishes and you get nothing. Except the satisfaction of having survived, that is. If DMF can't sell you an endowment policy, they may push their life assurance pretty hard and if they do, it may well be a 'with profits' policy in which there is an investment component (and an even larger charges component) to it. Decline it. You have the information you want, it is now time to make your excuses and leave.)*

DIRECT MORTGAGES FOR FOOLS. Thank you very much, I'll get that proposal out in the post to you today.

YOU. Thanks a lot, I appreciate it. Byeee.

There, it wasn't too bad, was it? And the reason is that you knew what you wanted beforehand and were in control throughout. Granted you've had to expend five weeks of unremitting misery to get to this point in the book, but it's starting to pay off. You now move on to the next likely-looking candidate in the magazine:

GERBILS PROVIDENT. Hello, Gerbils Provident – two hundred years of faithful service to rodents and other small mammals – how can I help?

We'll be honest here. This is going to take you a couple of hours one Saturday morning to sort out. Perhaps even a bit more by the time you've sorted through all the paperwork you're going to get sent and made your decision. But it'll be worth it.

Sorting out the special offers

One of the things you will find the most confusing is trying to sort out the various cashback and fixed rate offers. Financial advisers like to use this as the reason why the punter can't buy their own mortgage and needs their 'advice'. (The term is used here very loosely.) Don't roll over on your back and play their game, though. Briefly, what you're after is the cheapest mortgage for the longest period. Simple, hey? Nope, the mortgage companies were there before you. If you opt for a variable rate mortgage, then the interest rate on the loan – and hence the amount of money you have to pay back every month – will wax and wane as the Bank of England decides on where to set the Base Rate, or the rate at which banks are allowed to lend out money. This exposes you to the risk of interest rates moving up, but there is also generally no penalty imposed in the mortgage terms if you decide to switch mortgage providers and take your mortgage elsewhere.

Remember, the average mortgage rate has been 8.65 per cent since the war.

Suppose now that you opt for a fixed rate mortgage for five years. This means that the rate at which you pay back money is fixed at a predetermined rate, say, 8 per cent for that period. No matter what happens, even if the variable rate goes up to 10 per cent, you will still pay only 8 per cent. On the other hand, if mortgage rates drop well below 8 per cent, you're going to feel a little peeved and wonder whether you couldn't get a better deal elsewhere. Bingo! Enter the redemption penalty. This will usually be a fair whack (up to 5 per cent of the value of the loan) which the mortgage company will charge you for the privilege of switching to another company. It's their way of compensating for the upside risk they carry with a fixed rate mortgage and stopping you scooting off just when they look set to make a little profit themselves. There's a similar penalty period with cashback mortgages, where the mortgage company 'gives' you back a cash lump sum when you take out the mortgage. If you try to 'redeem' the mortgage within, usually, a five year period, you will have to pay the money back. There's nothing intrinsically wrong with redemption penalties as long as you don't labour under the illusion that you're getting something for nothing. You get what you hope is a good deal and the company has the guarantee of your business – or at least a big fat consolation prize if you move elsewhere – for as long as the redemption penalty period lasts. Always ask about them and always, always ask whether they extend beyond the end of the fixed rate period. A seven-year penalty period with only five years at the fixed rate can leave you feeling pretty exposed when mortgage rates shoot up and you still have a hefty penalty hanging over your head to stop you moving your mortgage to another company with a better rate. Know what you are getting yourself into is the motto, which stands pretty well for the rest of life, too. Simply apply the common sense you use in your other dealings to the issue of mortgages and you will be sailing home free, with a much better deal than any of your contemporaries.

The MIG

One more sting in the tail for house purchasers which it's worth knowing about is the Mortgage Indemnity Guarantee premium, or MIG. It can have other names, too, but whatever it's called, it's a one-off premium which can amount to £1500 or more which you generally have to pay if you are taking out a loan of more than 75 per cent of the property value. You see, the statistics tell the mortgage companies that loans of this kind of size are more likely to be defaulted on. Hmm, so that means the MIG insures you against not being able to repay the loan and you won't lose your house . . .? Sorry, it insures *them* against your not being able to repay the loan. They'll still repossess it, you'll still lose it and they'll still sell it on for whatever they can get for it. What's the point of it for the buyer, then? Good question. At the time of writing (early 1998), some companies are starting to abolish the MIG and it's a trend which we hope will continue. Good riddance!

Mortgages – the end

Sounding a bit complicated? Starting to wonder if it's all worth it? Don't! It's actually not all that complicated when you get into it and it's too late, anyway. You see, you may want to give all this over to someone else to manage, but you've ruined it. You now know too much. You've passed the point of no return and should have put this book back on the shelf in the shop immediately after you picked it up, silly Fool! For you now know that the people who are trying to sell you a mortgage are trying to make a fast buck, that some mortgages are far worse for your health than others and that if you're Foolish about buying property, you could be setting yourself up for a lifetime of healthy investment. You can't unlearn any of this stuff and while some say that ignorance is bliss, we say that when it comes to investment it carries a pretty hefty price tag and actually isn't all that blissful anyway.

Being ignorant and having to rely on others to make *your* financial decisions on their behalf is a little like one of those falling dreams when you tumble off a cliff and can see the ground coming towards you, but can't do anything about it. Sometimes you actually go on and hit the ground, but at other times you manage to wake yourself up with a start before you do, and that's what happened to you when you picked up this book on that fateful Tuesday afternoon in Bromsgrove. There's no going back and while that may feel a little burdensome at times, on the other hand the financial benefits are potentially enormous and the 'feel-good' factor is pretty strong too. You are now a fully fledged, card-carrying Fool, managing his or her own investments, captain of your fate and mistress of your soul. It's exhilarating, so savour it. After all, anyone who has got this far through a book on investment has earned it.

22

Pensions, Annuities and Endowments: The Foolish Story

O wombe! O bely! O stynkyng cod
Fulfilled of dong and of corrupcioun!
Geoffrey Chaucer, *The Canterbury Tales:* The Pardoner's Tale

Far better to learn from another's mistakes than your own and before we start talking about pensions, annuities and endowments, we have a confession to make. Actually, 'we' don't; David Berger has. Those of you who already own a computer will be aware of the need to back up your data at regular intervals to save it. This is so that if the computer breaks down, you don't lose for ever the letter you are writing, or the list of useful addresses you've compiled, or even the eight thousand words of the book chapter you happen to have been writing. *Eight thousand* words! 'Tis true: a knocking emanated from the computer and then all went black. Hair was pulled out, fists banged, lips bitten, imprecations to supernatural beings offered, but . . . nothing. The first draft of this chapter was lost for ever. It is tempting when writing a book of this kind to sprinkle it with exhortations like: 'If you learn nothing else from this book, learn XYZ.' Well, Foolish Reader, if you learn nothing else from this book, learn to back up your data.

But enough of this public confessional, cleansing though it be, and on with the book!

In the United States, people at parties discuss shares or mutual funds they own. Taxi drivers will comment on the level of the Dow. In Britain, people will occasionally talk about the windfall shares they received when their building society converted into a bank, but mostly investment doesn't really get discussed at all, beyond: 'I really must do something about my pension, but I don't understand a word my financial adviser says.' This is a shame, because if people did start discussing the investments most of them already own – endowments and pensions – and started to understand them, we might begin to get somewhere as an investing nation.

Really, though, it's not surprising that people don't discuss their endowments and pensions, as they have never received any education about them, they find the whole subject intimidating in the extreme and the last thing the professionals would like is for people to be considering these investments from a knowledgeable standpoint. Just why this is, we are about to see. Be warned that this chapter is a little more involved than most of the others, but if you own one of these investments or you're thinking you might buy one, it's worth ploughing through.

You've got to have a pension, haven't you?

Well, yes, and then again, no. Before we answer this in a slightly more helpful manner, let's take a Cook's tour of the different pension options available and also scoot Foolishly through the thorny issue of annuities. If you already have a pension yourself, our guess is that you'll be quite interested to hear what we have to say in this chapter. If you don't yet have one, then we hope it will also provide some food for thought, because sure as goldfish swim, the Pope is Catholic and the Shipping Forecast must mean something to someone somewhere, there is a financial adviser out there who is going to try and sell you one of these. Soon.

The State Pension

It is slowly being abolished, as we saw in Chapter 1. Slipping in a 2 per cent drop in growth was a shrewd manoeuvre by the Thatcher government in 1981. The Tories, in the aftermath of their 1979 landslide, realized that, since there was no investment fund out of which pensions were being paid (they are paid by the National Insurance contributions of those currently working), the rapidly ageing population was going to mean that pensions at the current levels were going to become too expensive. They therefore cut the rate at which pensions appreciated and so hastened the stranglehold on this country's old people. Whatever you think of the rights and wrongs of this, it is the case that by the time many people reading this book retire, they'll be lucky if the weekly state pension buys them a bottle of blue hair rinse and a packet of Mr Kipling's jam tarts. Do not factor the state pension into any of your retirement calculations.

Occupational Pensions

Forty years on the shop floor at Harding and Sedgewick ends with a handshake, a carriage clock and a generous pension to reflect the hard work and faithful service of a lifetime:

> *'Thank you, Higgins. Any plans for the future, my man?'*
> *'Well, sir, there's an allotment to dig and the cricket to watch. And may I say what a fine company this has been to work for over the years and what gentlemen you, and before you, your father have been. It has been an honour to work my fingers to the bone fourteen hours a day for a pittance of a weekly wage and a five shilling bonus every other Christmas. The outstanding growth in your personal wealth over that time and the way in which I was*

*allowed to shine your shoes on my birthday have been a source of great pride
to me. Truly a privilege, sir. Thank 'ee.'*

Yes, those were the days, the days of Mrs Miniver and Morris Eights, of
the Movietone News and good old British honesty and pluck and people
jolly well knowing their place. Those days, though, are largely gone. While
occupational pensions can provide a sound retirement income and should
generally be opted *for* rather than against, the picture is not quite so clear
as it was back then, when the sun always shone in June and we knew with
such certainty who the baddies were.

The best occupational pensions are to be found in the public sector. If
you are in the police force, your pension will be generous indeed and will
be paid for out of the organization's budget; there is no investment fund
out of which pensions are paid. Elsewhere, though, and especially in the
private sector, pensions are paid out of an investment fund into which
both employee and employer contribute. This fund will be invested in a
variety of things, although generally it is heavily weighted into equities.
That said, the equity investments are more likely to take the form of the
underperforming unit trusts we've already talked about. Occupational
pensions can take one of two forms:

Employees know exactly what they will get on retirement
In this option, employees contribute to a pension fund and the employer
also contributes up to 5 per cent of the employee's income. When the
employee retires, the pension paid will be calculated by a defined formula
based on salary and years of service. Not surprisingly, this type is known as
a *defined benefit* scheme or a *final salary* scheme. If the investments in the
fund underperform and there isn't enough money to pay the pension, then
the company will have to stump up the difference. The maximum you are
allowed to receive in a scheme of this sort is two-thirds of your final salary,
although in fact fewer than 4 per cent actually get this and the majority get
less than one-third. At the moment, the majority of company pension
schemes are 'defined benefit', but it is a risky business for the employer and
so they are stampeding to change to the next option.

The employee doesn't know exactly what to expect on retirement
Here, the employer still contributes up to 5 per cent, the employee makes
their contribution, too, and the money goes into the investment fund.
However, the employer is not obliged to make the pension up to any
defined amount if the investment fund fails to perform. This is called a
defined contribution scheme or a *money purchase* scheme and is much more
favoured by employers these days, as no risk at all attaches to them. If
things don't work out quite as planned and there isn't enough money to
pay the level of pension which might have been expected, then that is
tough for the employee and no doubt 'highly regrettable' for the employer,

but they are under no obligation to top it up. Employers, for understandable reasons, prefer this type of scheme to the first option.

What makes occupational pension schemes attractive is the contribution from the employer: free money, in other words. What makes them less attractive is the fact that they tend not to be portable. Since you are unlikely these days to be spending the whole 40 years of your career at Harding and Sedgewick – the average person changes job five times in their working lives and less than 5 per cent of men and 1 per cent of women stay in the same job for 30 years – this could leave you with a number of small pensions, each paying out not very much. If it is portable, you're still likely to lose out to some extent.

There are good things, then, and bad things about company pension schemes. As throughout this book, we don't seek to tell you what you should do and what you shouldn't do – that would be pointless; what we seek to do is give you the information to make informed decisions on your own behalf. What we hope you will take away from this short section is that, for most people, an occupational pension is probably not going to provide the single, all-encompassing answer to a prosperous dotage.

Avanti!

Personal Pension Plans

The late 1980s. Thatcher's generation of self-employed entrepreneurs is by turns quaffing lager and revolutionizing the British economy, but none of them, of course, has access to an occupational pension scheme.

> *Unfair, Nigel! These are my children. Go and DO something about it!' Roars the 'T', eyes ablaze with fury and index finger pointing to the door of the Cabinet Room.*
>
> *'Immediately, Ma'am,' ripostes Mr Lawson and scurries off to do the Leaderene's bidding.*

Thus, Fools, was an acronym born.

PPPs, or Personal Pension Plans, give self-employed people, or those working for small businesses without occupational schemes, a crack – as they like to say in the Sunday newspapers – of the pensions whip. Essentially, they are similar to the second type of occupational scheme, the *defined contribution* scheme. The PPP holder pays a percentage of their salary (rising from a maximum of 17.5 per cent at the age of 35 or below to 40 per cent at the age of 60 or above) into an investment fund, run by an investment or insurance company, into which the government also contributes the tax the investor would have paid. In other words, they get *tax relief* on their contributions, an undoubted advantage. The fund grows and then it is used at retirement to provide an income. Simple? No, definitely not.

First, it was with PPPs that the financial professionals got their knickers in a very painful twist in the late 80s and early 90s. By encouraging people to purchase their (expensive) plans and to abandon the perfectly good occupational schemes many of them were already in, they were giving disastrous financial advice, which would leave most of these people at a financial disadvantage in years to come. This has become known as the 'Pensions mis-selling scandal' and the precise reasons it arose (the companies involved were making a killing from selling these policies) will become painfully obvious as we consider the issue of investment charges in just one short paragraph from here. Suffice to say that some of the biggest names in financial services were implicated to the tune of billions of pounds of compensation which they are now having to pay to those they disadvantaged by their phoney advice. The issue was supposed to be in the process of being resolved in early 1998 (with some judicious prodding from Parliament and fines for those who were reluctant to pay compensation), when it all hit centre stage again. The government decreed in February of that year that the companies would have to investigate another 1.5 *million* cases, pushing the likely compensation bill from £5000 million to beyond £11,000 million at a single stroke. The minister responsible referred to this as 'an awful lot of money' and we're with him on that one. Now let's hear where this money is going to come from. In the July 1998 edition of *Money Management*, it was estimated that one company, Guardian, will have to pay up around £150 million. The magazine then went on to say:

> . . . this cost . . . looks set to have a material impact on policyholders' already poor bonus prospects. Under such circumstances, it is quite astonishing that, while policy holders suffered, Guardian Assurance plc saw fit to pay a bumper £165m dividend to its parent, Guardian Royal Exchange plc, which should then think it appropriate to return £190m of 'excess capital' to shareholders. Stale bread for the with profits policyholders but champagne for the proprietors (including share option owning directors); someone seems to have got the politics very badly wrong here.

The policyholders – in other words the people investing their *life savings* with this company – are going to pay for the wrongdoing of the company. Bare-faced cheek? This is a full-on moonie flashed to the policyholders!

Next, comes the thorny issue of charges. Let's cast our minds back for a moment to Chapter 2, 'The Miracle of Compound Interest'. There we saw how important it was, nay vital, to start on the investing trail as soon as humanly possible. Time and patience are the friends of the Foolish investor. What think you, then, Fool, of giving up 80 per cent or more of your first two years' contributions to a PPP in charges? This is money which will go not into your future, but into someone else's, either the financial adviser who sold you the plan, who takes it as his commission, or else the investment company itself. That's 80 per cent or more of the first two, *paramount* years: also an awful lot of very important money. (And are you still with us here?) It gets worse, breathtakingly so. Often, if you change the amount of your contributions, the company will *restart* the punitive charges schedule. Look at this e-mail from David Carter in 1998:

> *I increased my contribution to £300 [from £100] per month with effect from May 1st 1998. Then came the shock disclosure and here I do quote, because I was flabbergasted when I saw:*
> *'HOW MUCH WILL THE ADVICE COST?'*
> *'Company X will provide services and remuneration for arranging and servicing this increase [sic] to your plan amounting to £77.11 per month on average in the first year and a variable amount per month thereafter, being for example £64.50 on average in the second year, £15.28 in the third year and £24.28 in the final year. These amounts have been included in the deductions shown above and are determined by the size of the contribution increase and payment term.'*
>
> *Now, I've never been much of a jargon man myself. But to my simple thinking, this all adds up to a total of £2200 over four years just to service an increase to my premium – I even had to write the letter authorizing the increase to the company direct debit!*
>
> *I rang my Company X salesman (I've never accepted their term of 'advisor') who I've known for thirteen years. He was upset that I should question this 25 per cent (averaged over 4 years) charge. He compared it to my fees for recruiting staff for my clients (average: 20 per cent of first year's remuneration). I respectfully pointed out to him that I don't make any charges when a client increases someone's salary! (Anyway, isn't the first year's fee 40 per cent?)*
>
> *He's coming to see me tomorrow to try and sort it out. He asked me to find out whether other pension providers charge less – probably so that he can show me how well the Company X investment out-performs any other that I might choose. I don't want to play that game and told him that I shall not be doing any business with Company X again.*

Sadly, what happened to David happens to many people with personal pensions who think they're saving more and more for the future. Each time they increase their contributions, they don't realize they are paying directly into the pockets of the people who are running their policy.

Now, interesting things also happen when you stop paying into your Personal Pension Plan earlier than you'd planned. There could be a variety of reasons for this, which were nicely detailed in an article in the *Independent* on November 15th, 1997: Lincoln, a PPP provider, found that 45 per cent (!) of its pension premiums lapse within three years and, to their credit, commissioned research into why this was. This research revealed that 34 per cent lapsed due to unemployment, 23 per cent due to career breaks to raise a child and 20 per cent because people were offered a good occupational scheme – in other words 77 per cent of lapses were due to perfectly acceptable reasons, not just people jibbing out for no reason.

Let's turn for a moment to the pages of *Money Management*, effectively the industry magazine for those in the financial services industry. The November 1997 edition had some interesting intelligence and, in this instance, *MM* did a pretty good hatchet job of its own on our behalf.

Brace yourselves for the riveting story behind the paid-up value and the transfer value. If you decide to stop paying into your PPP, you can do one of two things: leave the money where it is or transfer it out. If you transfer it elsewhere you get (no great surprises here) the transfer value. If you leave it where it is, the company will credit you with a paid-up value that will then grow until the end of the term and you can take whatever benefits might be coming your way. So far, so good, but you won't be surprised to hear that some of the transfer values were truly appalling. Consider the case of a 30-year PPP with J. Rothschild Assurance, in which contributions of £200 per month were stopped after two years. Now, um, 24 × 200 equals, um, 4800, right? No, that can't be right, let's check it again, 24 × 200 equals . . .

(Sounds of head-scratching, whistling, pencil scribbling through long multi-plication sums)

. . . um, yes, 4800.

Now, in this case, the transfer value of the fund after two years is actually only £1473 – in other words 69 per cent *lower* than the contributions paid in. Just 69 per cent depreciation in two years: now, that's investment!

Fair enough, you might say (we wouldn't), they have to penalize people who decide to leave early, but take a look at their paid-up value: that's a whopping £4788. This is just about what you've paid in contributions and a definite incentive to leave the money where it is, rather than transfer it elsewhere. Not bad, you might think (we wouldn't): zero growth after two years. Leave it there and it'll grow nicely, you might think. Wrong! If we then move on to the maturity value of this £4788 at 30 years, we see that it is only £13,826, or equivalent to a return of around 4 per cent per year. The industry standard is to reckon on a 9 per cent per year predicted rate of return (far below, by the way, what you could hope for from an index tracker), giving around a 5 per cent penalty every year on this plan to account for ongoing charges.

Now, picture for a moment if you had had the misfortune to be sweet-talked into a Rothschild plan that you found you had to leave for one reason or another. The consequences are nothing short of catastrophic. For you, anyway. However, someone, somewhere is getting the benefit of all that compound interest on 4800 – 1473, or £3317 over 30 years. Nice work if you can get it, we say.

We'd like to give this as an isolated example, but it isn't. In fact, let's take a look at Lincoln itself, which commissioned the study into PPP lapses: both the 2-year transfer and paid-up values in their 30-year policies were a meagre £1346, less even than J Rothschild. Now reckon that it's not just the odd person here or there who is getting hammered by these poor transfer values – according to the July 1998 edition of *Money Management*, as many as 40% of pension planholders end up cancelling their contracts within five years, often as a result of what they describe as 'over zealous' selling by financial advisers.

When talking about charges, it can also be helpful to look at the effect of charges by the amount of pence in each contributed pound they eat up. This table has been taken from an article in *Money Management* in 1992, entitled 'Expenses and the Impact of Disclosure' and we think it speaks for itself:

Effect of charges on each pound paid into personal pension plans

	10 yrs	25 yrs
Lowest	10p	13p
Median	17p	20p
Highest	29p	31p

Numbers like these leave us with difficulty in believing that the professionals have our best interests at heart and little has changed since 1992. In a July 1998 survey of the cost of charges, *Money Management* still found a huge impact of charges, with our old friend, Lincoln, topping the bill at a cost of a whisker under £20,000 on a 25 year policy with contributions of £200 per month. In other words, the charges amounted to almost exactly one third of the total contributions! The last sentence of the November 1997 *MM* article sums it all up nicely:

No wonder the public places such little trust in the industry.

Couldn't have put it better ourselves.

We're not finished, unfortunately, because even when investors arrive at a stage where their contributions are actually being invested in something which earns money, they will have very little say over just what those investments are. It will almost certainly be into one of the underperforming unit trusts we have already heard about and the best they can hope for is to switch money between the unit trusts on offer by the pension plan provider. It is possible to get PPPs these days in which the investment fund is an index-tracking unit trust and we'll take a look at these a little later on. Alternatively, there are beasts called SIPPs – Self-Invested Personal Pensions – in which the person themselves makes the investment decisions, although is often still subject to quite significant charges. However, there is one very good reason why a PPP of any kind may not be such a good idea and it has to do with the way in which you finally draw an income from your investment fund when you retire. More on this in the 'Annuities' section, coming up in a short while.

Take cover! More acronyms on the way

Okay, it may be starting to look as if things are getting out of hand. Have the Fools gone mad, have they become . . . boring? Acronyms and jargon are flying hither and thither in this chapter, more so than anywhere else in the book. Perhaps you've been hanging on by the skin of your teeth so far. Perhaps you've just about got the Big Picture in your grasp, but if any more comes your way, the unstable edifice of Foolish knowledge you've managed to construct is going to come crashing down round your ears. If your over-loaded cerebrum is starting to shout 'Mercy!', then our Foolish advice is to act with compassion towards the grey cells and white cells which make your life so much richer than a simple choice between eating and sleeping. Take a break, have a cup of tea, put this book down, perhaps even resolve not to pick it up again until tomorrow.

This chapter is important and really not that difficult to grasp, given a little time and a little perseverance. Without an understanding of what the multi-billion pound financial services industry is trying to sell you, and why, it is going to be difficult to make rational, Foolish decisions and to place some of the other stuff we're putting over in context.

Back in the introduction, we quoted Winnie the Pooh on knowledge. Here's another thought from Francis Bacon, back, way back, in 1597: 'For also knowledge itself is power.' In the sixteenth century there wasn't a great deal of knowledge on general release and today, when it comes to finance at least, the situation hasn't changed much at all, with what knowledge there is around being far from evenly distributed. If you want to liberate yourself through the medium of knowledge, then redress this balance by *not* skipping over the rest of the chapter.

AVC and FSAVC schemes

You're back. Well done. We won't disappoint you.

If you have an occupational pension, which you don't think will provide enough when you retire and you want to top it up, then there are masses, no, *hordes* of besuited advisers out there, every one aching to sell you one of these beauties. 'AVC' stands for 'Additional Voluntary Contributions' and 'FSAVC' stands for 'Free-Standing Additional Voluntary Contributions'. The difference between the two is that every occupational scheme has a 'tied' AVC scheme option available for members. If a member chooses not to join the tied scheme, they can buy an AVC scheme from any one of the providers out in the marketplace – a Free Standing AVC. To all intents and purposes, they are the same species of animal, although the charges on FSAVCs are generally higher. For simplicity, we will just refer to AVCs from now on. But before we forge ahead, take a look at this quote from an article in the

Financial Times of April 25th 1998, in an article about AVCs (and which slams the selling of FSAVCs):

> *Bacon & Woodrow, one of the biggest pension analysts, warned recently that the stand-alone alternative to company-sponsored AVCs – free-standing AVCs (FSAVCs) – is being sold inappropriately.*
>
> *Indeed, B&W said this week that about a quarter of pension schemes contained members who had paid commission to a salesman, only to end up with an FSAVC identical to the in-house AVC – except for higher charges to cover the commission.*

AVCs are like Personal Pension Plans, but if you already have an occupational pension scheme, you're not allowed to have a PPP. AVCs are the next 'best' thing. They attract the same tax relief, they have similar, punitive charging structures, the kinds of underperforming investments that your fund will be channelled into are similar and they are sold by the same people. There are, however, two important differences. First, they do not pay out 25 per cent of your accumulated investment fund as a tax-free lump sum when you retire, which PPPs do. Secondly, they do not allow you to defer the purchase of an annuity until your seventy-fifth birthday, which PPPs do.

While it's obviously possible to see a disadvantage in the first of these differences (no holiday house in the South of France, or even a beach hut in Bournemouth) it is less easy to see one in the second. 'You can't defer purchase of an annuity until your seventy-fifth birthday with an AVC.' R-i-i-ght. Uh-huh. Hmm.

We would ask you to press the 'Pause' button on the second difference at this point and pass on to the next section, when all will shortly become clear.

Annuities

The government – and you won't be surprised to hear this – doesn't trust you a great deal. It doesn't trust you not to blow the entire amount of your retirement fund on General Montgomery at 50–1 in the 3.30 at Kempton Park. It doesn't trust you not to blow the whole caboodle on a two-week orgy of high-living in a pink Rolls-Royce with personalized number plate 'FOOL 1'. It doesn't trust you not to blow the lot on a dead-cert investment in an emerald mine in the Venezuelan interior or on Russian Ministry of Finance junk bonds. You see, if they did trust you not to do any of these things and you let them down, then they would end up having to feed and house you and that's why they make you buy an annuity with the money you have accrued in your PPP or AVC fund. It's a very sensible decision on their part, they see it as just return for their generosity in giving you tax relief on your pension contributions for all these years and it lets them avoid what could potentially be a whole lot of bother. For you, though, it may not be so good. Let's see why.

An annuity is the way in which you convert the money you have built up in your PPP or AVC fund into a regular income to see you through your retirement. It works broadly like this:

- You retire.
- You take the dosh in your PPP or AVC fund and use it to purchase an annuity, either from the company with which you already have your policy, or another company (for the privilege of which you may be charged a penalty by your original company).
- The annuity pays you out a fixed income until you die.
- The precise amount depends on how long you have left to live. Women, who live longer than men, receive less than men of the same age. Older people receive more than younger people. (And students of the macabre will note that with some companies, fat smokers can negotiate larger payments than slim non-smokers. We should have put a voucher for a large doner kebab and a packet of twenty Benson & Hedges at the back of the book. Enjoy them while you can!)
- Unless you have agreed to accept a substantially reduced initial annuity income, the amount you will receive will *not* increase with inflation.
- Unless you have agreed to accept a substantially reduced initial annuity income, your spouse may get nothing when you die.

Now, you and your spouse both die. *BIFF!*

- When you and your spouse are both dead, the annuity company pockets the money. Your relatives or favourite charity get nothing.

One of the problems with annuities is that these days we are living too long for them and the rate of inflation is just that little bit too high to make them last. People reading this book may be looking at 20, 30 or even more years of retirement. That may be a problem if you are going to be relying on an income derived from an annuity. Let's do a thought experiment to look at why annuities are not powerful investments:

Hermione is 50 years old and wins the lottery: £1,000,000 in cool, gleaming pound coins. She can't be bothered with thinking about all this tiresome business of investment, she has no relatives and all she wants is a steady income with which to enjoy herself, so she uses it all to purchase an annuity. At the rates prevailing in early 1998, this will buy her an annuity income of £70,000 per year. Whoopee! But remember, this will not increase with inflation. Assuming a long-term inflation rate of 3.5 per cent, then Hermione will enter her seventy-fifth year with an inflation-adjusted income of £28,725. Not bad still, but she's starting to have to think about whether she can really afford two cruises a year. She tightens her belt and this warhorse makes it to her eighty-fifth year. Now, she has an income equivalent of just £20,100 (by now her purchasing power has shrunk by over three times). If she has the misfortune to survive until the grand old age of 95, then her income will be the equivalent of £14,000, or less than one-sixth of her initial purchasing power. She can keep herself fed and warm in the winter, but a cruise? Forget it! And to think she was once a millionairess . . .

Suppose, now, that she decides she is not going to invest in an annuity. She is still cautious, however, and invests half of her £1,000,000 into bonds, returning, for the sake of argument, around 8 per cent per year and invests the other half into an index tracker. Her £500,000 in bonds gives her £40,000 a year. After five years in an index tracker, earning the 13.87 per cent which the Gartmore Index tracker has returned in recent years, her other 500K has doubled back up to a cool £1,000,000. Can you see what she's going to do now? She takes half of her £1,000,000 and buys more bonds with it, leaving the other £500,000 where it is. Now, at the age of 55, she has an income of £80,000 and still has £500,000 in the index tracker where it will hopefully double over the next five years. She goes on like this:

Age	Bonds	Income/year	Index tracker
50	£500,000	£40,000	£500,000
55	£1,000,000	£80,000	£500,000
60	£1,500,000	£120,000	£500,000
65	£2,000,000	£160,000	£500,000
70	£2,500,000	£200,000	£500,000
75	£3,000,000	£240,000	£500,000
80	£3,500,000	£280,000	£500,000
85	£4,000,000	£320,000	£500,000
90	£4,500,000	£360,000	£500,000
95	£5,000,000	£400,000	£500,000
95 (Inflation-adjusted)	£1,006,000	£80,500	£101,000

Compare this with the annuity at 95:

95 (Inflation-adjusted)	N/A	£14,000	N/A

Impressive, no? If you look at the numbers which take into account inflation, it turns out that the 'real' amount of capital she has at age 95 is just over £1,100,000 and that her 'real' income is just over £80,000, easily enough for a yearly world cruise, outside stateroom and paid companion to push her round the deck in a bathchair. She has preserved, and even increased, both her capital and her income in real terms. Compare this with the £14,000 in real terms she would be earning from the annuity and without the opportunity to leave any of the capital to the local Hedgehog Hospital.

Now, we make a few assumptions here and none of these calculations take into account tax. (Neither, though, do they take into account that you might save some of your £80,000 in real terms income every year.) They also assume a steady rate of growth from the index tracker, which will not occur. However, long-term this kind of return is likely and we will remember from the Bible of the Long-distance Investor (Chapter 4) that over ten-year periods or more, equities are *less* risky than gilts, and it is gilts on which annuity returns are based. Finally, ask yourself why, if you wouldn't put your stash of £1,000,000 into an annuity, you would put your stash of £100,000, or £10,000 into one?

Back to the two important differences between PPPs and AVCs. Remember them? *AVCs don't pay out 25 per cent of your accumulated investment fund as a tax-free lump sum when you retire, which PPPs do and AVCs don't allow you to defer the purchase of an annuity until your seventy-fifth birthday,* which PPPs do. Do they make a little more sense now? With an AVC, having to invest *all* your money in an annuity *immediately* you retire means no chance to let any of it grow, to let the Flower of Compounding bloom. An annuity is like a snapshot in time and all that can happen now is that the image will brown and yellow with the passing years, to eventually wither away. By allowing you to choose not to buy an annuity when you retire, a PPP gives you at least a chance to grow your stash of capital, while being allowed to draw income from it, before you buy an annuity and freeze yourself in time. However, this will cost you money in charges, you'll need a fund of at least £100,000 to make it worthwhile and when you hit 75, the music does finally stop and you have to put 75 per cent of your fund to purchasing an annuity.

And we're still not quite finished. The amount of return you will get from the annuity you are compelled to buy when you retire varies directly in relation to the rates on gilts (government bonds). These move up and down a great deal, such that £10,000 in mid-1996 would have bought a man of 60 an income of £900 per year, while earlier in the decade it would have been worth £1300. An AVC does not give you the option to wait until annuity rates are looking a little healthier before buying. Annuity rates happen to be low when you retire? Tough luck, friend.

To sum up on annuities, here's *Investors' Chronicle* in 1996, waxing lyrical on the insurers who sell them:

> *Insurers take their cut by investing your capital. They expect investment gains to more than pay your income. Therein lies a cautionary tale. If insurers can make more from investing your money than the income they are prepared to offer, so can you. In other words, if you don't have to buy an annuity, they are often best avoided.*

Quite.

Reprise: 'You've got to have a pension, haven't you?'

We feel a little more able to answer this now and the answer is 'Nope'. While it's probably a good idea to contribute to your occupational scheme

– as long as you don't switch jobs too often – in our opinion PPPs and AVCs are over-rated. Their exorbitant charges, inflexibility and the compulsion they bring to purchase an annuity counterbalance the undoubted advantage of the tax relief they attract. Let us remember, in addition, that you will still pay tax on the income you receive from your annuity, while you will not do so on any income you receive from a PEP or an Individual Savings Account. Further, a tax credit on dividends was removed from PPPs and AVCs in 1997, while it still remains on PEPs and ISAs until 2004. PPPs and AVCs are tax-*deferred* investments which attract tax relief to start with, they are not tax-*free* investments. While any sheltering from tax is attractive, we hope we have shown that tax advantages alone are not sufficient reason to choose one investment over another. In our book, the charges alone are enough to send you scooting away from most personal private pensions and AVCs, let alone the compulsion to buy an annuity.

In fact, if your investments do too well, you might be penalized with extra tax. There is a cap on the amount of pension you can have. Here, again, is an extract from the *FT* article of April 25th, 1998 on AVCs:

> *If you pay too much [in contributions], or the value of your investments grows faster than expected the final pension may exceed the maximum and you will be stung with what can amount to a hefty extra tax charge.*

There is, though, one overriding reason why you might want to open a PPP or AVC plan and that is if otherwise you wouldn't be able to keep your grubby paws off the capital. Most other types of investment will allow you to raid your funds before you really need them, before you really should. With a pension plan, you have to be at least 50 before you can use the money, no ifs, ands or buts. Be honest with yourself and if you're not going to be able to manage this, then start looking around for some halfway decent pension provision: an index-tracker based PPP or AVC is probably going to be your best bet. Alternatively, just resolve to sit on your hands for the intervening time, as good a solution as any.

The Foolish Pension Option: An Index Tracker

You know you wouldn't be able to keep your hands off the money if there was any way you could get at it and actually, when all's said and done, you really *do* prefer the idea of having a pension. You like the feeling of security it gives you, you love the idea of the upfront tax relief and only getting 25% of your invested fund as a tax-free lump sum doesn't particularly bother you. The fact that the other 75% will have to go – sooner or later – into purchasing annuity is of little interest, because since young Timothy totalled the car last Saturday night you've decided not to leave anything to your kids anyway. Also, you're a happy sixty a day smoker and are not planning to live long enough after retirement for inflation to eat significantly into your annuity income.

Okay, Fag Ash 'Lil, here's what you do. It's quite simple.

Get yourself (i.e. buy it directly from the company over the telephone and using no intermediaries) a personal pension plan in which the underlying investment fund is an index tracker. That way you pay no commission to a financial adviser, the upfront charges are peanuts, the yearly charges minimal and you'll outperform the majority of pension investments, while also benefiting from the undoubted advantage which tax relief on pensions provides. Easy.

But what if you're in an occupational pension scheme and decide you want to transfer your retirement funds into an index tracker? Well, if you're in a final salary or defined benefit scheme, you simply can't. In that case you have no say over where or how your money is invested and it's pretty well irrelevant to you anyway, since no matter how well the investments perform, your pension is fixed as a percentage of your final salary. If you're in a money purchase or defined contribution scheme on the other hand, then an index tracker may be one of the places into which you can invest your money, in which case that's great. If it isn't one of the options, then we suggest you write to the scheme manager asking why not and pointing out that the majority of actively managed unit trusts underperform the index over the long-term and that as a contributor to this pension scheme you're in it for the long-term, blah, blah, blah and by the way have they heard of this splendid little website called The Motley Fool UK . . .? (You know it all by now – no point us repeating ourselves.)

Finally, when you do hit retirement with this kind of personal pension plan, you will want to consider shopping around for the best deal on annuities. (In other words, don't necessarily buy it from the company with whom you've had your pension fund up to now.) Also, you will want to think about leaving some of your money *in situ* in the fund to continue growing at a rate above inflation, as we discussed a few pages back, and especially you will want to think about this if annuity rates happen to be low at the time you retire.

All facetiousness aside for a millisecond and despite our stance on them as a whole, personal pensions can be made Foolish if approached in the way outlined here. The key, as ever in investment, is to avoid those two evil horsemen from the DARK SIDE: overcharging and underperformance.

Endowments: last refuge of the Wise

For years and years, if you didn't have an endowment policy, you didn't have an investment. Endowment policies were the mainstay of the investment market and were commonly sold in conjunction with mortgages. You paid off the interest on the mortgage and a small amount also went into an endowment policy. When the mortgage term was up, the endowment policy matured and paid off the loan on the house. Neat. Easy. So neat and easy, in fact, that by the end of the 80s, 80 per cent of UK mortgages were backed by an endowment policy.

Before we go any further, let's hear a few comments about the life assurance industry in general (the people who sell endowments) from a former Deputy Chairman of one of the companies implicated in the pensions mis-selling scandal we've already heard about:

> . . . *for the last twenty years the big life assurance companies in this country have systematically been ripping people off* . . .

Steady on! He continues:

> . . . *the high turnover in salesmen, the commission system and the practice of front-end loading all lend weight to the accusation that there has been a massive distortion . . . by the life assurance companies . . . of the British retail savings market* . . .

Phew! Whose side is this fellow on? These comments were quoted in a book entitled *The Last Days of the Credit Culture* by Jonathan Mantle.

So what exactly is an endowment? It's a life insurance policy, combined with a savings and investment mechanism. Sounds innocent enough, but like so many things in this deceptive ol' Wise world, it isn't. Look back at the previous comments: 'Front-end loading'. We've seen that before, in the section on PPPs and AVCs. Yes, the same thing happens with endowments. The salesman largely creams off the first couple of years' contributions, pockets them and leaves you fighting to keep your head above water. Fighting so hard, in fact, that it is *seven* years before you break the surface again. The surrender value (i.e. what you'd get if you cashed the policy in) can take this long to even approach the value of the contributions paid in. In fact, let's not do our own dirty work, let's quote the industry's own magazine, *Money Management*, again. In a review of endowment mortgages in July 1997 they said: 'In most cases, even after seven years, . . . endowment surrender values do not even return premiums paid. The average yield on seven year surrender values is –0.9 per cent.'

Pardon us, but haven't we been here before? It can and often does take this long for the transfer or paid-up values of PPPs and AVCs to break even. We're starting to see some common threads emerging. Low returns, massive charges, inflexibility: all these things characterize the investments which people out there want to sell you. You know, sometimes we get financial professionals coming to our site and telling us we're misleading the public, that we're giving those fellows a bad name. Well, it seems to us like they've given themselves more than enough rope to do it themselves.

People are slowly starting to realize what these scams are about and the numbers speak for themselves. From 80 per cent of mortgages at the end of the 80s, endowments now support around a third of all mortgages. Has this come about because of an attack of conscience on the part of the financial professionals? We think not.

You might think it was convenient that you could combine life insurance and investment like this into one package. It may be, but it's very costly when compared with the most basic type of life insurance – simple, no frills, pay-the-money-if-you-die-but-get-nothing-if-you-don't, 'term' life insurance. Why not take it from the horse's mouth, the *Financial Times* of January 25th, 1992: 'Endowments are an expensive way to buy life cover.'

For years, many house-buyers have thought that their endowments *guaranteed* that they would be able to pay off the loans on their houses at the end of the term. Partly, this is due to ignorance – fostered of course by the professionals – but partly it has been due to unscrupulousness on the part of some of those professionals. Doesn't happen now, of course. No, definitely not! The fact is though, that as investments go, they really aren't much good. The Faculty and Institute of Actuaries has gone so far as to say that payments from endowments maturing in the future could be half those on policies taken out 25 years ago.

Endowment policies are often sold on the basis of impressive-sounding 'terminal' bonuses. In fact, one reason why the companies are able to offer these impressive-sounding bonuses may be because relatively few people ever get as far as the end of their policies and thus never collect them. So ashamed are the insurance companies of their surrender statistics, that 'very few companies supplied figures, making it difficult to draw conclusions' in a November 1997 study by *Money Management* into the subject, while in July 1998 the Financial Times Quarterly Review of Personal Finance reported that around 70% of policies failed to reach maturity. It is no surprise, then, that no less a body than the Office of Fair Trading has argued that the high sales commissions and early termination penalties result in endowments being a costly and inflexible product.

Endowments: No Surrender!

We could go on and on about endowment policies, but there are more fruitful ways to use up the ration of words our publisher has kindly allowed us in writing this book. The conclusion, if you are thinking of taking out an endowment policy is: 'At all costs, don't!' If you already have one, then bad luck. If you want to get rid of it then you may have some fairly complex mathematics ahead of you to calculate the pros and cons of whether it is now worth cashing it in or not. If you've had it for a significant length of time, you may well find that it is better to simply hang on to it. If you *did* decide you wanted out, because you thought you could do better elsewhere – or, of course, if you found you could no longer pay the monthly contributions – it would almost certainly pay you to sell rather than surrender your policy. Because we live in a world of markets and market makers, there are people out there who will *buy* your second-hand endowment policy off you and will *generally* give you a much better price than if you surrendered it. It's reckoned that about 60,000 people lose about £90 million a year by surrendering their endowments rather than selling them. You can get a free brochure on buying and selling second hand endowment policies from the Association of Policy Market Makers on 0171 739 3949 and if you want to be really Foolish – and we mean *really* Foolish – about selling your endowment policy read on.

First, get hold of the brochure detailed above and obtain quotes on your policy from a selection of market makers. Then contact H E Foster & Cranfield (0171 608 1941), an auctioneer which holds a second hand endowment policies auction on a weekly basis (and, incredibly enough, has done since 1843). Put your policy in for auction with them at a reserve price equal to the highest quote received from various market makers you contacted plus the auctioneer's fee. If it doesn't make the reserve price, you simply go back and sell it to the market maker who offered you that price in the first place. Either way, you can't lose, as there is no charge if the policy is not sold by the auctioneers. And there's more: even if no market maker wants to buy your policy, then you may still be able to sell it through the auctioneers for more than the surrender value.

One other thing. If you do sell your endowment policy it might be worth keeping a weather eye open for meteorites, hit-men and cunningly concealed open manholes on your regular walk to work. In fact, why not go the whole hog and employ a food taster? You see, even if you sell it on, the life assurance cover an endowment policy provides remains based on *your* life. If you die before the end of term, the new owner of the policy gets the money. Respectfully, therefore, we suggest you keep a close eye on your brake cables from here on in.

Let's summarize: endowments are inflexible, high expense, under-performing investments which line the pockets of the Wise at the expense of the public. If you want life insurance, buy just that – 'term' life insurance, no more no less, and put your money for investment into real investments, Foolish investments. If you want out it will almost certainly pay you to sell rather than surrender. Here, to end our consideration of endowments is an editorial quote from the *Daily Telegraph* of August 31st, 1991, at the height of the endowments boom:

> *It cannot be said too often that the advantages to the householder of an endowment mortgage are as nothing compared to the gain to the policy salesman, that life assurance has nothing to do with house purchase, and that savings-related life assurance is a waste of money.*

Conclusion

This hasn't been the lightest chapter in the book and it's possible you may have snored through half of it. In any case, the essential elements are these:

- Most occupational pension schemes are *probably* worth having, as long as you're not going to be switching jobs too often.
- PPPs and AVCs are generally overcharging, underperforming investments, but the most Foolish of this bunch are those in which the underlying investment is in a low-cost index tracker.
- Annuities – which you are forced to purchase by AVCs and PPPs – are poor long-term investments, which do not allow you to pass your hard-won savings on to the next generation.
- Endowments benefit primarily the person who sells you the policy.
- If you do want out of an endowment – and the pros and cons are not always clear – it will almost certainly pay you to sell it rather than surrender it.
- We believe that investments in PEPs and ISAs are in general a better way to save for your retirement than AVCs, PPPs and endowments.

We suggest you refer back to this chapter the next time an Independent Financial Adviser (salesperson) or a tied agent comes a-selling. That way you'll have a large number of awkward questions to ask them. If they can answer all of them to your satisfaction, then they *deserve* the huge commission you'll be paying them when you buy their product. We don't think there will be many who satisfy you, though, and our hope is that this chapter, this book and the ripples of our online world will result in a widespread and long-lasting commissions famine for unscrupulous financial advisers.

Rounding Up

23

Welcome to the End of the Beginning!

Now this is not the end. It is not even the beginning of
the end. But it is, perhaps, the end of the beginning.
Winston Churchill, Mansion House speech following
the first major German defeat of the war at El Alamein, 1942

Congratulations. If this is the first time you have dipped your toe in the murky waters of investment, you have now reached the end of the very beginning of your life as a Foolish, savvy, active investor. From now on, you can start to put your critical skills to good use in building for your financial future. To celebrate this new phase, we're going to take the opportunity to have one last shot at the world of Wisdom, and believe us, it's a real cracker. A week or so after the Motley Fool UK was launched in September, 1997, David B. received a phone call from a senior journalist, one of the worthies of financial writing at one of the UK's most respected newspapers. The encounter was so remarkable that he wrote about it later that day in the Motley Fool UK's daily missive, the *Daily Fool*. Here's an extract:

> *Over the last couple of days, one or two (250, actually) press releases have gone out to the Great and the Good of the British financial journalism world. Most have been filed straight in the paper shredder, but just a few, a very few have excited some interest.*
>
> *This afternoon, I found myself talking on the telephone to a senior City journalist on one of the national newspapers. It was an education in Wisdom and went something like this.*
>
> ME *(SQUEAKILY)*. Erm, hello, it's David Berger of the Motley Fool UK here.
>
> HE *(FOR HE IT WAS)*. Ah yes. I'm most concerned about this little scheme of yours.
>
> ME. Oh yes.
>
> HE. Yes, all this guff about index-trackers. I've written a lot about them myself and I don't know where you get this figure of 90 per cent underperforming the market. I am very concerned [that word again] about this. It's not true, you know.
>
> ME. Oh. It does come from a reputable source. In fact, I've read a lot about index-trackers in your newspaper, I'm sure. Although I think this is from a different source.
>
> HE *(BREAST PUFFING AUDIBLY OVER THE PHONE)*. Yes, what you've read in my paper was almost certainly written by me. I write a lot

about them and I'm very concerned [again] about this 90 per cent figure.

(D.B. flicks through past copies of the *Investor's Chronicle*.)

ME. Here we are, March 22nd, 1996, page 16. Of 203 UK unit trusts in existence for ten years, only fifteen outperformed the market over that period and that is even giving them an unfair advantage by disregarding initial charges. The source of the data is Micropal.

HE (*FOLLOWING A SHORT SILENCE*). Good God!

(I kid you not, he really said 'Good God!' I have filed this as one of my lifetime Golden Moments.)

HE (*SLIGHTLY OFF BALANCE, BUT RECOVERING QUICKLY*). Yes, well, I can see what they've done. But I'm very concerned about these message boards of yours. Won't people be able to cause a buying panic by posting unfounded rumours on your message boards? What's to stop that happening?

ME. Nothing, but we don't advocate buying on the basis of a single, hysterical tip. We stress buying on the basis of a sound analysis of a company's fundamentals. And anyway, anyone who believes an outrageous story on the basis of no obvious evidence merely because they want to, deserves everything they get. That's just stupid!

HE. Still, I am very concerned about this.

ME. Well, why don't you come and visit the site, or even better the American site where they have over 2000 message boards . . . ?

HE (*INTERJECTING, A TRIFLE IRRITADO NOW*). Oh, don't talk to me about computers. I don't know anything about computers!

(I kid you not, again. He said this. In 1997. In London. As a senior financial journalist.)

ME. More Foolish stuff.

HE. More Wise stuff.

ME. More Foolish stuff.

HE. etc., etc.

And so it went on for a few more desultory minutes. Later, he talked to a fellow Fool in the USA and came out with this:

HE. But your information is quite simple, isn't it? It's not very sophisticated.

THE FELLOW FOOL. Exactly.

It's hard to imagine a more succinct illustration than this snapshot for why there is a need for a sane, understandable alternative to the stuffy blather you so often find being purveyed as financial information these days. Of course, we hope that this book and the daily to-ings and fro-ings at our online areas go some way to meeting this need, but as of now it's in your hands, those of the reader, to judge.

Our aspiration is that even if you don't agree with everything written here and even if some of it seems incomprehensible – for which we blame no-one but ourselves – you will at least put the book down with the belief that it is *possible* for you to understand enough about investment to manage your own financial affairs. We don't expect everyone to rush off and suddenly become self-sufficient, amateur, stock market investors. The process of learning and understanding simply doesn't work like that. We do hope, though, that with a small chink of light showing at the end of a long black tunnel you may now be starting to question any and everything which is being sold to you in the financial world and scheming how *you* can do it better.

Hurry Up and Slow Down

Inspiration and panic make dangerous bedfellows and it's quite possible that by turns both of these will have accompanied the reader on your journey through these pages. Talk of endowments and other Wise investment plans may have caused you to fear that your best years are behind you, squandered on wastrel investments with huge charges and underperformance by way of return. Combine this with the breathtaking possibilities open to you in the stock market – from index trackers to the Obviously Great Investments to Beating the Footsie – and you may be inspired to rush out and transform all your investments into Foolish ones. Now. Right now.

But stop!

Go back.

Don't do it.

Precipitate, unthinking action is not the way to set yourself up for a lifetime of secure, profitable investment. Similarly, precipitate, unthinking *inaction* is not the right way either. Interestingly, we asked a selection of visiting Fools at our Fool UK focus group meeting / Pizza Express field-study trip, one evening in May 1998, what the hardest thing had been about starting in investment. Simultaneously, two answers were shot back. The first was: 'The hardest thing was buying my first share.' The second was: 'The hardest thing was *not* buying my first share.' Whichever of these categories you fall into, you need to think incrementally.

The only way you will be able to set up the habits for a lifetime of sensible investment is by approaching the whole subject cautiously, yet steadily. Don't rush out and cancel your endowment policy, AVC or personal pension plan. It is entirely possible that you will have passed the point where you were paying 80 per cent or more of your contributions in charges and it may pay you to hold onto it. You may decide not to increase the amount you put into it and instead divert those extra savings elsewhere, but that's another story entirely.

We suggest that the first thing you do is put down this book and have a good old think about your investment goals, the amount you can realistically save into an investment plan and where your interests lie. Where they really lie. It is easy to be inspired (which is a good thing) but inspiration alone is not going to carry you through a lifetime of investing. It requires persistence, too. Ask yourself if you're going to want to be the type of person who keeps an eye on their shares every few weeks and is prepared to put in a fair amount of graft to choose them in the first place. No? You're not? Then you don't want to be investing in a small-cap. company like Pizza Express, or an up-and-coming games retailer like Games Workshop. Are you going to be happy to have a peek at your shares every six months or a year? If so, then you might want to look at ferreting out some Obviously Great Investments, or knuckling under to a Beating the Footsie variant. If you think you'll just be able to muster enough interest to read this book and then forget about investment for the next 20 or so years, then an index tracker may be for you. Take a good hard look, too, at the investments you already have. Learn about them, about how well they've done for you and how much they might have cost you. If you decide to ditch one or any of them, make sure you do so after having weighed up the pros and cons carefully. From now on, you have no-one to blame but yourself. Similarly, when things go well, as they most assuredly will, if you approach investment sensibly and realistically, then no-one else will be standing in line to take the credit which will rightly fall to you.

Oh yes, debt. Almost forgot about that. That comes before any of the above. Pay down any non-mortgage debt as quickly as you can before you start investing and also aim to refinance any large chunks of credit card debt with a personal loan from your bank at a lower rate as quickly as you can. You knew that anyway.

When you've decided what strategy you might like to follow, then immediately do nothing. Nothing, that is, except track the progress of your strategy on paper, or in the financial planning software of your computer. After three months, six months, a year – yes, as long as that, or even longer – think about committing a small amount of your funds to your chosen strategy. Start with 5 per cent and work up as you feel comfortable. You're in it for the long haul and there's no sense in rushing into something you don't feel comfortable with and which you're going to bail out of at the first sign of market volatility. If you got yourself bitten badly in the stock market at the start, it'll be a long time, if ever, before you're back.

The Bottom Line

Several years ago, one of us (D.B.) spent a year working with a Frenchman: '*Mais*, Daveed, explain once more, what ees ze "Bottom Line"?' It does seem as if there is no equivalent expression in French (if you're a French scholar and you think there is, then you know where to e-mail us) and he never quite grasped the concept to his satisfaction. Of course, we know what it means and the expression we use in our daily lives ('Yeah, Snodbury United may have played well, but the bottom line is they lost twelve-nil') probably comes from company accounting, where the bottom line means after-tax profits. This is the money which remains to be divvied up between the company and its shareholders after all the froth and fury of the annual accounts has been played out. Often, it's the whole reason that investors have bought into the company and some would say the whole reason a public company exists. (We aren't going to get into that debate here, but if you're interested in a view from the other side of the 'Companies exist to make a profit / companies have a responsibility to society and their employees' fence, then get hold of a copy of *Downsize This!* by Michael Moore. It makes interesting, if rather vociferous reading, and that it's also published by Boxtree is irrelevant, apart from the fact that it never hurts to grease up to your publisher.)

'What's the bottom line?' is a question we should always ask, whatever endeavour we're about to embark upon. Of course, we hope that the process of reading this Foolish volume has encouraged you, nay, converted you, into a fanatical devotee of the bottom line when it comes to your investments and your financial future, but since you've now come to the end of it, it seems reasonable to ask what's the bottom line of the book itself and the Motley Fool as a whole? What have we been trying to say here? What are the crucial points we hope you'll take away from this book and which, in our opinion anyway, make it worth the purchase price? Okay, we think it's all pretty well encapsulated like this:

- Investment is not inherently difficult to understand.
- The average person is not as stupid as they are made out to be.
- Many types of investment on sale today overcharge and underperform.
- The people selling you those investments have interests diametrically opposed to your own.
- Investors should understand and have faith in the supremacy of shares as the long-term route to growing wealth.
- An understanding of the awesome power of compound interest is a prerequisite for any successful investor.
- The application of simple, commonsense rules and a small amount of knowledge can produce returns far exceeding those of the professionals.
- The Internet facilitates the spread of knowledge and information in a revolutionary and unprecedented fashion.
- Shareholders are uniquely placed to play an active role in modifying corporate behaviour for the greater good of society and of the world as a whole.
- Taking responsibility for your own investments and financial future need not be onerous and is one of the most lucrative, enjoyable and fulfilling activities open to you.
- The emphasis is on enjoyable.

That's it. That's our bottom line. The end of the beginning. We hope it pleaseth you.

Be Foolish, one and all!

DAVID BERGER
DAVID GARDNER
TOM GARDNER

We'd love to hear what you thought of this book, where we could have made it clearer, bits we should have put in, bits we should have left out and anything else you think of. Tell us what we ought to do to make personal investment in Britain easier to understand. In fact, tell us how to improve our business – we're always on the look-out for bright ideas and bright people. One thing, though: if you ask us to give you directive, individual advice about what to do with your own money, we'll neatly sidestep the question. Britain already has more than enough financial advisers. So, here's how to reach us:

E-mail   FoolUKbook@fool.com
Snailmail The Motley Fool UK
          3 Stevenstone Court
          Stevenstone
          Torrington
          Devon
          EX38 7HY

Acknowledgements

In most of mankind, gratitude is merely a secret hope for greater favours.
Duc de la Rochefoucauld, *Maximes*

David B.

Thanks first and foremost are due to David and Tom Gardner, valued co-authors of this volume and without whom not only would there be no Motley Fool UK, but no Foolishness whatsoever. I now understand the moral fibre it takes to receive an e-mail from a total stranger, suggesting that you transplant your cherished baby to the other side of the world – oh, and by the way, he'll look after it for you – and then to actually go ahead and do it. Near the start of this writing project, Tom offered some gentle and tactful advice, which (paraphrased) ran something like this: 'Dave, do you think it might be more positive *not* to try and beat the reader into a senseless pulp with a series of facts and figures and the supposed force of your rational arguments?' If I've failed to follow this guidance in many places, the fault is my own.

Specific Fools who have been invaluable in this project include Bruce Jackson, senior analyst at the UK Fool, for allowing his Rentokil toils to be published (as Appendix 1) and for shouldering so much of the daily burden of running our online world while I got on with writing. He also traipsed up to the newspaper library in North London where he spent several exciting mornings collating historical share prices to backtest Beating the Footsie. It is true to say that without Bruce there would be no UK Fool. Gabrielle Loperfido, our Motley Fool editor, has offered the most kindly encouragement and hand-holding to this novice writer. Also Erik Rydholm, our link man in the US, has been, well, simply a dear throughout. Tom Christiansen, Motley Fool numbers impresario, came up with the Beating the Footsie numbers, having been asked to do so a bare week before he left on holiday. Other Fools a-plenty know who they are.

Those Motley Fool readers who allowed their pieces to be reproduced here – Mark Kelly, Neil Fletcher, David Carter and Adrian Gill – have shown supreme candour in allowing their experiences to be published for the benefit of others. Yvonne Ravenhall, too, deserves special thanks for allowing her witty and original thoughts on several subjects to be published. Thanks also to the Foolish stockbroker from 'The Dark Side' who provided invaluable feedback on the stockbroking chapters. (He has to remain anonymous or else he may be court-martialled and shot.)

Many, many Motley Fool readers have also provided inspiration for much of the content of this book. I hope many people who have corresponded with me on the online message boards – and many whose contributions I have simply read and not responded to directly – will recognize the ripples of their sentiments in some part of this volume.

When it comes to the 'Vision Thing', no-one has more of it than our New York agent, Suzanne Gluck, her London counterpart, Gill Coleridge, or Adrian Sington of Boxtree, with whom the buck stopped when he dug his hand into his pocket and passed over an embarrassingly thick wad of used fivers as an advance. Now that, I humbly propose, took courage. Thank you for your faith, you three.

Jo Patterson designed a terrific book cover, Charlie Carman has been a splendid editor and all the staff at Boxtree have been helpful and smiling throughout.

My wife, Carol, has adapted to the role of Fool UK widow with a remarkable lack of protest. Without the support she provides in so many ways, I would long since have been carried away by a nasty deficiency disease. I owe her too much in too many ways to begin to list them here. My parents, Maurice and Gerry – there is truly no-one like them in the entire world. Individuals, both of you and the inspiration for any quirkiness I possess, I hope this work pleases you. My brother, Jon – okay, so this is sounding like an Oscar acceptance speech. Got a problem with that?! – I hope you can recognize some of the humour within these pages. Dora and the late Esther, two aunts of mine, both born in the early years of the century and both well ahead of their time, I hope it makes you chuckle too.

Two people who are long dead deserve a warm mention. I never met my maternal grandfather, Dr Heinz 'Hunnickl' Schmeidler, society doctor in 20s Berlin, thriller writer, sexologist, and later scrap metal merchant in Egypt. Nor did I meet Sarah Berger, my paternal grandmother, by all accounts a woman of great humility and kindness. She reportedly showed tremendous resource and courage when forced into earning a livelihood at an advanced age in Britain, her second country of refuge. I know I owe them both a huge amount and I will never be able to thank them.

The late Dr Laurie Payne who used to teach personal finance courses in the South of England was the person who first inspired me to get educated about investment. In retrospect, his courses were Foolish from start to finish.

Peter Noble kindly proof-read the manuscript in the week in which he was meant to be writing up his PhD. He told me of Samuel Johnson's aphorism that the most crucial step in writing a book is to take out the bit you like the most and throw it away. It was hard, Peter, but I finally did it!

Max Saenger, biathlon skier, man of letters and bum first introduced me to the Motley Fool way back in '95. Before that, long before that, he'd also introduced me to the joys of powder skiing, kissing girls in cable cars and riding a skateboard pulled behind a moped. And that's *all* I'm saying.

The staff of Brannam Medical Centre in North Devon have been supportive of my bizarre double life far above and beyond the call of duty. Dr John Marston (he'll snort at this) is a beacon of humour and humanity in a downtrodden world, and out of Dr Bob Bunney's psychedelic, Electric Kool-Aid Acid Trip mind spring some of the most wonderful ideas. (*He'll* snort at that.)

I'd also like to thank the chaps at Heatstore for making such a splendid Power Shower. If anything I have written in these pages is funny or true, it was conceived under a steaming jet of hot water and with Carol banging on the bathroom door to make sure I hadn't soaked to death.

I have surely missed out many people deserving of an individual mention and if you're one of them, I can only hope I've already thanked you in person.

Where it all goes from here, I simply don't know, but so much fun can't be scheduled to end any time soon.

Permission Acknowledgements

Permission to use existing material:
We thank PanMacmillan for permission to quote from the *Hitchiker's Guide to the Galaxy*. We also thank Michael Hughes, formerly of Barclays, currently of Baring Asset Management, for permission to quote him personally. And we are very grateful to Brian Martin of Barclays for permission to use that marvellously sloped graph, along with incredibly compelling numbers from the Barclays Capital Gilt-Equity Study. And finally, thanks to Gartmore.

Foolish Glossary of Investment Terms

'When I use a word,' Humpty Dumpty said in a rather scornful tone,
'it means just what I choose it to mean – neither more nor less.'
Lewis Carroll, *Through the Looking Glass*

None of us likes complicated words and many of us are distinctly allergic to them. Often it seems as if they are bandied about simply to confuse. However, like most things in life, it's not quite that simple. Using specialist terminology can be a useful aid to communication and means that you don't have to go into long-winded explanations every time you want to explain a particular concept.

But don't take it from us, take it from Sir David Attenborough:

> *The first time I travelled in the forests of Borneo, I knew no Malay. My guide, a Dyak hunter who, with his blowpipe, regularly collected birds for the local museum, knew no English. So, to begin with, we had some difficulty – to put it mildly – in sorting out where we should go and what we should do. On our first day out together, we were paddling up a river in a canoe, when I heard a sonorous* tok-tok-tok-tok *call echoing through the trees. I cupped my hand round my ear and raised my eyebrows towards my guide. He then, for the very first time in our acquaintance, spoke words that I precisely understood. 'Caprimulgus macrurus', he said and I knew immediately that I was listening to the voice of the long-tailed nightjar. It was a nice demonstration that those cumbersome Latin names, sometimes mocked by the ignorant as pretentious obfuscations invented by scientists to prevent others understanding what they are talking about, do indeed constitute a truly international lingua franca.*
> (Foreword, *Oxford Dictionary of Natural History*)

To the accompaniment of a gentle 'Lap, lap, lapping' along the side of the canoe, the ever present 'Drip, drip, dripping' of huge droplets from the dark, forest canopy overhead, eerie shrieks from the impenetrable green tangle on the banks and the occasional 'Thwoop!' as your Dyak guide spits another wad of betel nut into the river, please feel free to consult our Foolish glossary of investment terms.

Additional Voluntary Contributions (AVCs) Many try and enhance their OCCUPATIONAL PENSION schemes by paying into one of these plans. Watch out for the hefty charges and dismal underperformance, though.

Like PERSONAL PENSION PLANS, they attract tax relief.

Advisory Stockbroker Stockbrokers which offer advice on which shares to buy and sell. We don't favour using them. See EXECUTION-ONLY STOCKBROKER and CHURNING.

Alternative Investment Market (AIM) AIM opened in 1995 for small, growing companies. It's less difficult to be listed here than on the LONDON STOCK EXCHANGE and shares are higher risk and more likely to be difficult to buy and sell. See LIQUIDITY.

Analyst A financial professional who analyses securities to determine a 'fair' or 'intrinsic' value for those securities. The term is generally applied to almost any professional investor who does research of some kind.

Annualize Taking an item measured over a certain period and restating it on an annual basis. For instance, if it costs £10 million every month to run a factory, the annualized cost is £10 million × 12, or £120 million, since there are 12 months in a year.

Annual Percentage Rate (APR) When you borrow money, this rate should always be quoted to you. It's the percentage rate which your loan will cost you each year, *including* all charges. Incredibly, APRs for credit cards can run at around 22 per cent.

Annual Report A yearly statement of a public company's operating and financial performance punctuated by pictures of families enjoying the firm's products and/or services.

Annuity The investment you purchase with your pension fund which will provide you with a regular income in your retirement. They are intrinsically poor investments.

Appreciation Increase in the price (or value) of a share or other asset. Appreciation is one component of total return.

Australian-type Mortgage As it sounds, a type of mortgage common in Oz. Interest due is calculated daily as opposed to yearly, which can make a significant difference to the cost for those on a REPAYMENT MORTGAGE. Also more flexible and allows periods of both under- and over-payment of the mortgage to suit the borrower's changing financial circumstances.

Balance Sheet An important financial report regularly issued by companies. It provides a look at a company's assets, debts and shareholder equity at one particular point in time.

Bank of England Set up in 1649, the 'Old Lady of Threadneedle Street' has responsibility for regulating the banking industry and since 1997 sets interest rates to help the government meet its inflation targets. The stock market hangs on the Bank's interest rate pronouncements.

Bankruptcy When a company owes more than it can pay, or when its debts exceed its assets, it's bankrupt.

Bear So you think that the market is headed south? You're bracing yourself for a crash or correction? You feel that share XYZ will soon be taking a tumble? Guess what – you're a bear! Bears are investors with pessimistic outlooks, as opposed to BULLS.

Beating the Dow The US grand-daddy of our very own BEATING THE FOOTSIE.

Beating the Footsie A mechanical investment strategy, based on buying large-cap. shares with a high DIVIDEND YIELD on a regular, rotational basis. Like BEATING THE DOW, it has been historically very successful.

Bid-Offer Spread The difference between the bid price (at which the holder can sell shares) and the offer price (at which the holder can buy shares). On occasion this can be quite large and depends on the equity's underlying price, LIQUIDITY, volatility and a number of other factors. Many UNIT TRUSTS also have a bid-offer spread and effectively this amounts to an EXIT CHARGE when the investor sells.

Big Bang The first big shake-up of the stock market in October 1986, when computers were introduced into the trading process for the first time. This was followed in 1996 by the introduction of CREST and then in 1997 by BIG BANG II.

Big Bang II October 20th 1997. The use of a computer-driven trading system to cut out the middlemen in share trading, who match buyers and sellers. Initially, this was just for FTSE 100 shares, but is likely to be extended to the FTSE 250. Bid-offer spreads, rather than being reduced as was thought, actually *increased*, especially during trading early in the day.

Blue Chip A share in a large, safe, prestigious company. Marks & Spencer is a blue chip, so is the Hong Kong and Shanghai Bank Corporation. Many of the shares making up the FTSE 100 are blue chips.

Bond A bond is essentially a loan. Bondholders lend money to governments or companies and are promised a certain rate of interest in return. Interest rates vary depending on the quality or reliability of the bond issuer. Government bonds, or gilts, for example, carry little risk and thus offer lower interest rates. Company bonds offer higher interest rates, with the riskiest companies' (or governments') bonds offering the highest of all and being called junk bonds.

Bonus issue Or, in the US, a STOCK SPLIT. Whenever a company believes that the price per share of its stock has risen to a point where investors may erroneously perceive it as 'expensive', they will split the stock, reducing the price but increasing the number of shares outstanding. For instance, if Huge Fruit plc. trades at £60 a share with 3 million shares outstanding and decides to split its stock two-for-one, this means that each share will now trade at £30 but there will be 6 million shares outstanding.

Broker One who sells financial products. Be it in insurance, pensions or shares, most brokers work under compensation structures that are at direct odds with the greatest good of their clients. (Also see INDEPENDENT FINANCIAL ADVISER, EXECUTION-ONLY STOCKBROKER, ADVISORY STOCKBROKER, STOCKBROKER.)

Bull Are your glasses rose-colored? Do you see nothing but blue skies ahead for the stock market or a particular security? Then you're a bull – an optimistic investor – as opposed to a BEAR.

Building Society A mutual organization, owned by the people saving money in it and borrowing money from it. Increasing numbers have converted to banks in recent years, paying windfall profits to the owners. See DEMUTUALIZATION.

CAC 40 French INDEX of – wait for it – the 40 major French companies.

Capital A business's cash or property, or an investor's pile of cash.

Capital Gain You bought a share and later sold it. If you made a profit, that's your capital gain. If you lost money, it's a capital loss. If you make enough of a capital gain outside your tax-sheltered accounts (PEPs, ISAs or TESSAs), you'll be liable for Capital Gains Tax (CGT). The amount of profit you can make without paying CGT is £6800 for the 1998/9 tax year.

Capped Rate Mortgage The mortgage interest rate cannot go above a certain level if mortgage rates rise, but can fall as rates drop. Ain't no free lunches, though, and if you want to extricate yourself from the mortgage during the capped rate period (say, three or five years), you'll have to pay a REDEMPTION PENALTY.

Chief Executive The Chief Executive is the highest executive officer in a company, rather like the captain of a ship. He or she is accountable to the company's Board of Directors and is frequently a member of that Board. The Chief Executive participates in setting strategy with the Board and other officers and is responsible for the tactics in meeting the company's goals.

Churning The unconscious or conscious over-trading by a STOCKBROKER in a customer's account. Since stockbrokers are generally compensated by the number of transactions made on a customer's behalf, there is a temptation to trade for the sake of it. It's illegal, but hard to prove.

The City London's financial district, which encompasses the square mile of the old City of London, bounded on the south by the Thames, on the west by the Law Courts, on the east by the Tower of London and in the north by Billingsgate Market.

Commission The way a STOCKBROKER or an INDEPENDENT FINANCIAL ADVISER is compensated. When he or she makes a transaction for a customer, the customer pays a commission.

Common Stock A US term for SHARES.

Compound Interest The investor's best friend. One hundred pounds invested in the stock market in 1918 would be worth £884,714 today. Now *that's* compound interest!

Correction A decline, usually short and steep, in the prevailing price of shares traded in the market or an individual share. Any time that commentators cannot find a reason for an individual stock or the entire market falling, they call it a correction. It sounds better than a 'Crash'.

CREST Introduced in 1996, this is a computerized system to settle up share purchases. No more bits of paper passing hands any more.

Cum-Dividend *Cum* means 'with' in Latin. If you buy shares cum-dividend, you are buying them at a time when you will be entitled to receive the next dividend. This is as opposed to EX-DIVIDEND. If restrictions on entitlement to dividends didn't exist, people would simply buy shares the day before the dividend was due, collect it and then sell them the day after.

Dax German index of major companies, broadly equivalent to the DOW-JONES INDUSTRIAL AVERAGE.

Day Trader A US term. Day traders are in and out of the market many times during the course of one trading session and may not even hold a position in any securities overnight. This approach tends to generate a lot of expenses in the form of commissions and denies the day trader the ability to participate in the long-term creation of wealth through compounding that is possible if you own the shares of a quality business.

Defined Benefit Scheme See FINAL SALARY SCHEME.

Defined Contribution Scheme See MONEY PURCHASE SCHEME.

Demutualization The process building societies go through when they convert to banks and thus go from being owned by their members (the borrowers and savers of the society) to being a PUBLIC LIMITED COMPANY owned by shareholders. There are pros and cons and the arguments rage on . . .

Derivatives If SHARES are assets, derivatives represent contracts to buy a particular SECURITY at a given point in the future for a particular price. OPTIONS and FUTURES are derivatives. They can be used to lessen investment risk, but often their main attraction is that they are highly geared (see GEARING) and can thus offer spectacular profits . . . and spectacular losses. We do not advocate their use.

Disclosure Since 1995, INDEPENDENT FINANCIAL ADVISERS and TIED AGENTS have been forced to disclose the level of commission they will earn from selling financial products to clients. It's a good thing, but the investor still isn't able to compare the levels of commission between investments. STOCKBROKERS also have to tell you of any financial interests they have in SECURITIES they are recommending.

Discount Broker The US term for EXECUTION-ONLY BROKER.

Discounted Rate Mortgage A mortgage with a guaranteed reduction in the variable mortgage rate (say, 2 per cent below the variable, whatever it may be). Generally lasts for an agreed period and if you change mortgages within that time, you will pay a REDEMPTION PENALTY.

Dividend A distribution from a company to a shareholder in the form of cash, shares, or other assets. The most common kind of dividend is a distribution of earnings. See DIVIDEND YIELD.

Dividend Yield The dividend over the current share price, expressed as a percentage. Different companies have different policies on the size of their dividend payouts. See BEATING THE FOOTSIE.

Dow-Jones Industrial Average The 30 companies chosen by editors of

Dow Jones & Company that are supposed to epitomize the very best American corporations and reflect the landscape of corporate America.

Dow Dividend Approach Another name for BEATING THE DOW.

Earnings The money a company puts in the bank after all of the costs of delivering a product or service have been accounted for. See EARNINGS PER SHARE.

Earnings Per Share (EPS) Net income divided by the current number of shares outstanding. This is one of the principal elements used in determining at what value the shares should trade.

Endowment A life assurance and savings and investment policy, classically sold to back an INTEREST-ONLY MORTGAGE. The key word here is 'sold'. No-one in their right minds would 'buy' one of these overcharging and underperforming abominations these days. See WITH-PROFITS INSURANCE and SURRENDER VALUE.

Equities A concept that comes from 'equitable claims'. Equities are essentially shares of stock. Because they represent a proportional share in the business, they are equitable claims on the business itself.

Ex-Dividend A share sold without the right to receive the dividend payment which is marked as due to those shareholders who are on the share register at a pre-announced date. These shares have 'xd' next to their price listings in the *Financial Times*.

Execution-only Stockbroker Stockbrokers who offer fewer of the services championed by ADVISORY STOCKBROKERS, but charge cheaper trans-action fees. Basically, you tell them to buy or sell a particular share and they get on and do it with no frills and no hassles. Often they hold your shares in a NOMINEE ACCOUNT. Execution-only brokers are ideal for do-it-yourself investors – that's you. They are called discount brokers in the USA.

Exit Charge A sales charge paid for redeeming a unit trust or other investment. See FRONT-END LOADING.

Fair Value The theoretical price at which a company is 'fairly valued', meaning that it would not be reasonable to assume that the shares will rise. Fair value at any given point is derived from a number of qualitative and quantitative aspects of the business.

Final Salary Scheme Most occupational pension schemes still calculate the pension as a percentage of final salary (maximum 40/60ths), also known as a DEFINED BENEFIT scheme, although they are changing more and more to MONEY PURCHASE SCHEMES.

Financial Services Authority (FSA) The top investment watchdog. Contact them on 0171 638 1240, but if you have a problem with a financial adviser or insurance company, contact the PERSONAL INVEST-MENT AUTHORITY. If you have a problem with a stockbroker, contact the SECURITIES & FUTURES AUTHORITY.

Fixed Rate Mortgage The interest rate on the mortgage is pegged at a set level for an agreed number of months or years. Pull out before the end of that period and you'll end up paying a REDEMPTION PENALTY.

Flotation See NEW ISSUE.

Fool One who exhibits a high degree of FOOLISHNESS.

Foolishness The state of being wry, contrary, canny and capable of looking after your own investments. Fools believe in shares as the long-term path to wealth creation and believe in buying and holding good companies for the long haul based on their fundamental financial and business strengths. Also see WISDOM.

Foolish Four The Fool's variation of the Beating the Dow strategy. The Foolish Four has you buy two portions of the number two positioned stock and one portion of stocks three, four and five. The stocks are positioned by first determining what the ten highest yielders in the Dow-Jones Industrial Average are and then ranking these high yielders by price, with the lowest-priced stock being number one. (Also see BEATING THE DOW and DOW DIVIDEND APPROACH.)

Front-End Loading A sales charge paid when a PPP, AVC, ENDOWMENT or other investment is purchased. It can amount to the whole of the first two years' contributions.

FT 30 For many years, the FT 30 was the INDEX most often quoted in relation to the LONDON STOCK EXCHANGE. It was originally conceived as being the UK equivalent to the DOW-JONES INDUSTRIAL AVERAGE, but is little quoted now. (Except by Fools intent on BEATING THE FOOTSIE.)

FTSE All Share Index An INDEX containing the 900 largest companies on the LONDON STOCK EXCHANGE. Either the FTSE-ASI, or the FTSE 100 are the indices generally tracked by index trackers (see INDEX TRACKING UNIT TRUST).

FTSE 100 An INDEX containing the 100 largest companies by MARKET CAPITALIZATION on the LONDON STOCK EXCHANGE. Came into being in 1984 and largely superseded the FT 30.

FTSE 250 An INDEX containing the 250 largest companies by MARKET CAPITALIZATION on the London Stock Exchange, created in 1992.

Full-Service Broker The US name for an ADVISORY STOCKBROKER.

Futures A type of DERIVATIVE that allows you to bid for the right to pay a future value on either an index option or a commodity. Futures are a great way to lose 100 per cent of your investment, because if they expire worthless you get nothing. Futures have a fixed duration and normally only last for one year at the most.

Gearing Buy a house for £100,000 with a deposit of £10,000 and the rest as a mortgage. Six months later, sell it for £150,000 and you've made 400 per cent profit on your original profit – that's gearing. Of course, it can work the other way too (see NEGATIVE EQUITY). Gearing can be expressed as the ratio of debt to assets and is used by companies and investing individuals to enhance their profits, as well as homeowners to allow them to buy a home.

Gilts When the government needs to borrow money, it sells you these.

They are government BONDS and as a rule the interest is paid GROSS (i.e. free of tax). They are very safe and their US equivalent is the Treasury bill, or 'T-Bill'.

Gross The payment of any form of income (interest or dividend payout) without the prior deduction of tax.

Independent Financial Adviser A financial adviser who is not employed by a particular company to market their products. They may be paid by COMMISSION, which in our view amounts to a conflict of interest, or else by agreed fee. We like to call these people Independent Financial Advisers (salespeople). See PERSONAL INVESTMENT AUTHORITY.

Index Groups of shares mathematically reworked to be representative of the current level of the market or of different sub-groups of companies within the market. See FTSE 100, FTSE-ASI, FTSE 250, FT30.

Index-linking Something which increases at the rate of inflation is index-linked. Some gilts are index-linked and the old age pension is index-linked.

Index Tracking Unit Trust The only type of unit trust that makes sense to us. While most unit trusts are actively (mis-)managed, index trackers are generally computer-driven and designed to mimic the performance of a given stock market index such as the FTSE 100 or the FTSE ALL SHARE INDEX.

Individual Savings Account (ISA) ISAs start in April 1999 and are replacing PEPs and TESSAs. In the first year you'll be able to invest £7000 and thereafter £5000 per year into a wide variety of investments. They are very attractive to FOOLs.

Initial Public Offering (IPO) The US name for a company's first sale of SHAREs to the public. In the UK we call it a NEW ISSUE.

Inland Revenue Come on, you know who these people are! You probably don't know their very helpful website, though http://www.open.gov.uk/inrev/irhome.htm

Insider Dealing This is when you buy or sell a share and at the same time possess privileged information which would move the price if it were widely known. It's illegal, but is also widespread and there are few prosecutions for it.

Institutions Institutional investors include pension funds and unit trusts. These are the big players in the stock market as they have a lot of money to invest and as major shareholders they often have a say in company decisions.

Interest-only Mortgage Monthly payments to the lender are made up simply of interest. You don't pay off any of the CAPITAL of the mortgage during the term of the mortgage, but do so at the end, having – hopefully! – accrued a large enough amount of money in an investment fund. Classically, these investment funds have always been ENDOWMENTS, but increasingly they are PEPs of one sort or another.

Investment Club Group of investors which meets regularly to discuss which shares to buy and sell out of a common fund. See PROSHARE.

Investment Trust A public limited company which makes investments into a variety of other companies. Notwithstanding several important differences to UNIT TRUSTS, these are also pooled stock market investment funds.

ISEQ The Irish stock market INDEX.

Large-Cap. See Market capitalization.

Leverage The US term for GEARING.

Life Insurance See TERM LIFE INSURANCE and WHOLE OF LIFE INSURANCE. (By the way, life *in*surance means the same as life *a*ssurance.)

Listed Company A PUBLIC LIMITED COMPANY (PLC), listed on a STOCK EXCHANGE.

Liquidity The easier it is to turn an asset into cash, the more liquid it is. Shares are very liquid as they can be sold any weekday at any brokerage. Works of art and homes are not nearly as liquid because you need to find an interested buyer. Since every buyer needs a seller and vice versa, PENNY SHARES, which are very thinly traded, are more *illiquid* than larger capitalization shares.

London Stock Exchange The place where shares in the 2,000 UK public companies are bought and sold. It is in the CITY.

Margin 1. Borrowing money to use specifically for buying securities of any kind in a brokerage account. 2. A measure of profitability of a company, like profit margin, operating margin or gross margin.

Market Capitalization The total market value of all of a firm's outstanding shares. Market capitalization is calculated by multiplying a firm's share price by the number of shares outstanding. Large-cap., medium-cap., small-cap. refer to shares in decreasing order of market capitalization.

Medium-Cap. See MARKET CAPITALIZATION.

MIG Mortgage Indemnity Guarantee. If you borrow more than 75 per cent of the value of your house, you'll probably get stung with one of these. It insures the lender against you being unable to pay. Even though it's you that pays this premium, it still won't stop you ending up at the Salvation Army soup kitchen.

MIRAS Mortgage Interest Relief at Source. Currently the government gives you 15 per cent tax relief on the first £30,000 of your mortgage repayments.

Money Purchase Scheme Pension schemes where you build up a pot of cash, out of which your pension will be generated, also known as a DEFINED CONTRIBUTION scheme. PPPs and AVCs work on this kind of system, as do an increasing number of OCCUPATIONAL PENSION SCHEMES.

Mortgage A loan to buy a home, where you put up the property as a security against you paying back the loan.

Mutual Fund The US equivalent to our UNIT TRUST.

Nasdaq National Market A national US stock market where trades are made exclusively via computers. The second largest market in the country, the Nasdaq is home to many high-tech and newer firms, including Microsoft. It now has its own website for UK investors http//www.nasdaq.co.uk.

Negative Equity Bought a house for £80,000 and now it's only worth £60,000? Bad luck – that's £20K of negative equity you're sitting on there. See GEARING.

New Issue The first time a company is floated on the stock market. Selling your company, or a part of it, to outside investors is a way to raise money for expansion plans.

New York Stock Exchange (NYSE) The largest and oldest stock exchange in the United States, this Wall Street haunt is the one frequently featured on television, with hundreds of traders on the floor staring up at screens and answering phones, ready to trade stocks upon command from their firms.

Nominee Account A type of account in which EXECUTION-ONLY STOCKBROKERS tend to hold shares belonging to clients, to make buying and selling of those shares easier. It does mean, however, that any shareholder perks are unlikely to be enjoyed by the investor.

Occupational Pension Scheme Contribute to your firm's pension scheme and get a maximum of 40/60ths of your final salary. Few, very few, get this much, though. Your occupational pension may well not be enough for your retirement. See FINAL SALARY SCHEME and MONEY PURCHASE SCHEME.

OEIC See OPEN ENDED INVESTMENT COMPANY.

Open Ended Investment Company These are going to replace unit trusts and indeed many UNIT TRUSTS are already converting to them. Ostensibly, they will be simpler for investors to understand and the charges will be lower as there will not be a BID-OFFER SPREAD between the buying and selling prices. In practice this will likely be replaced by a 'Dilution levy'. *Plus ça change . . .*

Options Contracts that give a person the right to buy or sell an underlying share or commodity at a set price within a set amount of time. The majority of options expire worthless.

Paid-Up Value If you stop paying into your AVC or PPP, but leave the money where it is, this is the amount of money which will be left to grow in the investment fund. In the first years of the plan, this is generally much less than the amount you have put in. See TRANSFER VALUE.

Penny Share A share of very low MARKET CAPITALIZATION (often a few million pounds) trading in multiples of just a few pence. They are very volatile, subject to extreme price fluctuations on the flimsiest of rumours and not at all the thing for the long-distance FOOL. See LIQUIDITY.

Personal Equity Plan (PEP) Started in 1987. Up to April 1999 you'll be able to put up to £9000 per year into equity-based investments in one of these and allow it to grow tax free. They're being replaced by ISAs.

Personal Investment Authority The people who regulate INDEPENDENT FINANCIAL ADVISERS and indeed anyone marketing retail investment products to the general public. You can contact them on 0171 538 8860.

Personal Pension Plan (PPP) A private (i.e. non-state, non-occupational) pension. Charges can eat dramatically into what is often, in any case, poor investment performance. PPPs receive tax relief. See Capitals, AVC.

Portfolio Management Give all your money over to the STOCKBROKER and say 'Here, go manage this.' It's one step up even from an advisory service. See ADVISORY STOCKBROKER.

Price/Earnings Ratio (P/E) A measure of a share's price in relation to its trailing twelve months earnings per share. Often, the higher the sustainable growth rate of a company, the higher its price-to-earnings ratio.

ProShare A pressure group representing the interests of the private investor. They publish a magazine called *The Investor*, and also have a useful information pack on how to set up an INVESTMENT CLUB. Contact them on 0171 600 0984.

Public Limited Company (PLC) As opposed to private, a company is public after it issues partial ownership of itself, in the form of shares, to the public. Only PLCs can be listed on the LONDON STOCK EXCHANGE or the ALTERNATIVE INVESTMENT MARKET.

Quarterly reporting In the US after each quarter year a company is required to file a report providing investors with juicy details on how the company is doing. In the UK equivalent reports are seen only every six months.

Redemption Penalty If you try and bow out of a CAPPED RATE, DISCOUNTED RATE or FIXED RATE MORTGAGE early, you'll be liable for one of these.

Repayment Mortgage The monthly repayments pay off both the interest and the capital on the mortgage. Early on, the majority of the monthly payment goes towards the interest. See AUSTRALIAN-TYPE MORTGAGE.

Revenue The money a company collects from a customer for a product or service. See EARNINGS.

Rights Issue When a public company creates new shares. Existing SHAREHOLDERS are generally offered the right to purchase a certain number at a discount to the market value. In the US, a rights issue is a form of secondary offering.

Securities Securities is just a blanket way to refer to any kind of financial asset which can be traded.

Security & Exchange Commission (SEC) The United States agency charged with ensuring that the US stock market is a free and open market. All companies with stock registered in the United States must comply with SEC rules and regulations, which include filing quarterly reports on how well the company is doing.

Securities & Futures Authority (SFA) The people who regulate your STOCKBROKER. Phone number 0171 378 9000.

Securities & Investments Board (SIB) Now called the FINANCIAL SERVICES AUTHORITY.

Share A SECURITY which represents part ownership of a company.

Shareholder If you buy even one SHARE in a company, you can proudly call yourself a shareholder. As a shareholder you get an invitation to the company's annual meeting, and you have the right to vote on the members of the Board of Directors and other company matters.

SIPP Self Invested Pension Plan. Like a PPP, but the plan holder calls the shots in terms of which investments fill the plan.

Small-Cap. See MARKET CAPITALIZATION.

Stamp Duty A tax you pay on buying shares (0.5 per cent) or buying properties (1 per cent). In the latter case, stamp duty starts to be charged at £60,000.

Standard and Poor's 500 Stock Index (S&P 500) An index of 500 of the biggest and bestest companies in American industry.

Stock Exchange A place where stocks and shares are bought and sold. The LONDON STOCK EXCHANGE serves this function in the UK.

Stock Split US name for a BONUS ISSUE.

Stock The same as a SHARE and used more commonly in the US. A share of stock (confusing, yes – just use the two interchangeably; everyone else does) represents a proportional ownership stake in a corporation. Investors purchase stock as a way to own a part of a publicly traded business.

Stockbroker A middleman who buys and sells shares on your behalf and earns commission on the transactions. Considered by many to be the fifth-oldest profession after prostitutes, pimps, tax collectors and accountants. See ADVISORY STOCKBROKER, EXECUTION-ONLY STOCKBROKER, PORTFOLIO MANAGEMENT and SECURITIES & FUTURES AUTHORITY.

Surrender Value If you cash in your ENDOWMENT before its time, this is what you'll get. On average, it takes more than *seven* years for the surrender value to equal the money you've put in.

Symbol An abbreviation for a company's name which is used as shorthand by share quote reporting services and various online sites.

Tax-Deferred When you invest in something like an AVC or PPP, you receive an initial tax refund from the government and are then deferring taxes until you withdraw money in the form of ANNUITY payments, when you will be liable to income tax.

Tax-Efficient AVCs, PEPs, PPPs, TESSAs, ISAs – we have many, many ways in this country to invest with a minimum tax penalty. Some are far better than others.

Term Life Insurance A no-nonsense life insurance plan where you pay low annual payments (premiums) that will increase as you get older. See WHOLE OF LIFE INSURANCE.

TESSA Tax Exempt Special Savings Account. Being phased out after 1999 and replaced by the INDIVIDUAL SAVINGS ACCOUNT. Keep your money in this bank deposit account investment for five years and you won't pay any tax. For the long-term investor, TESSAs are an irrelevancy, as the stock market provides much greater returns.

Tied Agent Less independent even than an INDEPENDENT FINANCIAL ADVISER. These are company salespersons, trying to sell you the products of the company they work for. Buying from them is a fool's, not a FOOL's game.

Transfer Value If you stop paying into your AVC or PPP, and decide to take the money out, this is what you'll be left with. In the first years of the plan, this is generally much less than the amount you have put in. See PAID-UP VALUE.

Treasury The government's finance department. They have a natty little website: http://www.hm-treasury.gov.uk/

Underwriters The STOCKBROKERS who help a company come public in a NEW ISSUE. They underwrite (vouch for) the stock. When a company has been brought public, the shares have been underwritten.

Unit Trust Your money is invested with thousands of others in one pooled fund. Presiding over the fund is a manager or managers responsible for achieving the fund's stated investment objective. Most unit trusts underperform the INDEX and have high charges. They are going to be replaced by OPEN ENDED INVESTMENT COMPANIES. INDEX TRACKERS are the only form of unit trusts we advocate.

Valuation The determination of a fair value for a security. If you don't use some reasonable method, then you have what is technically called a 'guess' or a 'hope'.

Wall Street Also known as 'The Street' in US cocktail-party patter, this is the main drag in New York City's financial district.

Whole of Life Insurance This will cover you until you die, whenever that may be, unlike TERM LIFE INSURANCE. Don't think, though, that you'll pay the same premiums for the rest of your life – they'll be revised upwards every ten years or so!

Wisdom The state of being Wise. These are the people who seek to sell you inherently underperforming investments, hobbled even further by heavy charges. See ENDOWMENTS, FOOLISHNESS, INDEPENDENT FINANCIAL ADVISER and TIED AGENT.

With-profits Insurance Insurance policies which have both an insurance cover element and an investment element. Endowments are a form of 'With-profits' policy. Remember that quote in the pensions chapter from the *Daily Telegraph* about endowment mortgages? It goes well here: 'It cannot be said too often that the advantages to the householder of an endowment mortgage are as nothing compared to the gain to the policy salesman, that life assurance has nothing to do with house purchase, and that savings-related life assurance is a waste of money.'

Yield See DIVIDEND YIELD.

Zymurgy The pre-epileptic state a non-Foolish investor enters when the market drops 10 per cent in a day.

Appendices

APPENDIX 1
Diary of a Share Purchase

Rentokil Initial PLC has already been featured as an example of a Less Obvious Obviously Great Investment. It was in fact the first share to be bought by the QualiPort, the Motley Fool UK's online, fully accountable portfolio. What follows is the basis for that buy decision. Every week from Thursday, October 7th, to Friday, December 12th, 1997, Bruce Jackson, senior analyst at the Fool UK, set out his thoughts at our online area on Rentokil Initial, their current valuation, their business, their management and future prospects. He goes into quite a lot of detail at some points, but he's an accountant, so we'll forgive him that. We hope, though, that his reasoning will be clear even to the novice investor and that if you choose to read through this series, it will make some of the principles of share valuation plain to you. There is nothing magical to what you are about to read; it all follows logically and makes good sense. We don't suggest that you have to go into detail like this with every company you buy and you may not even agree with everything he says, but as an educational experience, we think it's valuable and so did many of the people following Bruce's thoughts week after week.

Right at the end, we have tacked on a report written in March 1998 when Rentokil Initial announced company results for 1997 which were once more bang on the nail – 20 per cent annual growth in earnings per share. At the time of writing, Rentokil's share price is hovering around the 400p mark, an increase of over 50 per cent since we bought it in December 1997, just five short months ago. It's hard to justify a valuation like this and it seems probable at least that the market will have taken some of the wind out of Rentokil's sails by the time you read these words. We don't mind: if Rentokil returns us 'just' 20 per cent every year for the next ten years we'll be more than happy. We don't ask for more.

If you have any questions or queries about this series, you can e-mail Bruce at FoolUKBook@fool.com. He'll be thrilled to get a deluge of e-mails when this book is published and undertakes that he will answer every one personally within fifteen minutes of receipt, or else will take a voluntary 20 per cent cut in salary.

Enjoy!

Tuesday, October 7th, 1997

Rentokil Initial *An Investment Opinion by Bruce Jackson, a Fool*

Background

'Rentokil Initial is an international service company whose consistent objective is to provide for its shareholders growth of at least 20 per cent per annum in profits and earnings per share, whilst not detracting from long-term growth prospects.'

So begins Rentokil Initial PLC's [http://www.rentokil.co.uk] 1996 annual report and accounts. And the 1995 report. And probably the 1980 report too. This is no idle statement. Rentokil Initial has fulfilled its very public objective for a staggering fourteen years in a row.

Sir Clive Thompson is the man much credited with Rentokil's success. As Chief Executive, he is one of only two executive directors, the other being C. T. Pearce, the Finance Director. Having been Chief Executive since 1983, Sir Clive has presided over most of the company's rapid growth and its proud record. No wonder he is known in the City of London as Mr 20 per cent. He uses slogans like 'Management is Success' and the company has been voted 'Britain's most admired business' (or so it says on the side of the Rentokil vans and lorries).

This great British company, with a consistent growth record second to none, is well worth considering as a founding member of the Fool UK Quality Portfolio (Qualiport). It operates in over 40 countries and employs some 140,000 people. With its share price currently standing at 256p, it has a market capitalization of over £7300 million.

We know that Rentokil Initial is a service company. But, what do they really do? Let's have a look at their last two published annual reports, for 1996 and 1995. I couldn't find them on the Internet, although the latest interim report is available at their website.

The first thing to notice is the company's name change. This all came about as a result of Rentokil's £2300 million take-over of BET PLC. The bid, originally announced on February 16th, 1996, was acrimonious to say the least. Mud-slinging was one of the more pleasant pastimes practised by the two sets of directors. Eventually, after increasing their initial (no pun intended) offer of £1900 million, Rentokil got their prize when 60 per cent of BET shareholders voted in favour of the take-over.

Before then, Rentokil had a market capitalization of around £3400 million. The BET deal would increase that by two-thirds. Clearly, the successful integration of the BET businesses was vital to Rentokil's continued growth prospects. As a sign of their commitment, one of the first things the management did was change the name of the combined company to Rentokil Initial, in recognition of BET's biggest and best-known brand.

Even some of Rentokil's existing businesses were transferred to the Initial brand.

Apart from building the world's biggest services group, the take-over also meant that comparisons between the annual reports of 1995 and 1996 become somewhat difficult. For example, take a look at the following numbers, with increases from 1995 shown;

Turnover	*£2,339.7m*	*(+168%)*
Pre-tax Profit	*£318.0m*	*(+48%)*
EPS	*17.13p*	*(+21%)*

The interesting numbers are the percentage increases. The first thing to notice is that margins must have reduced (the smaller percentage increase in pre-tax profit) and the number of shares in issue must have increased significantly (the smaller percentage increase in Earnings Per Share). We'll look more closely at the underlying numbers a bit later, but, needless to say, the BET acquisition, finally completed on April 29th 1996, had quite an impact on the company.

The Business

Before they tacked the 'Initial' onto their company name following the hard-fought take-over of BET, Rentokil were best known for their pest control business. The word 'Rentokil' immediately conjures up images of giant mousetraps, rat poison and sticky flypaper. In fact their pest control business is a little more sophisticated than that, and they are still the largest commercial pest control company in the world. But, as we shall see, there's a little bit more to their business these days.

Rentokil Initial splits itself into six major business areas, being, in order of 1996 turnover:

- Hygiene and Cleaning
- Plant and Distribution
- Security Services
- Property Services
- Personnel Services
- Pest Control

Rentokil Initial must have been so successful at eradicating pests all over the world that, by turnover, its pest control business is now the smallest part of their group! Talk about putting yourself out of business. But, pests have an amazing resilience and, through experience, I know 'they'll be back'.

Hygiene and Cleaning now makes up the biggest portion of their business both in terms of turnover and profit contribution. Let's check the numbers.

	1996 £m	1995 £m
Turnover	728	326
Pre-tax Profit	130	86
Operating Margin	17.8%	26.4%

Included in this division are washroom hygiene services, which includes daily cleaning, linen towel systems, soap dispensers and warm air hand-dryers. This is the most recognizable part of Rentokil Initial's entire business. At work, in the pub, at restaurants, and in most public places, the name plastered all over the rest rooms is 'Initial'. Take a look next time you're out. Initial is the dominant brand name in toilet hygiene.

You may think that this is hardly an inspiring business to be in. I bet Rentokil Initial are glad you think so. I also reckon they'd be happy if any potential competitors think that way too. They'll just keep on servicing as many public and office loos as they can, and keep on raking in the steady income and profits. Uninspiring it is, but Rentokil Initial is not complaining. It's an essential service and one that is unlikely to be subject to huge technological advances.

Also included in the Hygiene and Cleaning division are various hospital services, textile services, deep cleaning services to the catering industry, and daily cleaning services including for IT equipment. The word 'services' crops up throughout this division. Rentokil Initial fulfils customers' essential needs.

The drop in the operating margin, from 26.4 per cent to 17.8 per cent, looks, on the surface, a bit worrying. This fall, as we shall see, is pretty universal across all of Rentokil Initial's divisions. The BET take-over is the main reason for this fall. One of the major attractions of BET for Rentokil was their low margins. Through its lean management structure, and administration and general office rationalization opportunities, Rentokil saw an opportunity to substantially increase BET's margins. So, whilst margins in the Hygiene and Cleaning division have dropped in 1996, there may be opportunities to increase these again as the BET business is fully integrated into the Rentokil fold.

Thursday, October 17th, 1997

Rentokil Initial – Qualiport or Bust – Part II

Last week we started looking at Rentokil Initial, the international services company that has grown profits and earnings per share by at least 20 per cent for the past fourteen years. Of their six major business areas, we looked at the biggest one by turnover, Hygiene and Cleaning. Now we'll look at the other divisions, starting with Plant Services and Distribution. Here are the numbers.

	1996 £m	1995 £m
Turnover	536.7	39.3
Pre-tax Profit	67.6	10.6
Operating Margin	12.6%	27.0%

Without looking any further than these figures, it is easy to see from the massive jump in turnover that the Plant Services and Distribution business is mostly made up of ex-BET divisions. Initial Plant Services supply and hire equipment like scaffolding, aerial work platforms, cranes and lifting equipment, accommodation units and offshore crane services. Also included in this division is City Link and A to Z couriers, Rentokil's own express parcels delivery service

This is hardly the type of business you expect a company with a great long-term growth record such as Rentokil to be in. It is cyclical, capital intensive, linked to the fickle building and construction industry, is traditionally highly competitive and therefore subject to low margins. A lot of this division's turnover comes from the US plant hire business. Rentokil have been quizzed by investors about whether they would sell this part of the business, freeing up cash to fund further, 'better fit' acquisitions. But, as Rentokil prides itself on its lean management structures and tight cost control, I suspect they'd like to try and weave the Rentokil magic on the cash generative plant hire business before they considered selling it off. After all, if they were to sell the business in a year's time after a nice profit increase, they may get a better price for it.

Security Services	1996 £m	1995 £m
Turnover	366.1	146.6
Pre-tax Profit	24.8	11.8
Operating Margin	6.8%	8.0%

This division provides security personnel in many situations, including static guards, mobile patrols, airport security and special events. Next time you're at work, a concert, a sporting event or Heathrow, have a look around to see if you can see any Rentokil badges. I know I never have to look too far to see them. They are not the only major security providers, however, and it is a highly competitive business, with many players involved. The low margins for this division as a whole are not surprising.

Rentokil Initial is also a provider of electronic security. This includes alarms, access control, fire alarms and closed circuit television (CCTV). This part of the division has grown the most quickly. Although there isn't a breakdown, I suspect it also may have higher margins, whilst remaining in a highly competitive market.

Improving the margins in this division may hold the key to any substantial future increase in profits. This is a constant thread, and is one of the reasons why Rentokil took over BET. Their track record suggests this is something they do well, and as the ex-BET businesses become more fully integrated into Rentokil, margin improvement will help fuel future growth.

Property Services	1996	1995
	£m	£m
Turnover	277.8	152.8
Pre-tax Profit	35.9	32.4
Operating Margin	12.9%	21.2%

How's that for an erosion of margins?

This is a hotch-potch of service functions – basically anything Rentokil does to look after properties, whether they be office, school, factory or holiday resort. Included are services like office machine lease and rental, catering, and specialist property care (woodrot, damp, roofing and timber preserving).

Rentokil Tropical Plants fits into this division. It is the world's largest provider and maintainer of decorative trees and indoor plants. Companies love to have their corporate offices looking great, with lots of tropical plants strewn about the place. They also love the idea of someone else looking after them. After all, how many times has your office plant been killed by lack of watering, sunlight or just plain neglect? (I must confess – sorry). This has been an area of substantial growth in the past for Rentokil and is the type of service that promotes lots of repeat business. A nice little earner for the company.

The huge divisional drop in margin from 1995 to 1996 surely can't all be down to the BET acquisition this time. Apart from the tropical plants, this division is struggling, but contains mostly cyclical types of activities. Rentokil must hope the cycle is about to turn upwards.

Next week, in Rentokil Initial Part III, we'll be wrapping up our overview of the business and will have a look at the company's 1997 interim report to see how they've progressed since the year end.

In the mean time, pose these questions to yourself:

- Is Rentokil one of the top 10 companies in the UK?
- Will they be able to grow at a rate of 20 per cent for the next fourteen years?

- Can they improve margins?
- What will happen if/when Sir Clive Thompson retires?

Monday, October 27, 1997

Rentokil Initial – Part III

Rentokil Initial is one of the companies we are looking at as a potential founding member of the Fool UK Quality Portfolio, or QualiPort as it is affectionately known around here. For those who don't know, the QualiPort aims to stick six to ten of the best British companies in a portfolio and sit back and watch them grow and grow over the next five, ten and twenty years. What could be easier?

In the first two instalments of Rentokil Initial, I started looking at the six divisions that make up the company. Part I gave an overview of its business and concluded by looking at its largest division, Hygiene and Healthcare. Part II concentrated on the Plant Services and Distribution, Security Services, and Property Services divisions. Today we will complete the set by examining Rentokil Initial's two smallest divisions by turnover, Personnel Services and Pest Control.

Personnel Services	1996	1995
	£m	£m
Turnover	226.3	5.9
Pre-tax Profit	13.8	0.5
Operating Margin	6.1%	8.5%

As with most of the year-on-year comparisons, the Personnel Division numbers are almost completely useless. Like the Plant and Services division, this unit is made up almost entirely of BET-acquired businesses.

Initial Personnel Services makes up the bulk of this division. It is a largely US-based recruitment agency but has some UK exposure too. I personally have never heard of it in the already crowded and highly competitive UK market. IPS provides temporary, contract and permanent staff in addition to messenger services and mailroom management. The 1996 annual report states that margins have improved in the eight months since the business was acquired whilst admitting this was starting from a low base. Also included in this division is the UK-based training and education business. Once again, according to Rentokil's annual report, this unit 'showed excellent growth'.

It will be interesting to look at the 1997 interim report to see if the very low 6.1 per cent operating margins have improved at the half-year stage.

Now that I know a little bit more about Rentokil and its emphasis on lean management structures, I'll put my money on these margins moving up.

Pest Control

As we found out in Part 1, this is now, surprisingly, the company's smallest division by turnover. Talk about re-engineering your business! It's almost like Coca-Cola's diversification into shrimp farming being a success and the prawn division becoming bigger than their fizzy drinks business. Okay, maybe it's not quite comparable to that, but who would have thought that Rentokil and its rat-catchers would be overtaken by temporary personnel agencies?

	1996 £m	1995 £m
Turnover	204.9	203.9
Pre-tax Profit	67.3	66.6
Operating Margins	32.8%	32.7%

Out of all six Rentokil divisions, this is the only one that truly compares like with like. It is a BET-free zone, with Rentokil-type margins. But what's happened to the revenue growth?

Rentokil Pest Control is the largest commercial pest control company in the world. It will try to eradicate all types of nuisances, and not just the rats I keep referring to. It even has a go at stopping the pigeons landing and doing what comes natural on my cousin's 6th floor London balcony. If its bird control systems sub-division ever gets the job of removing the millions of pigeons from Trafalgar Square, I suspect this division's turnover will get a much-needed boost.

It concentrates on 'green' pest control, placing special emphasis on environmental safety. Also nestled in this division are special services that reduce or eliminate the use of toxic materials – not to be understated in this environmentally conscious world we supposedly live in.

Pest control operates in all the company's 40 countries, but has struggled in the more mature UK economy. Europe was a disappointing region for this and most of Rentokil's other divisions. It seems most European economies are somewhat behind in terms of recovery those of the UK, US and Asia. Whilst pest control may have the best margins of all Rentokil's divisions, it is probably the most mature and will therefore not have the growth potential of the other divisions.

The performance of this division gives us some insight into why Rentokil launched its massive bid for BET in February 1996. With its original businesses reaching maturity and with margins having been improved almost as much as they could be improved, Rentokil needed something big to keep its 14-year record of 20 per cent growth in profits and earnings per share intact. Chief Executive Clive Thompson and his fellow directors saw BET as the answer.

We have now learnt all about Rentokil Initial PLC and what it does. An international service company sums it up in three words, but as we have seen, it is made up of many businesses within its six main divisions. As I've been running through this round-up, the one thing that strikes me is that, without its excellent past growth record and its stated 20 per cent growth objective, I probably wouldn't be looking at this company as a potential QualiPort member. Rentokil Initial is involved in relatively unexciting and mostly highly competitive businesses, but it is obviously an extremely well managed company. High quality management usually means a high quality business. Rentokil Initial has an enviable past record that alone makes it worth consideration for the QualiPort.

Next week, we'll be looking at Rentokil Initial's 1997 interim report. If it is weaving the famed Rentokil magic over the ex-BET businesses, we should expect to see an improvement in margins. Also, that report will be the first where the BET businesses are included for the full length (i.e. all six months) of the accounting period. That should allow us to have a better look at the structure and growth prospects of the company as it moves forward.

Before then . . .

As Innings so rightly pointed out in his posting to the QualiPort messageboard, we haven't yet looked at the market valuation of Rentokil Initial PLC, or indeed at the balance sheet its level of debt. These are all things investors need to know about before considering parting with their hard-earned money. Learning about and evaluating a company is a long process, but one that shouldn't be avoided. Knowing why one did or even didn't invest in a company is essential, especially if and when the share price takes a tumble. If you can be sure the company itself hasn't changed, any temptation to panic-sell because the share price drops will be avoided.

As usual, please post all thoughts and comments to the *QualiPort* message board. In particular, and picking up on Innings's post, I'd like to see comments about Rentokil's current market valuation. As of this writing, its share price is 246p and trailing EPS are 9.37p, putting it on a trailing p/e of 26. Quality doesn't come cheaply!

Friday, November 7th, 1997

Rentokil Initial – The 1997 Interim Report

The history of Rentokil Initial continues today with Part IV in the series: looking at the company's latest reported results. Being a UK-based company means we have to look at their half-year results to June 30th, 1997. If the company were based in the US, we would instead be looking at their 3rd-quarter results for the period ended September 30th, 1997. But that's another story. For those of you who have missed the first three parts in this series, check out The Quality Portfolio area.

For fourteen and a half years in a row, Rentokil Initial achieved their aim of growth of at least 20 per cent in profits and earnings per share. Interim pre-tax profits jumped by 44 per cent to £194m and EPS by 20.3 per cent to 4.74p. (Note that on May 19th, 1997 the company split its shares in two. The 1996 comparative EPS has been re-stated to reflect that split.)

Because all turnover and raw profit figure comparisons for Rentokil Initial are distorted by the April 1996 take-over of BET, looking at their operating margins is the only way we can get a reasonable comparison of how the integration of Rentokil and BET is progressing.

	6 mths to 30 June 97	2 mths to 31 Dec 96
Hygiene and Cleaning	19.5%	17.8%
Personnel Services	7.3%	6.1%
Pest Control	34.4%	32.8%
Plant Services and Distribution	12.1%	12.6%
Property Services	12.7%	12.9%
Security Services	8.9%	6.8%

When comparing margins over different time-periods like this, we need to be careful to remember that some of the businesses are cyclical and their results can be skewed by seasonal factors. Retailers are especially cyclical as their results invariably depend on the vitally important Christmas trading season. Whilst Rentokil Initial's divisions aren't subject to the vagaries of the seasons as, say, Boots and Dixons are, they do undoubtedly have some cyclical parts to their business. For example, Initial Leisure Services provides resort management in ski and beach locations, and we all know that no-one goes skiing if there ain't any snow!

Ignoring the seasonal factors completely, it's pretty clear from the above numbers that Rentokil Initial are weaving their management and margin magic over the combined company. Four out of the six divisions are showing improved margins with only Plant Services and Distribution and Property Services letting the team down. Even so, margins in those two divisions fell by only a relatively small percentage, especially when compared with the percentage increase in margins in the other four divisions.

The only division where we can compare year-on-year numbers is Pest Control. This is the only part of the original Rentokil that is almost completely unaffected by the BET take-over.

	6 mths to 30 June 97 £m	6 mths to 30 June 96 £m
Turnover	96.1	102.8
Pre-tax Profit	33.1	35.6
Operating Margin	34.4%	34.6%

As we found out in Part III of this series, Pest Control is the company's most mature business and therefore unlikely to grow at the same pace as the other divisions. However, the above numbers are obviously disappointing, negative growth never being a great thing for share price appreciation. The company says that both turnover and profits would actually have been higher at constant exchange rates. Even great companies like Rentokil Initial are seemingly not immune to the continued strength of sterling.

The fall from grace of the Pest Control division is again an indication of why Rentokil Initial needed the massive BET acquisition to continue its fantastic growth record. Rentokil on its own had probably stretched margins and organic growth almost as far as they would have gone. BET gives it the opportunity to start that process all over again.

So far, we have looked backwards at Rentokil Initial. We've dissected and analysed the business so that we understand exactly what they do, what their operating margins are and we've worked out their strategy for growth. I think we've got a pretty good understanding of their business.

Next we shall look at their balance sheet and in particular at their debt. At June 30th, 1997 they had negative shareholders funds of £22.9m and net debt of £454m. Things we will be addressing are:

- Will the high level of debt be a drag on their growth going forward?
- Are they reducing their debt?
- Are they cash flow positive?

Monday, November 17th, 1997

Rentokil Initial's BET Debt A QualiPort Investment
Opinion by Bruce Jackson (TMFGoogly)

The fifth in the Rentokil Initial Series.

As of December 31st 1997, Rentokil Initial PLC's net debt was £509.9m. The year before, they had a net cash position of £97m. The April 29th, 1996 acquisition of BET PLC for a total consideration of £2,221.7m, of which £568.5m was satisfied in cash, had a considerable impact on the new company. By June 30th, 1997, the date of that last published set of Rentokil Initial accounts, their net debt had reduced to £454.2m.

A householder when buying a new dwelling takes on a certain level of debt. Mortgage companies allow a family to borrow up to a certain limit based on the income of the family members. This is often something like $2\frac{1}{2}$ times combined salaries. The reason the lender sets this limit is so that they can be sure the family has sufficient income to pay them back the principal and interest thereon.

With a company, the principle of borrowing is very similar. It's up to the company's bankers and its management to decide what level of debt is manageable. The challenge for investors also is to assess that level of debt in relation to a company's ability to pay interest on it and capacity for paying it back to the bank.

One way to assess a company's level of debt is by its interest cover. This is a measure of how many times a company can pay its interest charge out of its profits. The calculation is:

$$Interest\ Cover = \frac{Pre\text{-}tax\ Profit\ plus\ Gross\ Interest\ Expense}{Gross\ Interest\ Expense}$$

The higher the ratio, the more times the company can pay its interest bill. For a company with little debt in comparison to its profits, the interest cover number will be very high and the company will usually be in a sound financial position. Conversely, a company that finds most of its profits eaten up by a high interest charge will have low interest cover. Such a company will often be in financial difficulties. A classic example is Eurotunnel, whose net interest paid in 1996 was £645m on turnover of £448m and pre-tax losses of £685m. No wonder that most of the 225 banks that financed the project have already written off their investment in Eurotunnel. As for an absolute number that investors would feel comfortable with, there is no set rule. However, I personally wouldn't feel comfortable investing in a company whose interest cover was much below 2.

Luckily for me, this isn't the case with Rentokil. Taking their full year 1996 numbers we get:

Pre-tax Profit   £318.0m
Gross Interest   £43.7m

$$Interest\ Cover = \frac{318.0 + 43.7}{43.7} = 8.28\ times$$

Rentokil have covered their interest bill over eight times by profits. It would take a huge rise in interest rates coupled with a big deterioration in their profits for them to have any major problem meeting their interest charges.

Because UK companies don't have to produce a comprehensive set of accounts at the interim stage, it's impossible to exactly calculate the interest cover for the six months ended June 30th, 1997. We are given the net interest payable of £16.3m, but this is not broken down into interest paid and interest received. Making an educated guess, I'll say that interest received is about £12m and interest paid £28.3m. With pre-tax profits of £193.9, that gives Rentokil interest cover for the first six months of the financial year of 7.85 times. This is little changed from December 31st, 1996 and still at a very comfortable level.

More important, however, is that the level of net debt has decreased in the six months to June 30th, 1997 from £509.9m to £454.2m, indicating the company is generating sufficient actual cash to help pay off its borrowings. This is important because accountants, legitimately using non-cash charges, can to some extent manipulate profit levels of a company. But cash is cash is cash, and a company cannot vary its cash balances from what is actually in the bank or owed to the bank.

In the next instalment of Rentokil Initial, I'll take a look at another measure of a company's level of debt – its gearing. As usual, I'll finish this round-up with a couple of questions.

Who are Rentokil Initial's competitors? Rentokil is a somewhat unique company in that they probably have lots of competitors in each of their six different divisions. Chief Fool US analyst Randy Befumo, looking for just one company, suggested ServiceMaster of the US, which is owned by none other than investment guru Warren Buffett.

Will the currency and stock market turmoil of the Far East affect Rentokil Initial's growth prospects?

Friday, November 21st, 1997

Rentokil – Gearing Up For A Decision A QualiPort Investment Opinion by Bruce Jackson (TMFGoogly)

The sixth in the Rentokil Initial Series.

As at December 30th, 1996, Rentokil Initial had net debt of £509.9m. This can be broken down into cash of £189.8m and borrowings of £699.7m. Gross debt is the £699.7m.

Gearing, or leverage as it is known in the US, is a way of measuring a company's level of debt in comparison to total shareholder's funds, or capital employed. It is most commonly calculated as:

$$Gearing = \frac{Debt}{Equity\ Shareholders\ Funds}$$

In the case of Rentokil, as at December 31st, 1996, they had negative shareholder's equity of £130.3m. Luckily for us, that doesn't mean that shareholders owe the company money. Here in the UK when a company makes an acquisition, all sorts of techniques are used to account for that acquisition. Without getting into too much detail, the thing we need to know is that of the £2,221.7m total consideration paid by Rentokil to acquire BET, a whopping £2,132.9m was considered goodwill. Under UK GAAP (Generally Accepted Accounting Principles) this amount may be deducted from shareholder's equity, hence the negative £130.3m on Rentokil's balance sheet. In the US the goodwill cost of the acquisition would be shown in the assets section of the balance sheet, under intangible assets.

To calculate a meaningful gearing figure, we first need to add back the total goodwill reserve to shareholder's funds. As at December 31st, 1996:

$$Gearing \ = \ \frac{£699.7m}{(£130.3m) + £2,459.2m} = 30\%$$

The same calculation, using net debt of £509.9m as the numerator, gives net gearing of 21.9 per cent. Neither of these numbers seems too demanding.

Another popular measure of debt is Debt-to-Capitalization. This is calculated as:

$$\frac{Debt}{Market\ Capitalization + Debt}$$

Where market capitalization = shares outstanding × share price
For Rentokil, it is:

$$\frac{£699.7}{(2,857m \times £2.40) + £699.7m} = 9.26\ per\ cent$$

The percentage is getting lower all the time!

The last ratio we will look at is Debt-to-Revenues. This is the ratio that they (meaning Randy and Jeff) prefer to use over in the States at the Motley Fool. Its attractiveness stems from the fact that sales are completely independent of external factors, like a share's current market capitalization and the way a company deals with intangible assets such as purchased goodwill. It's a great ratio for company to company comparisons. It is calculated very simply as: Debt ÷ Sales. For Rentokil, the ratio is £699.7m ÷ £2,270m = 30.8%. Uncannily, this is very close to the first number we calculated: gearing. In comparison, pub operator Regent Inns has a debt-to-revenue ratio of 46 per cent, and acquisitive transport company Stagecoach's ratio is a whopping 79 per cent. I would have calculated the ratio on more suitable companies, like Glaxo Wellcome or Hays, but I haven't got their annual reports to hand, and I can't get the information off the Internet. Perhaps we'll get there one day.

A Debt-to-Sales ratio of 30.8 per cent is nothing to get too concerned about, especially as we have seen that Rentokil are reducing their debt level while increasing sales. Doing a bit of guesswork about their gross debt as at June 30th, 1997, I calculate their debt-to-sales ratio to be about 22.8 per cent. I'd expect it to be even lower at the end of this year.

I think we've now covered Rentokil's debt. Basically, they are in debt, but not excessively. They can easily cover their interest payments, and their overall level of gearing is acceptable.

Just before leaving cash, I'd like to touch on something I spotted in the company's cash flow statement that gave me reason for a little concern. Capital expenditure is exceeding depreciation in 1996 and the first six months of 1997. I'd like to make sure that the capital expenditure is not all spent on replacing old assets, but some is being spent on genuine expansion. There's a big difference between the two. If it's the former, the company may be using a lot of cash just to keep going. Spending cash on new plant and equipment that will increase profits over a period of time is a more preferable use of the money as far as shareholders are concerned.

In the next bulletin, I promise, we will look at the share price and its valuation. At 240p, Rentokil Initial trades at a trailing p/e of 25.6. The company hopes to grow at 20 per cent per annum.

Friday, November 28th, 1997

Rentokil – The Final Countdown, Part I *A QualiPort Investment Opinion by Bruce Jackson (TMFGoogly)*

Before we get to the final decision about Rentokil Initial, I thought it would be a good idea to do a summary of the relevant numbers and criteria. I'm going to unashamedly steal the format that Randy and Jeff are using for their *Drip Portfolio* analysis of food companies. It will be split over two instalments, the first one today, the next on Monday.

Description

'Rentokil Initial is an international service company whose consistent objective is to provide its shareholders growth of at least 20 per cent per annum in profits and earnings per share, whilst not distracting from long-term growth prospects.' This is a straight quotation from the company's 1996 Annual Report. The business is split into six divisions:

- Hygiene and Cleaning
- Plant and Distribution
- Security Services
- Property Services
- Personnel Services
- Pest Control

Major Brands

Rentokil for pest control, security and tropical plants. Initial for hygiene, cleaning, personnel services and plant services.

Core Moneymaker

In profitability and turnover terms, Hygiene and Cleaning is by far the biggest of the divisions. Of the company's 1996 pre-tax profit of £318m, that division contributed £129.6m, or 40.7 per cent. As a reminder, the Hygiene and Cleaning division includes the Initial branded washroom hygiene services. Next time you're in the loo, take a look around and see if you can spot the Initial brand and logo. The next biggest division is Plant and Distribution with profits of £67.6m, or 21.3 per cent of the company's pre tax profit.

Valuation and Growth

Rentokil Initial have fulfilled their stated aim of 20 per cent growth in profits and earnings per share for the last fourteen years in a row. Although analysts are currently forecasting growth of less than that figure for the next two years, I think it's safe to say that the company will confound the critics and achieve their growth target. With 1996 trailing earnings per share of 8.57p and a share price of 250p, that has Rentokil Initial trading at a price earnings ratio (P/E) of 29. This is well above their future growth rate.

Using the most up-to-date information we have available, we can work out the trailing EPS up until June 30th, 1997. This comes from the company's 1997 Interim Report. In the US you'd have this information at your fingertips. Here, we have to get the old abacus out.

EPS

12 months to 31/12/96 (from 1996 Annual Rpt):	8.57p
less 6 months to 30/6/96 (from 1997 Interim Rpt)	−3.94p
equals 6 months to 31/12/96	4.63p
plus 6 months to 30/6/97 (from 1997 Interim Rpt)	+4.74p
equals 12 months to 30/6/97	9.37p

Rentokil Initial's P/E based on trailing EPS of 9.37p is 26.7, still above their stated future growth rate of 20 per cent. The current 1997 full-year EPS consensus forecast stands at 10.3p, giving growth of 20.2 per cent based on 1996 EPS of 8.57p. The Hemmington Scott site (http://www. hemscott.com) has 8.91p as the normalized 1996 EPS, which gives growth of 15.6 per cent. On these figures it appears Rentokil is not going to meet its stated 20 per cent growth target. Shock, horror, mark down the shares. Sell, sell, sell.

Hang on a minute. Although for most companies we would usually take the normalized EPS as the base when calculating growth, for Rentokil Initial this is not appropriate. When the company states that its aim is to increase earnings and profits by 20 per cent per annum, it doesn't add to that statement 'and oh, by the way, that growth will be based on normalized profits after adding this, subtracting that and removing the other'.

Some years Rentokil will have exceptional losses, other years they will have exceptional gains (as they had in 1996, which gives them the higher normalized EPS of 8.91p), but the swings and roundabouts will even themselves out. Fool UK applauds Rentokil Initial for being consistent and for taking into account all costs of running the business every year when applying their growth target.

Interestingly, the current consensus EPS forecast for 1999 is 12.2p, which is growth of 18.4 per cent over 1998's forecast of 10.3p. It seems analysts, as ever, seem to doubt Rentokil's ability to deliver their stated growth target. Sir Clive Thompson will derive great pleasure from proving them wrong yet again.

Tuesday, December 2nd, 1997

Rentokil – The Final Countdown, Part II A QualiPort Investment Opinion by Bruce Jackson (TMFGoogly)

We're almost there. Today, we conclude the summary of Rentokil Initial, our first potential QualiPort buy. For those who missed it, here's a link to *Part I* of the Final Countdown.

A ratio we didn't look at in our run-down of the company was price-to-sales ratio (PSR). It is calculated as:

$$\frac{Market\ Capitalization}{Trailing\ Sales}$$

With a market cap. of £7167m and trailing sales of £2819.6m (calculated using the same technique as EPS), Rentokil has a PSR of 2.54. If the PSR was calculated on 1996 full year sales of £2339.7 it would be 3.06. This compares with Glaxo Wellcome's PSR of 5.4, Reuters 3.8, British Airways 0.70 and British Steel 0.45. The average FTSE 100 stock trades at about 1.6 times sales.

Another new concept is the enterprise value of the company. It simply takes the market capitalization of the company, subtracts cash and adds debt. The enterprise value is effectively the price someone would have to pay to take over the company. They would not only get the assets and brand names of the company they were acquiring, but also would get the cash and assume the debt.

At December 31st, 1996, Rentokil Initial had debt of £699.7m and cash of £189.8m. Adding debt and subtracting cash to their current market capitalization of £7167m gives you an enterprise value of £7676.9m. That gives them a 1996 enterprise value PSR of 3.28, and based on trailing sales it is 2.72. Because of their debt, the PSR based on enterprise value is higher, but still not excessive. Coca-Cola trades at a PSR of over eight times sales and is the richest Dow-Jones Industrial stock by this measure.

Margins

Because the BET take-over distorts the 1996 figures, we'll look at the 1997 interim report when calculating Rentokil's margins. Operating margins are calculated by dividing revenue by operating profits. For the six months ended June 30th, 1997, this is 15.4 per cent. Net profit margins arguably are the only ones that we should ultimately consider as they take into account the interest and taxation charges. Net profit margins are currently 9.9 per cent.

These margins are nothing to write home about; however, net profit margins of 10 per cent or more are often considered to be quite good. In the full year to 1996, operating margins were 14.9 per cent and net margins 9.7 per cent. As a comparison, Glaxo Wellcome has operating margins of 37.5 per cent, Reuters 22.3 per cent, Hays 14 per cent and Marks & Spencer 13.2 per cent.

In 1995, the last full year before the BET take-over, Rentokil's operating margins were 25.5 per cent, up from 24.6 per cent in 1994. Net margins were 16.5 per cent, up from 15.9 per cent in 1994. These are margins normally associated with a well-managed company in a strong competitive position. I reckon by March next year when we finally see their results for 1997, Rentokil's net margins will be above that magical 10 per cent figure.

Gearing

Gearing is a way of measuring a company's level of debt compared with total shareholder's funds. With 1996 gross debt of £699.7m and adding back the goodwill reserve to shareholder's funds, we get gross adjusted gearing of 30 per cent. See the section on Rentokil Initial's BET Debt for this and the various other ways we can look at debt. With adjusted gearing at 30 per cent and with their interest charged covered 8 times by earnings, Rentokil has a very manageable amount of borrowings. Strong operating cash flow is helping pay off that debt, reducing the interest charge and allowing them to continue with their small acquisitions.

Capital Allocation

Prior to the BET acquisition, Rentokil was a true service company, which largely had people as its assets and therefore had relatively little in the way of operating assets. The BET take-over changed that to some extent, especially as the Plant and Distribution division was concerned. In the 1996 fiscal year, excluding the actual BET acquisition, the company spent a net £163.9m on new capital. As we've said previously, we have to be sure that this expenditure is for actual expansion of the business, and not just replacing old clapped-out assets. However, given Rentokil's exceptional record and its proven cash management expertise, this is not something to get too concerned about.

Like so many UK quality growth companies, Rentokil operates a progressive dividend policy whereby they increase dividends in line with the longer term, underlying trend in earnings per share. As that rate has been 20 per cent or more in the past fourteen years and is expected to continue at that level, it is safe to assume that the dividend will also continue to rise at about 20 per cent per annum. The trailing dividend for Rentokil Initial is 2.68p. At 250p, this gives a yield of 1.1 per cent, which is quite low for a UK company. We're definitely looking for share price appreciation rather than relying on the dividend pay-out for growth for Rentokil Initial.

Whilst their stated and very public aim of 20 per cent per annum growth stays in place, Rentokil will probably look for another big acquisition in the next few years. There would appear to be at least two to three more years worth of 20 per cent growth to be stretched out of the BET acquisition, if not more.

BET looks like it has turned out to be a perfect take-over target with lots of opportunities for rationalization of existing business, the most obvious being the Initial brand. The danger with any acquisition is di-worse-ification. With no single UK-based competitor standing out as a future possible take-over target, Rentokil may look abroad for a suitable company. Having six established divisions allows Rentokil to consider picking off smaller companies which will fit well within their existing businesses.

The Rentokil Initial Snapshot

>Recent Share Price: 250p
>Trailing 12 months sales: £2819.6m
>Trailing 12 months net profits: £265.1m
>Trailing 12 months EPS: 9.37p

1997 EPS estimates: 10.3p
1998 EPS estimates: 12.2p

Valuation:
Enterprise value to sales: 2.72
Current P/E: 26.7
Forward P/E: 24 on 1997 estimates, 20 on 1998.
Long-term expected growth rate: 20%
Yield: 1.1%

Conclusion

At 250p, Rentokil Initial is not cheap. As we have seen over the course of this epic, they are a very well managed company with an enviable track record. Fiscal 1997 is almost over, and you can bet your bottom dollar that Rentokil will at least meet the estimated EPS of 10.3p. This is one of the beauties of the company – they're so consistent and predictable.

Once they hit their 1997 estimate, they will be trading at a forward P/E of 20, which exactly equals their growth rate and stated aim. Looking at the share price valuation in that light puts the rich P/E this quality growth company currently trades on into some sort of perspective.

Before we make the final decision about Rentokil Initial's potential entry into the QualiPort, I want to have a look at the risks and opportunities of investing in the company at this share price. Until then, I urge you to post your thoughts on whether we should be buying Rentokil Initial into the QualiPort message board.

Friday, December 12th, 1997

Rentokil Initial – Fool UK Buys
A QualiPort Investment Opinion by Bruce Jackson (TMFGoogly)

The aim of the Fool UK QualiPort is to have a fully accountable online portfolio that buys quality companies at reasonable prices. Our journey through Rentokil Initial has confirmed that this is in fact an excellently managed company with an enviable track record. In this last piece of the jigsaw, we shall look at the risks and opportunities of buying this company with a trailing price earnings (P/E) ratio of 27 and an expected long-term growth rate of 15–20%.

One of Warren Buffett's investing tenets is, when investing in a company, think as if you are buying the whole thing, not just a small part ownership. Think big. If you could raise £7000 million, would you buy Rentokil Initial? If the answer is yes, the company is yours. You cannot sell it voluntarily, as there may never be a willing buyer. You have to be prepared to hang on to it for five, ten or more years. Buffett rarely sells.

Reality, of course, is different. If we wanted to, we could buy the shares on one day and sell them the next. The great thing about thinking really long-term is that it allows us to move away from the accepted City practices of concentrating on earnings in six-monthly blocks, in tune with when companies are required to report their figures. In the US if a company misses its quarterly earnings figures by even a penny, shares in that company are often severely marked down. It doesn't happen to the same extent here in the UK, but it does and will happen.

Rentokil Initial has stated that its aim is to grow profits and earnings per share by at least 20 per cent, 'whilst not detracting from long-term growth prospects'. Although they've achieved this fantastic record for fourteen years in a row, it would be foolish (small 'f') of us to simply assume they will do it for the next fourteen years. Even the next five years may be asking too much. No company can physically grow by 20 per cent indefinitely.

The 1997 calendar year is almost over. I need not remind you that there are very few shopping days till Christmas. Rentokil Initial's 1997 fiscal year also ends on December 31st and current earnings per share (EPS) estimates are at 10.3p, giving them growth of 20.2 per cent for the year. If that estimate is met or beaten, and there's no indication as to why it shouldn't be, Clive Thompson will be chalking up year number 15 in a row of 20+ per cent growth. It will take the accountants and auditors a couple of months to add up all the numbers, double- and triple-check them, and release them to the public. But, regardless of when Rentokil Initial actually reports their results, the numbers will be up to December 31st, 1997. As our decision as to whether to buy them or not will be so close to that date, we will use January 1st, 1998 as a base for our calculations when looking at the returns we can expect from holding the shares over the next ten years.

We will assume base EPS of 10.3p, being the current 1997 estimate. If Rentokil Initial were to continue growing at 20 per cent for the next ten years, it would earn 63.8p in the year ended December 31st, 2007. Over the past five years, Rentokil Initial has traded at P/E ratios of between 18 and 36. It is not realistic to think that the company will trade at a P/E of 36 ever again, so we won't even consider at what price the shares may trade at in ten years' time based on that P/E.

(I couldn't resist it. At 20 per cent growth for ten years and a P/E of 36, the shares would trade at 2297p for an annualized growth rate of 24.8 per cent. Wow! Now that's impressive.)

Because of their fantastic growth record over the years, Rentokil's shares deservedly trade at a premium P/E. That premium is usually something in the order of 20 per cent above their long-term growth rate. For example, at today's price of 250p, based on the 1997 EPS of 10.3p, the shares trade on a P/E of 24, which is a 20 per cent premium to their 20 per cent growth rate.

The Conservative Valuation

Going forward, let's assume Rentokil can continue to grow EPS at 20 per cent for the next three years. For the year 2000, that would give them EPS of 17.8p. After that, let's assume they reduce their stated growth aim to 15 per cent and achieve that for the next five years. EPS in 2005 would be 35.8p. And then, shock of all shocks, if they reduce their aim even further to 12 per cent, and grow at that rate for the next two years, 2007 EPS would be 44.9p.

Although this is not the 'worst case' scenario, it certainly isn't the best one. With their growth rate having slowed to 12 per cent in 2007, it would be only fair to give the shares a multiple of 14.4, being 20 per cent above their current growth rate. The shares would then trade at 647p (44.9p x 14.4), giving annualized growth over the ten years of 10 per cent. But what about the dividend? This forms part of the overall return. Over the years, Rentokil Initial has adopted a progressive dividend approach. They have raised their dividend by roughly the same percentage as the growth in their earnings. The 1996 full year dividend was 2.53p. We would expect this to increase by 20 per cent in 1997, giving a starting point of 3.04p. At the same rate of growth as I've assumed for EPS, by 2007 the total dividends paid should total 82.03p.

The table below summarizes.

Year No.	Year	Market Cap.	Growth	EPS	Div	P/E	Future Price
0	1997	7,167	20%	10.3	3.04	24.0	–
1	1998	8,600	20%	12.4	3.64	24.0	297
2	1999	10,320	20%	14.8	4.37	24.0	356
3	2000	12,385	20%	17.8	5.25	24.0	427
4	2001	14,242	15%	20.5	6.03	18.0	368
5	2002	16,379	15%	23.5	6.94	18.0	424
6	2003	18,835	15%	27.1	7.98	18.0	487
7	2004	21,661	15%	31.1	9.18	18.0	560
8	2005	24,910	15%	35.8	10.55	14.4	516
9	2006	27,899	12%	40.1	11.82	14.4	577
10	2007	31,247	12%	44.9	13.24	14.4	647

Total Dividend: 82.03

Adding the total dividends received of 82p to the 2007 share price of 647p gives a total return of 729p. For the share bought at 250p, that is a profit of 479p per share over the ten years. The total annualized return is 11.3 per cent, which is about the percentage the stock market as a whole has returned over the past 60-odd years. For comparison, the risk-free rate of return for government bonds at the moment is around 6.5 per cent.

A Possible Valuation

The above table awards Rentokil Initial a P/E of 14.4 in 2007, based on the company growing at 12 per cent per annum at that time. We have optimistically looked at a valuation based on the company growing at 20 per cent per annum for the next ten years and being valued at a P/E of 36. That just won't happen. But it is conceivable that the company will keep on growing its profits and earnings by 20 per cent for the next ten years. It has done it for the last fourteen years, so it's not inconceivable. If Rentokil were to succeed, their EPS would be 63.8p in 2007. Put a P/E of 24 on that and you've got a share price of 1531p. Add on the total dividend of 98p and that gives you a total return of 1629p and an annualized growth rate of 20.6 per cent. Even if the shares were given a P/E of 20, the total return would be 1373p for an annualized growth rate of 18.56 per cent.

The Risks

Rentokil Initial has grown over the years both organically and by acquisition. Before the big BET take-over, they only made relatively small niche acquisitions. BET was the first big, high-profile acquisition and was done specifically to keep the 20 per cent growth dream alive. It has and will hope to continue fulfilling this goal in the next few years. There should be a few more years of stretching those BET margins yet.

The 20 per cent organic growth of the original Rentokil business is a thing of the past. The same will happen to the old BET businesses as the years roll by. As the company gets bigger and bigger, the organic growth becomes harder to generate. The solution to continued growth is to do so both organically and by acquisition. This is something Rentokil Initial have successfully achieved in the past and are doing now with BET. But, if they are to keep on growing at 20 per cent per annum, the next take-over may need to be bigger still. And the bigger the acquisition, the harder it is to manage.

It has been rumoured recently that Rentokil Initial may be interested in taking over food services company Compass. The company would fit reasonably well into their Property Services division. This is only rumour, and Fools never buy or sell companies on rumour alone. Any acquisition is risky. They could be forced into overpaying or find the business doesn't quite fit as management expected. A company that relies on acquisitions for its growth can be a risky company.

Clive Thompson is one of the most respected Chief Executives around. His track record says it all. If he were to leave the company in the next ten years, it would certainly have a detrimental effect on the share price. We would hope that any replacement would come from within the company, someone who is familiar with the Rentokil management culture. No-one is indispensable.

The above conservative valuation table has the share price remaining static between years 3 to 5. That's two years without any share price appreciation, caused by the P/E and growth rate contracting. The risk here is that investors may be tempted to sell the shares as they may become disillusioned with the lack of progress in the share price. This is something anyone who invests in such a high-growth company must be prepared to accept.

The recent shenanigans in Asia may have an effect on the company's profitability. In 1996, 7 per cent of Rentokil Initial's turnover and 17 per cent of their profit came from the Asia Pacific and Africa.

And finally. When 1997 full year results are released in March next year, Rentokil Initial may miss their 20 per cent growth target. Unlikely, but nevertheless possible. The shares would almost certainly lose a lot of their premium P/E rating. Another option is that they scrap their 20 per cent growth aim sooner than we thought, which would certainly knock the shares down. Volatility is part and parcel of buying shares with a trailing P/E of 27.

The Decision

Fool UK buys £4000-worth of Rentokil Initial shares! Welcome to the QualiPort. The founding share. A defining moment in UK Fooldom.

Over the past couple of months, we have dissected the company into as much detail as we possibly could. We know what they do, about their management and their record. We know the risks, and the potential rewards. We don't suggest for one minute that you go out and buy Rentokil Initial just because we have. We've done our homework and are comfortable purchasing a part-ownership in this company at the current valuation.

We expect gains of between 11.3 and 20.6 per cent a year over the next decade. Being conservative, we're taking the lower figure as our expected rate of return. However, if everything went to plan, we could expect returns of 18.5 to 20.6 per cent.

Over the next five days, in accordance with the *Fool's buying policy* we will be buying 1600 shares in Rentokil Initial. With the share price currently standing at around 250p, this will cost us about £4000 plus brokerage and stamp duty.

This is a real money portfolio. The Fools are stumping their own money to buy shares in this company. We will be riding the highs and cursing the lows, just as any investor would. We'll also be looking forward to those dividend cheques rolling in over the years. It won't be much money, but they will all be gratefully accepted.

The overall aim of the QualiPort is to produce a portfolio of about five shares and watch that produce market-beating returns over the years. We will be putting a total of £20,000 into the portfolio, and we see Rentokil Initial as being the ideal first entrant. It serves the dual purpose of being a large capitalization company and of also being a fast-growing company. In the near future (once we've re-mortgaged Fool UK HQ) we aim to buy the four other companies that will make up the initial QualiPort. We will consider adding some medium- and smaller-sized companies, as they will make an ideal foil to our large capitalization shares like Rentokil Initial.

Although the QualiPort is largely going to be using a buy-and-hold strategy, we won't be averse to selling shares. This will usually happen when something materially changes about the company we originally bought (for example, a loss of confidence in the management), or we find a better business in which to invest our money.

So that's it. Go Rentokil Initial – here's to the next ten years!

And then came the 1997 results:

Wednesday, March 11, 1998

Rentokil Results Day
Did the QualiPort share maintain its 20 per cent growth record?

Sure did. For those few Fools who don't already know, Rentokil's stated objective is to 'increase profits and earnings per share by at least 20 per cent every year as long as it is not at the expense of long-term growth'. The objective has been in place, and achieved, for the past sixteen years. To put that in some perspective, if you had invested £5500 on January 1st, 1980, it would now be worth over £100,000.

Here are today's headline figures.

Turnover	£2875m	+22.9%
Pre-tax profit	£417m	+31.1%
EPS	10.32p	+20.4%
Dividend	3.06p	+20.9%

At first glance, it looks like Rentokil have only just achieved their objective. That is true if you are looking simply at the EPS growth figure. The target for exactly 20 per cent growth was 10.28p, so 10.32p is cutting it mighty fine. The market responded by marking down the shares by 5p to 308p in the usual bout of post-results fright. This ritual has been consistently re-enacted every six months as analysts doubt whether Rentokil can keep on delivering.

For me, today's numbers were bang on expectations. I'm an accountant by trade, and am supremely aware that, through the perfectly legitimate use of provisioning, a profit target can be hit almost exactly on the head. In future *Daily Fool* articles, I will attempt to impart some of these techniques to you, but for the moment believe me when I say it is true.

A big feature of the QualiPort's Rentokil buy report epic was their margins. I am a big fan of investing in companies that have strong and increasing margins. However, that's not the first thing I calculated following today's results. I flicked straight to the cash flow statement to make sure that operating profits are being at least reflected by a corresponding increase in cash. This is often where you can spot whether some really creative accounting has been at work, as a company can sometimes massage its profit figures but not its cash flow. The good news is that an operating profit of £447m resulted in a cash inflow from operating activities of £552m. If this is over your head, don't worry, as it will all be explained in an easy-to-follow format in the future.

Next, naturally, I turned to the margins. This usually gives a good indication of a company's competitive strength. QualiPort Fools will remember that, having completed the acquisition of the BET business in early 1996, Rentokil saw its full year operating margins fall from 24.5 per cent in 1995 to 13.6 per cent in 1996. Suddenly, Rentokil went from a business with market-beating operating margins to one with very average margins. When finally deciding to invest in Rentokil, one of the key deciding factors was that we thought there was scope to improve the margins, perhaps not to the heady days of 1995, but certainly to stretch them up above the 15 per cent mark.

The fact that turnover grew by 22.9 per cent and pre-tax profits by 31.1 per cent sort of gives the game away. Operating margins must have increased. In fact they went from 13.6 to 14.5 per cent, with every division bar the hotch potch Property Services business area showing an improvement. The highlight was the competitive Personnel Services division, which increased profits by 109 per cent and stretched margins from 6.1 to 8.4 per cent.

I'm not going to bore you with the numbers for too much longer. We already know Rentokil Initial is a great business with a fantastic track record. But that is all in the past – we want to know what the future holds and whether their 20 per cent growth objective still stands.

Most companies use their annual report to give investors an update on their current year trading (remember, we are over two months into the new financial year) in the area labelled 'Future Prospects'. Investors often see this as the most important section of the report, and the share price can rise or fall significantly on the words in this statement more than on the actual results themselves. The prospects section of the Rentokil report uses exactly the same simple words as ever. 'The board expects further good growth in 1998.'

Some may see those few words as unhelpful and unfair. As shareholders and, therefore, part-owners in the company, perhaps we should expect more. To this particular shareholder, those words are in fact very meaningful. They mean that the 20 per cent growth objective still stands. If it didn't, this is where Sir Clive Thompson would tell us.

For a moment, I'm going to put my super-duper City analyst hat on. I'm going to crunch as many numbers as I can get my hands on, work out the expected exchange rate movements of the 40-plus countries in which Rentokil operates and visit them all (wouldn't that be great), and finally come up with my 1998 forecast EPS.

And here it is: 12.40p. How's that for speed? Tomorrow's papers will tell me how close I am to the Wise. I'm sticking my neck out and saying that Rentokil Initial's 1998 earnings growth will be 20.2 per cent. Spookily, that's the exact same number I came up with in the final Rentokil *buy report* back in December last year.

In a remarkably candid press briefing, Sir Clive Thompson today said that 'there is sense in Rentokil looking at least at ISS . . . Compass . . . and Securicor' as take-over possibilities. Now that the BET acquisition is bedded in, the group no longer faces financial and managerial constraints on its acquisition policy.

I suspect that Rentokil won't go chasing the big BET style take-over in the next twelve months. There's still some mileage left in the existing businesses for margin improvement, and the odd two or fifteen bolt-on acquisitions will complement that. Although borrowings are now relatively low again, another year of consolidation could be in order. However, management will have their eyes firmly on the 20 per cent growth objective, and will act quickly and decisively should it look like it is in jeopardy.

With the share price at 303p, are they still a buy? With 1997 EPS of 10.32p, that leaves them trading on a trailing P/E of 29. This is historically high for Rentokil, but far from out of kilter with some of the valuations of other mere mortal companies that are knocking about at the moment. A forward P/E of 24 versus a growth rate of 20 per cent makes them look a bit more attractive. The QualiPort is very happy to hold.

APPENDIX 2
A Fool's (Brief) Guide to the Internet

Never surfed the Net? Confounded by all that jargon? Not sure if you have an anorak suitable to a new life as a Web surfer? Read right on, for this chapter is just for you. Everyone else who knows their URLs from their ISPs and their search engines from their homepages, you'll find some links and descriptions of potentially useful investment sites at the end of this chapter.

The Internet is an extraordinary phenomenon and, given the chance, we would wax lyrical once more about the mind-expanding opportunities it offers us all. Sadly, our publisher will not allow us that chance (although we'll be pleased to discuss them with you online) and this chapter is dedicated to the nitty-gritty of the Internet and how it can help you as an investor.

What Exactly *is* the Internet?

It's a network of computers, linked through the phone lines and was developed by the US government to be a communications system which would still work even if a large chunk of it was vaporized in a nuclear war (there might be no-one left to work it, but the network would still be there). Each computer on the Net is linked to a myriad of others and messages between two computers sent one after the other will likely follow totally different paths to reach their destinations.

Your computer is connected to the telephone line using a black box thingamyjig called a modem. The telephone number which the modem uses (generally a local charges number), will take you to an 'Internet gateway'. The people who run these gateways are the people to whom you pay your subscription for Internet access and are called Internet Service Providers, or ISPs.

I've Heard of Them, But What Exactly *Are* Email and the World Wide Web?

E-mail is like writing a letter, only better. You send and receive e-mail as you would letters, with the difference being that the 'letter' goes directly from your computer to another computer. This doesn't happen instantaneously and messages generally take up to a few minutes. They can take a few *days* to reach their destination, although this is unusual and does suggest something somewhere has gone wrong. (It has always baffled us just what these messages get up to when they go AWOL. Does the wayward e-mail pass through a computer in the Caribbean and say to itself, 'Mmm, nice here. I think I'll sun myself for a bit'? Or does it take the wrong turning at Tunbridge Wells and end up peeling spuds for a couple of days in a computer in one of the former Russian Republics?) In general, though, the immediacy of the medium means that people sometimes carry on e-mail 'conversations', in which they exchange just one- or two-line e-mails a number of times in a day. E-mail, in our opinion, has signalled a rebirth in the use of the written word as a communication medium between individuals. We think this is a Good Thing.

The World Wide Web is very different and was dreamed up by some nuclear physicists at the CERN particle accelerator in Geneva one wet Tuesday afternoon when Pascal the lab assistant tripped with the bucket of protons and they all disappeared down a crack in the floorboards. Since they had nothing to do for a couple of hours, they came up with the World Wide Web, instead of just twiddling their thumbs. (Actually, we don't know if the stuff about a bucket of protons is true, but the Web, as we Net jockeys call it, *was* invented at CERN.) For most purposes, the World Wide Web means 'The Internet' and vice versa for those of us who aren't programmers or nuclear physicists (that's us and probably you, too). At its simplest, the World Wide Web allows you to display pages of information to anyone, anywhere in the world with the means to access the Internet. This could range from Dennis's homepage in Accrington Stanley, with a catalogue and pictures of his fascinating collection of Accrington Rovers F.C. ticket stubs 1945–78, to altogether more useful sites like the Motley Fool UK, your daily newspaper, the daily surf report (the wet kind), snow report (the cold kind), or just about anything you can think of. (We know, when somebody tells you to 'think of something, anything' your mind goes blank. Ours do too, but there is an awful lot of very useful and interesting stuff out there.)

Think of a website as a physical place. It has different areas, which at their most basic might be simply pages of text. To get between different areas of a website and between different areas of the Web itself, you click on areas of underlined, coloured text called hyperlinks. You'll recognize them as soon as you see a website. You'll just *have* to click on them. Hyperlinks are magical because they allow you to move as the spirit takes you and they make surfing the Net the liberating, uplifting experience it is.

What Do All These Strange Addresses Mean?

While you'll send any e-mail queries about honey to the e-mail address winnie.pooh@poohcorner.co.uk, you'll stop by http://www.tiggershome-page.co.uk to view a list of what Tiggers like to eat (not thistles, you'll remember). The address, http://www.tiggershomepage.co.uk, is known as a Universal Resource Locator (URL). A URL will take you to a particular location on the Web (in reality a chunk of space on a computer somewhere linked to the Net). Your Internet software will then display the main page of the site whose URL you have typed in.

When you connect up to the Internet, you will receive an e-mail address – freddie.widget@home.co.uk – but will not receive a URL, because you won't automatically have a Web page. Unless you desperately want to make photos of your collection of size 12 Hush Puppies available for the world to view at their leisure, or you really do have something you think other people might be interested in, you probably won't go to the trouble of setting one up either.

What's the difference between an ISP and an Online Information Service?

There are two basic means of getting access to the Internet. One is by means of an Internet Service Provider, plain and simple. These companies provide a gateway to get out onto the wide oceans of the Internet and that's about it. The other way is to use a company which bills itself as an Online Information Service. These companies provide not only full access to the Internet, but also content which is unique to themselves and which is accessible only by subscribers to that service. Unlike the Internet, it is edited, policed, of a standard format and guaranteed to be user-friendly. AOL is one of these online information services and CompuServe and Microsoft Network are two others. The charges to subscribe to an Online Information Service are generally a little higher than for a basic Internet Service Provider, but then you're getting more for your money.

How Do I Connect Up and How Much Will It Cost?

It's easy to get hold of free CD-ROMs offering Internet access, as they are given out by lots of high street shops. If you stick one into your computer with attached modem, it will take you straight to the sign-up procedure. To find alternative companies to use, leaf through one of the Internet magazines in the newsagents and you should find one of them has a table of all the different Internet Service Providers in the back.

What? You don't have a computer with attached modem?! Okay, no problem, it will cost you somewhere around £1000 at current prices to buy a system capable of connecting you up to the Internet, but with microchip prices halving every six months, this will probably have decreased by the time you read this.

Where's the Internet Going?

Not only are computers getting cheaper and more powerful than they ever were, but the Internet itself is advancing at a staggering rate. We are convinced that in a very few years the Internet will be available via far more outlets than it currently is and that the memory of paying local phone charges to be connected will seem like a bizarre dream. The Internet will come streaming into our lives and people won't even know they are using a computer to access it. The Internet will be so freely available and so easy to use (it's pretty easy already) that the very idea of needing to be 'computer'-literate to use it will seem ludicrous. The Internet will change the way we shop, invest, interact, everything. Take an example: in 2010 you decide to renew your car insurance. Instead of phoning up one car insurance firm after another you pick up the TV remote control, type in a few details about your car and yourself (three points for doing 45 in a 30 mph zone? Tsk! Tsk!) and then make a cup of tea while a computer program trawls the Internet for the cheapest deal.

If It's All Changing So Quickly, Why Not Wait for the Technology to Advance Before Joining Up?

Bad move. There are immense advantages to being connected right now and there will never be a 'perfect' time to get connected. There will always be an earth-shattering advance just around the corner. Knowing what the Internet is and having an idea of its huge potential will allow you active participation in this revolution and will allow you to maximize the opportunities on offer.

In 1998 double the number of people were using the Internet in the UK as compared to 1997: six million people, or 11 per cent of the population. It's only going one way from here.

Sorry, did we hear you say you ran a small business? Then get online this instant! There are great opportunities out there for small businesses. Now, we don't usually give tips – and you'll have noticed there's no propaganda icon next to this, because we don't even know who these people are and we certainly don't get any commission from them – but if you think your business might be able to sell its products over the Internet, stop by this website: http://www.actinic.com. There you'll find low-cost software to set up online ordering systems, allowing people to fill in a form detailing which of your products they wish to order.

What About Security?

Security is understandably a big worry for many people, but for most of us it isn't an issue. There aren't millions of hackers out there waiting to jump into our computers and extract our household accounts. Viruses are a little bit of a worry, but even then the risk from them is overblown. At the worst, they will corrupt the files on your computer, making all the information on them unreadable, but good virus-scanning software should keep you trouble-free. In any case, they are not as common as made out.

People worry about giving out credit card details, but we cannot see how this is more dangerous than giving out those same details over the phone. In fact, with the new encryption software, we think it is probably far *less* dangerous.

What About Nasty Stuff?

It's out there, but you have to actively seek it. Most of the material on the Net is harmless at worst. If you're worried about your kids getting access to things you'd rather they didn't, then there is a whole range of software products on the market which will allow you to limit the kinds of sites to which they have access.

Will I Enjoy It?

That's up to you. As with everything, it's what you make it. But the *potential* for usefulness and enjoyment is far, far greater than anything else which has rolled along these last 30 years or so. See you online!

A Few Useful Websites

Two good search engines

Yahoo
http://www.yahoo.co.uk

Altavista
http://www.altavista.digital.com

These are places you go to look up whatever subject happens to interest you on the Internet. Simply type in your search query and off you go.

Investment sites

Moneyworld
http://www.moneyworld.co.uk
This is a useful UK-based financial directory service.

Hemmington Scott
http://www.hemscott.co.uk
Provides good basic information about UK-listed companies.

Yahoo Finance
http://finance.yahoo.co.uk
Good general finance information and news. (Instead of using the search engine, simply click on the link to the investment area.)

ESI
http://www.esi.co.uk
Cheapish, subscription-based investment information service. Very popular, take a look.

The Motley Fool UK
http://www.fool.co.uk
'Nuff said.

The Motley Fool
http://www.fool.com
'Nuff said.

Some Financial Calculator Sites

The Financenter
http://www.financenter.com/calcs.html

Kiplinger Calculators
http://www.kiplinger.com/calc/calchome.html

Hugh's Financial Calculators Page
http://www.interest.com/hugh/calc/index.html
These are US sites which allow you to do calculations for just
about any financial situation you can think of while you're online.
Simply substitute the dollar signs for pound signs in your mind.
Have a browse – it's good fun.

A Magical Mystery Site

http://ussubs.com
Things change quickly on the Internet, but if this website is still
there then it will provide a fine idea for what to spend some of
your millions on. Sorry, did we say millions? We meant *tens* of
millions! (If it's vanished, e-mail us at FoolUKBook@fool.com
and we'll let you know what it was all about.)

APPENDIX 3
How the Fool Makes Money

I'm tired of Love: I'm still more tired of Rhyme.
But Money gives me pleasure all the time.
Hilaire Belloc, 'Fatigued'

We've spent the rest of this book telling you how everyone else makes money out of you, so it seems only reasonable to devote a couple of lines to telling you how we make an honest shekel.

We're a group of free-marketeerin', free-bootin', free-lovin' [*Hang on, that wasn't meant to be in here. Ed.*] capitalist Fools, so we *do* like to make money. Here's how:

Advertising

Our sites carry banner adverts from a variety of financial and non-financial advertisers. Each time the fizzing photons from an advert hit your retina, the cash register rings, as we get paid by the advertiser. This is our major source of income – 80 per cent in fact.

E-mailed reports

Some Foolish content – only at the US site, currently – is available to be e-mailed to your mail box every day for a small charge. Of course, if you want to turn up at the site and view it for free, you can do that too.

Software

Portfolio tracking and more besides.

Knick-knacks

Caps, ties, T-shirts, that kind of thing.

AOL Usage Fees

We get paid a small amount by AOL each time someone visits the AOL online area, although the individual does not get charged directly.

Syndicated Newspaper Column and National Radio Show

In the United States.

Books

Buy one of these, ask us to sign it and watch us smile!

And that's pretty well it. If you can think of any other ways of making money which won't have us capitalizing directly off the profits you make from investing, or exploiting the consumer, the poor, or the environment we'll be pleased to hear of them: FoolUKbook@fool.com

APPENDIX 4
Publications You Should Like

The possession of a book becomes a substitute for reading it.
Anthony Burgess in *The New York Times* Book Review, 1966

Many of our readers have asked us for a short list of things to read on money and investing. Below, you'll find a selection of our favourites. You don't have to read them all, but one or two is probably worthwhile. If you've enjoyed and understood this book, you're going to find most of these pretty accessible.

Saturday's *Financial Times*

This is well worth reading for anyone interested in finance and has a good personal finance section, along with a good spread of non-finance content, too. If you become really interested in shares, you'll become one of us sad people who read the daily edition as well.

Investors' Chronicle

Weekly magazine about investing in shares. If it would have seemed incomprehensible to you before reading this book, go and browse it now on the shelves of your local newsagents and you might have a big surprise – you can understand most of it! It's not a bad read, with much useful information, but don't fall into the trap of reading their two-paragraph share recommendations in the back and rushing out and buying them. You're more Foolish than that now. Aren't you?

Investment Made Easy, The Zulu Principle, Beyond the Zulu Principle – A series of books by Jim Slater

Jim Slater's books are well worth reading and written specifically for the British market. *Investment Made Easy* is a simple introduction to investing in Britain and a very useful reference book. The 'Zulu' books examine investment yardsticks and share screens and Jim is a fan of the 'PEG' ratio for selecting shares or, as we know it in Fooldom, the 'Fool' ratio.

A Guide to Stockpicking – by Gillian O'Connor

Gillian O'Connor is the personal finance editor of the *Financial Times* and has written a well-informed, fair overview of the UK share buying scene. This analyst says 'BUY' and picks out the bits relevant to you.

The Warren Buffett Way – by Robert Hagstrom

A very readable book outlining Mr Buffett's market-beating approach to investment. This is one to take to the beach. Or else . . .

Warren Buffett's Letters

Read the great man's annual 'Letter to shareholders' for the past fifteen years at his website: http://www.berkshirehathaway.com. He comes out as someone of great humour and his yearly missives are well worth a read.

Beating the Street – by Peter Lynch

As fund manager of Fidelity's superbly performing Magellan fund in the 80s, Peter Lynch attained guru status in the US. In this book he gives good insight into his stockpicking methods and writes clearly and well.

Common Stocks and Uncommon Profits – by Philip A. Fisher

This is an investment classic and a wonderful guide to understanding a company's core business and the importance of becoming familiar with the people that run it. Fisher provides a number of ways to better understand what these companies do and why, who they are, and whether you should continue to invest in them.

The Intelligent Investor – by Benjamin Graham

A simple analytical framework for investors as well as a definition of what investing really means, which is to say 'investing' shouldn't be confused with 'trading'. It's another classic.

Beating the Dow – by Michael O'Higgins

The landmark book on high yield investing. It's somewhat dated now, but gives a good feel for what it's all about. The numbers in the book aren't entirely accurate, however, and you'll find more accurate numbers at the US Fool's Dow Dividend area (AOL Keyword: FOOL or website http://www.fool.com).

What Works on Wall Street – by James O'Shaughnessy

If you're serious, really serious, about Beating the Footsie, you'll enjoy this book. The author tested a variety of mechanical stockpicking approaches on different groups of US shares ('universes' he calls them) over the last 45 years, coming out in favour of the dividend yield ratio and the price-to-sales ratio, two Foolish favourites. It makes interesting reading and we wish we had similar information available in the UK. Also, it has an illuminating section near the beginning on the psychology required to be a long-distance investor.

The Unemotional Investor – by Robert Sheard

Robert Sheard runs the US Fool's Dow Dividend area, from which our own Beating the Footsie is derived. If you're into mechanical strategies, this one has to go in the shopping basket along with *What Works on Wall Street* and *Beating the Dow*.

Interpreting Company Reports and Accounts by Geoffrey Holmes and Alan Sugden

Gripping it's not, but a gold-standard reference it certainly is. Well-researched and thorough, this British investment classic will help the UK Fool plough through some of the obfuscation surrounding company accounts.

Accounting for Growth – by Terry Smith

Terry Smith throws some interesting light on the devious ways in which companies spruce up their balance sheets. Not a reference work like Holmes and Sugden, but not necessarily the kind of thing you'd take to the beach either.

The US Fool Books: *You Have More Than You Think, The Motley Fool Investment Guide, The Motley Fool Investment Workbook* by David and Tom Gardner

What can we say? We won't go into great detail here, but we hope the US bias of these books doesn't detract from their basic message, which is applicable anywhere there's a decent stock market. Look out for more books from FoolPublish UK and in the meantime, if you catch us looking a little too po-faced, self-righteous or undermining your efforts to save and invest, then flame us at FoolUKBook@fool.com.

You can buy all these books and more at the Foolish investment bookshop, hosted by Global Investor: http://www.global.investor.com/tmf/.

APPENDIX 5
Issues to Clarify When Choosing a Broker Worldwide

Yvonne Ravenhall, a Motley Fool UK reader based in Portugal, offers these guidelines for choosing a broker anywhere in the world. Ask these questions and have them answered satisfactorily and you won't go far wrong. If you can't find a broker who satisfies these criteria, then you probably shouldn't be trading in that country anyway.

1. Is the broker covered by meticulous regulation in his country of operation?

    The USA and UK have strict regulatory systems; other countries can be woefully lax. More to the point, does your broker belong to the appropriate regulated bodies?

2. Is the broker compelled to insure clients against his own demise?

    What happens if Swindle & Churn go to the wall – is your portfolio safeguarded?

3. What is the limit of that insurance; does it cover the size of your account?

    If the obligatory insurance falls short, ask if additional cover is available.

4. What is the cost per trade?

    A flat fee sounds simple, but is a little misleading. You have to average all charges (trading, subscription, annual fee, custody, etc.) over your estimated annual trades and portfolio size to arrive at a true, per-trade cost.

5. What statutory charges are there, on top of the broking fees?

    Some countries have mandatory taxes, e.g. UK's 0.5 per cent Stamp Duty; Lisbon's 0.03 per cent Bolsa tax. If you don't ask, you may not be told.

6. Does the standard broking fee encompass all types of trading that interest you?

    There may be a premium for limit orders, for unfulfilled orders, or for dealing on external markets.

7. Can the broker provide custody of titles? In other words, is the broker set up to allow you to hold the share certificates of the shares you own?

Of course, you may not wish to hold certificates – it can complicate the sale of stocks.

What is the charge for this service?

8. Does the broker offer only nominee accounts?

You may prefer that anonymity; however, you won't get any shareholder perks.

More importantly, is the nominee account ring-fenced, insulated from Swindle & Churn's company assets should they go under? See notes below on pooled and designated nominee accounts.[1]

9. Will the broker collect dividends on your behalf?

Virtually all brokers will, but some make a charge for it.

10. What if you want to change your broker?

Some brokers charge for accepting titles, or for delivering titles elsewhere.

11. Is there any charge on transferred funds?

There may be a charge on funds received from foreign banks, even though the currency of the transfer is the same as that of the broking account.

12. How frequently will you receive trading and/or portfolio statements?

A month is a long time to wait to learn if, and at what price, a stock was bought/sold.

13. Finally, try phoning your broker (if you're not going to be trading online) at busy times to make sure you can get through.

---

1 Pooled/Designated nominee accounts. A pooled account is where the broker has, say, 100 clients holding the same stock (ABC PLC). On the shareholder register the holding would appear as only one holding in the broker's name. This means that the broker's internal record keeping has to be very good as that is all that identifies who owns what. A designated account is where the holding in ABC would be shown under the broker's name but with every single client identified on the register by an account designation that does not identify them to outsiders but shows their unique number at the brokerage. This makes the client less vulnerable to an internal record-keeping breakdown at their brokers. It can be very important in a 'worst case' scenario situation! *(This information kindly provided by a stockbroker who regularly visits the Fool UK and signs himself 'From the Dark Side'.)*

APPENDIX 6
The Y2K Problem

The scouts' motto is founded on my initials, it is: BE PREPARED, which
means, you are always to be in a state of readiness in mind and body . . .
Robert Baden-Powell, *Scouting for Boys*

You've probably realized by now that our interest in great disaster scenarios
began and ended with *The Towering Inferno*. We just don't really take them
seriously. We believe the world probably will keep turning, that the asteroid
probably won't hit and that the terrorists of the twenty-first century probably won't be organized enough to wipe us all out with anthrax without
wiping themselves out first. This contribution, though, from a Motley Fool
UK reader in Portugal in early 1998, Yvonne Ravenhall, struck us as not
only eloquent, but deserving of some mighty serious consideration.

Most people will have heard of the Y2K problem by the time this book
is published. Back, way back, in the 70s and 80s, computer programmers
had a problem. They didn't have sufficient memory to cope with recording
years in four figures, so they chose to record all dates in the format
12/11/82 rather than 12/11/1982. Back then, they didn't really think their
programs and machines might still be running at the end of the century, or
maybe they did, or who knows, but whatever happened they didn't think
about any potential problems. The problem will come at one second past
midnight on the first of January 00, or rather, 2000. At that time, any
computers or computer programs which are not Y2K-compliant will think
it is 1900, not 2000 and will start to become very confused indeed. They
will spit out diodes, chew up data, go blank, refuse to switch on again and
cause a great deal of confusion.

In theory, everyone should be getting ready for this event and the
changes required to individual machines are generally not that difficult or
time-consuming or complex to perform. In theory, it should all get sorted
out. In practice, with computers these days linked to one another as never
before, it may not be that simple.

Just how much chaos there will be and what it will mean for the
individual, no-one knows. Some pessimistic souls are even predicting the
mother of all stock market crashes. Of course, we may all wake up (if we
went to bed) on 1/1/00 to a world which is purring along just as it was in
the old century; and that was the opinion of a couple of software Fools
who followed up the open invitation we made on our site to have dinner

with us (Pizza Express, of course) in early May 1998. If you're the cautious type, though, and like to have everything sewn up, you may want to pay serious attention to the severely Foolish advice below.

Take it away, Yvonne:

What are you doing about Year 2000? The immutable march of time and/or your celebratory cruise to Hawaii are not what I refer to. Current estimates suggest that only 25 per cent of British businesses are actively taking appropriate measures to address the looming problem. Tony Blair feels obliged to put money where the governmental mouth is – you can thus assume that the issue is both serious and too long neglected. If you were about to de-tune, thinking this has scant relevance to your investments, READ ON! Enlightened self-interest is imperative at this juncture.

You may be sleeping easily, confident that the Wise – administration departments, company registrars, programmers, bureaucrats – will ensure that the doomsayers' predictions come to naught when time ticks round to 00:00:01 on January 1st, 2000. Don't you believe it! Globally, there's more work still to be done than can be fitted in before 23:59:59 on December 31st, 1999. Some organizations will not make it.

This is where self-interest impinges: your prime concern is that your chosen suppliers (bank, insurance company, building society, shareholdings, fund manager, pension provider, government departments, broker, solicitor, doctor, et al.) will be amongst those who meet the deadline.

It isn't just that computers must have 2000-compliant BIOS; all the software used must also be compliant. That's a murky region, because much sector-specific or specially commissioned software was written a while back, with no cognizance taken of the import of the forthcoming millennium. A further complication is that many companies are as reliant on the systems and software of their suppliers as they are on their own in-house computing resources.

Think about one possible scenario. It's January 3rd, 2000. You have a buyer for your house, he's proffered a deposit, and you're anxious to get the process under way.

Alas, your solicitor's records are in disarray. He is ingratiatingly reassuring: a Hexium 99 computer is on order; retired employees will be drafted in to reconstitute the database. In the interim, with no computer reference, you're a beige needle in a manila haystack, wherein lie the documents needed to facilitate the sale. The database of Outer Shires Bank PLC has gone awry, too, so the Client Account is inaccessible – he can't accept the deposit cheque. But come back at the end of the month . . .

Cut to the next scene. With a new residence identified, you need mortgage approval, pronto. A call to your Building Society reveals that there is a small administrative problem. To interpret the PR-speak of their functionary, there is no record that you are a client, nor how much is outstanding on the old mortgage, much less whether you can be offered a mortgage on the new property. If you could ring next week . . .

You decide to be Foolishly self-reliant, and garner relevant documentation. In your present home, the woodworm was exterminated in 1994 by a prominent company giving a 25-year guarantee; the garage roof was resurfaced in

1998 with space-age technology of like warranted duration. A call to the roofing company elicits that they cannot trace doing work on your garage in 1998 – if you have the quotation and invoice, and could send them copies . . .

I don't think I have to tread the remaining painful steps for you, do I? Unless you're a compulsive hoarder of paperwork and can thereby prove chapter and verse, you've overnight become a nonentity – and the onus of proof will be on you, rest assured.

Make a list of every company, institution, Government department that you've ever had contact with, and expect to hold your records, should you need recourse to them after Year 2000. Use lateral thinking – could a new job hinge on a University attesting that you graduated in 1990 with an MSc (Information Technology)?

If you've got offspring, you'd be well advised to involve them. They'll be more free-thinking and might provide pointers you would otherwise overlook (school? library? ISP? game programs?). Turn off the TV and make it a family enterprise: compile a list of all external entities which do/could/might affect the life of you and your nearest and dearest. Better still, turn over the whole kit-and-caboodle to the kids and offer a generous pocket money premium based on list length – the best investment you'll make this side of Year 2000.

Next, draft a brief letter, headed with your postal address (forget phone, fax or e-mail: you want a reply in legally enforceable black-and-white), which includes the following items:

- *A space for the Reference Number (of your account/policy/certificate/etc.)*
- *A request that the organization confirm that:*
  (a) All computers they access (internal or external) are Year 2000 compliant
  (b) All software they access (internal or external) is Year 2000 compliant
- *A demand that, if they cannot presently guarantee this, they specify the date on which they will achieve it.*

Nip to the nearest copy shop for the photocopies. Complete the 'Ref. No: _____' line with the number of the insurance policy, bank account, share certificate, broker's account, private health plan, National Insurance, Premium Bond, registered software, or whatever, and consign the letters to the postbox.

Monitor the responses. Anyone who doesn't reply, or whose response is vague, is suspect. If it's feasible, divest yourself as rapidly as possible – checking first that the alternative supplier is up to scratch! If government departments, like the DHSS (or whatever is the current acronym), should be amongst the voiceless, all I can suggest is that you make your local MP's life miserable.

Even from here, I detect the rumble of protestation. Wait!! I, like you, have a full-time job, a home life, and myriad claims on what remains of spare time. Similarly, I have investments that I expect to cushion my future. If you can't fit in this Foolish little chore – 'taking charge of your own affairs', remember? – so be it. Come Year 2000, should there be messages on Motley Fool boards to the effect that certain organizations have inexplicably rendered you invisible, I shall be Foolishly, smugly unsympathetic and retort, 'Told you so, way back in 1998!'

APPENDIX 7
Major UK Index Trackers

Name	Telephone Number
Barclays Uni FTSE 100 PEP 5% initial charge 1.25% annual	0181 534 5544
CF Net PEP Tracker http://www.netpep.co.uk. (No phone number) 1% initial 0.3% annual	
Direct Line FTSE 100 Tracker PEP No initial 1.1% annual Exit 0.5%	0117 925 9099
Equitable UK Index Tracking PEP No initial 1% annual	01296 393 100
Fidelity Moneybuilder Index PEP No initial 0.5% annual	0800 41 41 61
Gartmore UK Index PEP No initial 1% annual	0171 623 1212
Guardian UK 100 Index Tracking PEP No initial 1.17% annual	0800 28 28 20

HSBC Footsie Fund   0171 955 5050
PEP
No initial
1% annual
Exit 0.5%

HSBC UK Index   0171 955 5050
No PEP
No initial
0.5% annual
Exit 0.5%

Kleinwort Benson UK Index   0171 956 6600
PEP
No initial
1% annual

Legal & General UK Index   0500 11 66 22
PEP
No initial
0.5% annual

Lloyds Bank FTSE 100   01634 834 000
PEP
6% initial
1% annual

Marks & Spencer UK 100 Cos Acc   0800 363 451
PEP
No initial
1% annual

Midland FTSE 100 Index Acc   01392 602 000
4% initial
1% annual

Morgan Grenfell UK Ind Trk INC   0171 545 6000
PEP
3% initial
0.75% annual

NatWest UK Tracker   0800 200 400
PEP
No initial
1% annual
0.5% exit

Norwich UK Index Tracking   0345 73 83 93
No PEP
5% initial
0.9% annual

Royal Life UK Index Tracking   01277 842 601
No PEP
5.25% initial
0.3% annual

Scot Widows UK Index   0345 678 910
PEP
No initial
0.5% annual

Virgin UK Index Tracking   0345 900 900
PEP
No initial
1% annual

APPENDIX 8
Execution-only Stockbrokers

Listed at the top are the major UK online brokers and then below is a more comprehensive list of execution-only brokers, most of whom do not support online dealing. At the time of writing, there is also a useful list of stockbrokers on the Internet at the *Investors' Chronicle* site http://www.investorschronicle.co.uk/pubs/mags/ic/site/broker/b_do.htm, and another at the *Moneyworld* site http://www.moneyworld.co.uk.

Torrie & Co.	http://www.torrie.co.uk	0131 225 1766
Charles Schwab Europe	http://www.sharelink.co.uk	0121 200 2242
ESI	http://www.esi.co.uk	
Infotrade	http://www.infotrade.co.uk	
Xest	http://www.xest.com	
The Share Centre	http://www.share.co.uk	0800 800 008

Firm	Service Provided By	
Abbey National	Charles Schwab	0121 233 2333
Bank of Ireland	Charles Schwab	0121 200 4603
Barclays Stockbrokers	Barclays Stockbrokers	0800 55 11 77
Barratt & Cooke	Barratt & Cooke	01603 624 236
James Brearley & Sons	James Brearley & Sons	01253 21474
Brewin Dolphin Bell Lawrie	Brewin Dolphin Bell Lawrie	0131 529 0101
Cheshire Building Society	Dealwise	0800 243 278
CityDeal Services*	CityDeal Services	01708 742 288
Darlington Building Society	Dealwise	0113 243 4477
Durlacher Traded Options	Durlacher Ltd	0171 628 4306
First Direct	Midland Stockbrokers	0345 100 100
Gall & Eke	Gall & Eke	0161 237 9443

Hargreaves Lansdown Stockbrokers	Hargreaves Lansdown	0117 980 9800
Henderson Crosthwaite	Henderson Crosthwaite	0345 125 719
Killik & Co.	Pershing Securities	0171 345 6123
Lambeth Building Society	Waters Lunniss	01603 219 993
Lloyds Bank Stockbrokers	Lloyds Bank Stockbrokers	0345 888 100
Midland Stockbrokers	Midland Stockbrokers	0800 100 250
Nationwide Building Society	Charles Schwab Europe	0121 200 7711
NatWest Stockbrokers	NatWest Stockbrokers	0171 895 5018
Options Direct Europe	Options Direct Europe	0171 638 0100
P H Pope	PH Pope	01782 202 154
Redmayne-Bentley	Redmayne-Bentley	0113 243 6941
Albert E Sharp	Albert E Sharp	0121 200 2244
Skipton Building Society	Dealwise	0191 201 3800
Charles Stanley	Charles Stanley & Co.	0171 739 8200
TSB	Lloyds Bank Stockbrokers	0345 888 100
Walker Crips Weddle Beck	Walker Crips Weddle Beck	0171 253 7502
Waters Lunniss & Co.	Waters Lunniss & Co.	01603 622 265
Yorkshire Building Society	YorkSHARE	01274 736 736

* not currently taking new business

APPENDIX 9
Companies Offering Direct Mortgages

You won't find an exhaustive list here, but it's enough to be going on with. Where available, we've included the website. Websites are being added by the thousands every day, so by the time of publication some of the Internet-naïve companies without websites listed here will have seen the light. At the time of writing, in mid-1998, Paragon Mortgages has an especially useful site, with a number of mortgage calculation tools which you can download for free. The *Moneyworld* site (http://www.moneyworld. co.uk) has the current best-value mortgage offers listed and you'll also find a useful selection in the Saturday edition of the *Financial Times*.

Company Name	Phone Number	Opening Hours	Weekend Hours
Abbey National Direct http://www.abbeynational.co.uk	0800 555 100	8 a.m.–9 p.m. Mon–Fri	8 a.m.–4 p.m. Sat
Bank of Ireland Mortgages http://www.bank-of-ireland.co.uk/mortgage	01734 510 100	9 a.m.–5 p.m. Mon–Fri	Closed weekends
Bank of Scotland Mortgages Direct http://www.royalbankscot.co.uk	0800 810 810	8 a.m.–10 p.m. Mon–Fri	8 a.m.–10 p.m. w/ends
Birmingham Midshires http://www.birmingham-midshires.co.uk/bmbs			
Bristol & West http://www.bristol-west.co.uk			
Bradford & Bingley Mortgages Direct http://www.bradford-bingley.co.uk	0345 852 852	8 a.m.–8 p.m. Mon–Fri	8 a.m.–12 p.m. Sat
Chelsea Direct	0800 291 291	8 a.m.–8 p.m. Mon–Fri	9 a.m.–1 p.m. Sat
Cheltenham & Gloucester Mortgages Direct http://www.cheltglos.co.uk	0800 454 305	8 a.m.–8 p.m. Mon–Fri	9 a.m.–1 p.m. Sat
Churchill	0800 0800 30	8 a.m.–7 p.m. Mon–Fri	9 a.m.–2 p.m. Sat
Colonial Direct	0800 828 500	8 a.m.–8 p.m. Mon–Fri	Closed weekends

Commercial Union
http://www.commercial-union.co.uk

Derbyshire Direct	01332 207 666	9 a.m.–5 p.m. Mon-Fri (9.30 a.m. Wed)	Closed weekends
Direct Line	See Yellow Pages	8 a.m.–8 p.m. Mon–Fri	9 a.m.–5 p.m. Sat
First Direct	0345 100 103	7 a.m.–midnight	7 a.m.–midnight
FirstMortgage	0800 080 088	8 a.m.–7 p.m. Mon–Fri	10 a.m.–3 p.m. Sat

http://www.first-mortgage.co.uk

Halifax
http://www.halifax.co.uk

Hinckley & Rugby Building Society	0800 774 499	9 a.m.–5 p.m. Mon–Fri	Closed weekends
Household Mortgage Corporation	01494 459 100	9 a.m.–5 p.m. Mon–Fri	Closed weekends
Legal & General Mortgages Direct	0800 664 444	8 a.m.–8 p.m. Mon–Fri	9 a.m.–5 p.m. weekends

http://www.legal-and-general.co.uk

Lloyds Bank
http://www.lloydsbank.co.uk

Market Harborough BS
http://www.mhbs.co.uk

Midland Bank	0800 494 999	9 a.m.–8 p.m. Mon–Fri	Closed weekends

http://www.midlandbank.co.uk

Mortgage Express	0500 111 130	8 a.m.–8 p.m. Mon–Fri	10 a.m.–2 p.m. Sat
Mortgage Trust	0800 550 551	9 a.m.–5.30 p.m. Mon–Fri	Closed weekends

http://hyperlink.com

Nationwide Direct	0800 302 010	8 a.m.–8 p.m. Mon–Fri	9 a.m.–6 p.m. weekends

http://www.nationwide.co.uk

NatWest Mortgages	0800 400 999	8 a.m.–8 p.m. Mon–Fri	10 a.m.–4 p.m. w/ends

http://www.natwest.co.uk

Newcastle Direct	0191 244 2468	8 a.m.–8 p.m. Mon–Fri	9 a.m.–1 p.m. Sat

http://www.newcastle.co.uk

Northern Rock	0800 591 500	9 a.m.–5 p.m. Mon–Fri	10 a.m.–3 p.m. Sat

http://www.nrock.co.uk

Paragon Mortgages
http://www.paragon-mortgages.co.uk

Sainsbury's Bank Direct	0500 700 600	8 a.m.–10 p.m. Mon–Fri	8 a.m.–10 p.m. Sat

Scottish Widows Bank Direct	0345 829 829	8 a.m.–9 p.m. Mon–Fri	Closed weekends
Sun Alliance http://www.sunalliance.co.uk/sunalliance			
The Direct Mortgage Business	0800 454 662	9 a.m.–8.30 p.m. Mon–Thu 9 a.m.–5.15 Fri	Closed weekends
TSB Phonebank	0500 758 000	8 a.m.–9 p.m. Mon–Fri	9 a.m.–5 p.m. weekends
UCB Direct	0500 401 400	9 a.m.–5.15 p.m. Mon–Fri	Closed weekends
Woolwich Direct http://www.woolwich.co.uk/woolwich	0645 757 575	8.30 a.m.–9 p.m. Mon–Fri 10 a.m.–2 p.m. Sun	9 a.m.–3 p.m. Sat

APPENDIX 10
Home Insurers

Here you'll find a few companies offering home insurance directly over the phone. There are others, but this isn't a bad list to start with.

Company Name	Phone Number (Direct)	Opening Hours
Barclays	0800 151 617	8am–8pm Mon–Fri 9am–5pm Sat
Churchill Insurance	0800 200 3459	8am–9pm Mon–Fri 9am–5pm Sat
Colonnade Direct	0800 678 678	8am–9pm Mon–Fri 8am–9pm Sat
Commercial Union	0171 283 7500	9am–5pm Mon–Fri Closed on Sat
Cornhill Direct	0800 60 70 70	8am–8pm Mon–Fri 9am–5pm Sat
Direct Line	0181 686 8877	8am–8pm Mon–Fri 9am–5pm Sat
Eagle Star Direct	0800 333 800	8am–10pm Mon–Fri 9am–2pm Sat
General Accident Direct	0800 121 004	8am–9pm Mon–Fri 9am–5pm Sat 10am–4pm Sun
Homeguard	0800 137 107	9am–5.30pm Mon–Fri 9am–1pm Sat
The Insurance Service	0800 878 787	8am–8pm Mon–Fri 9am–5pm Sat
Jardines	0800 445 444	8.30am–8pm Mon–Fri 9am–1pm Sat
Landmark Express	0800 45 45 45	8am–8pm Mon–Fri 9am–1pm Sat
Legal & General Direct	0800 282 404	8am–8pm Mon–Fri 9am–1pm Sat

Lloyds Bank Insurance Direct	0800 750 750	8am–8pm Mon–Fri 9am–2pm Sat
Midland Direct	0800 277 377	8am–8pm Mon–Fri 10am–2pm Sat
Norwich Union Direct	0800 888 222	6am– 10pm Mon–Fri 8am–4pm Sat
Prospero Direct	0800 747 576	8am–9pm Mon–Fri 9am–6pm Sat
Prudential Direct	0800 300 300	8am–8pm Mon–Fri 9am–5pm Sat 10am–2pm Sun
Sun Alliance Connections	0800 300 800	8am–8pm Mon–Fri 8am–5pm Sat
Touchline Insurance	0800 207 800	8am–8pm Mon–Fri 9am–2pm Sat
Willis First Response	0800 22 44 22	8.30am–8.30pm Mon–Fri 9am–1pm Sat
Zurich	0800 868 686	8am–8pm Mon–Fri 9am–1pm Sat

APPENDIX 11
The Pan-galactic Gargle Blaster

For those of you who are wondering just what is in the Pan-galactic Gargle Blaster, the 'best drink in existence' to which we alluded in the introduction, then read on:

> *Here's what the* Encyclopaedia Galactica *has to say about alcohol. It says that alcohol is a colourless volatile liquid formed by the fermentation of sugars and also notes its intoxicating effect on certain carbon-based life forms.*
>
> The Hitch Hiker's Guide to the Galaxy *also mentions alcohol. It says that the best drink in existence is the Pan-galactic Gargle Blaster.*
>
> *It says that the effect of drinking a Pan-galactic Gargle Blaster is like having your brains smashed out by a slice of lemon wrapped around a large gold brick.*
>
> The Guide *also tells you on which planets the best Pan-galactic Gargle Blasters are mixed, how much you can expect to pay for one and what voluntary organisations exist to help you rehabilitate afterwards.*
>
> The Guide *even tells you how you can mix one yourself.*
>
> *Take the juice from one bottle of that Ol' Janx Spirit, it says.*
>
> *Pour into it one measure of water from the seas of Santraginous V – Oh, that Santraginean sea water, it says. Oh, those Santraginean fish!!!*
>
> *Allow three cubes of Arcturan Mega-gin to melt into the mixture (it must be properly iced or the benzine is lost).*
>
> *Allow four litres of Fallian marsh gas to bubble through it, in memory of all those happy Hikers who have died of pleasure in the Marshes of Fallia.*
>
> *Over the back of a silver spoon float a measure of Qualactin Hypermint extract, redolent of all the heady odours of the dark Qualactin Zones, subtle, sweet and mystic.*
>
> *Drop in a tooth of an Algolian Suntiger. Watch it dissolve, spreading the fires of the Algolian Suns deep into the heart of the drink.*
>
> *Sprinkle Zamphuor.*
>
> *Add an olive.*
>
> *Drink . . . but . . . very carefully . . .*
>
> The Hitch Hiker's Guide to the Galaxy *sells rather better than the* Encyclopaedia Galactica.
>
> *From* The Hitch Hiker's Guide to the Galaxy *by Douglas Adams (Pan, 1979).*

The Motley Fool UK would like to add that it accepts no liability for anyone following the directions above. All claims to be addressed to Douglas Adams.

Your work is both good and original.
Unfortunately, the parts that are good aren't original,
and the parts which are original aren't good.
Samuel Johnson, to an aspiring author

Index